Indian Summer of the Heart

Indian Summer
of the Heart

DAISY NEWMAN

Boston

HOUGHTON MIFFLIN COMPANY

1982

In memory of
George Selleck
and for
Bruce and Rosalind Simonds

Library of Congress Cataloging in Publication Data

Newman, Daisy.
Indian summer of the heart.

1. Quakers — Fiction. I. Title.
PS3527.E87715   813'.52   82-6226
ISBN 0-395-32517-X   AACR2

Printed in the United States of America

P 10 9 8 7 6 5 4 3 2 1

Years have passed on, and left their trace . . .
Yet hath thy spirit left on me
    An impress Time has worn not out . . .
    The shadows melt, and fall apart,
And, smiling through them, round us lies
The warm light of our morning skies, —
    The Indian Summer of the heart!

      — John Greenleaf Whittier, *Memories*

PART ONE

Oliver

1.

I N THE SUMMER of his seventy-ninth year, Oliver
Otis of Firbank Farm fell in love, not circumspectly, as an
elderly widower might properly do — to secure companionship
and decent cooking — but wildly, without design, head over
heels.

The preposterous situation frightened Oliver. It was un-
seemly.

At thy age! he reproached himself a dozen times a day.

He could think of little else.

Every morning, sitting quietly in his study, cultivating his
spirit, as he always did before going out to cultivate the stony
Rhode Island soil, Oliver reviewed his condition. Later, when
he thought he was working in his garden, he'd discover that
he had just been leaning against the hoe, lost in dreams. On
First Days, enveloped in the silence of the Friends Meeting
at Kendal, he waited anxiously for insight. But the turmoil
persisted.

I'm ordinarily calm, Oliver argued with himself. All my life,
my emotions have been pretty dependable. How did they get
so out of control?

One minute, they soared elatedly; next they nosedived. And,
all too often, Oliver simply floundered uncertainly, somewhere
in between.

He told no one, naturally.

At times, he suspected that Serenity and Peter Holland, who lived with him, had a tiny inkling. They seemed to regard him more tenderly these days, almost in sorrow, as if they feared that his judgment was impaired.

For *their* sake, Oliver thought, closing the door of his study after breakfast on the morning of the autumnal equinox — for *their* sake, I ought to explain; assure them that I'm not senile, only in love.

Yes, he'd tell them, but not right now. This was his time for solitude, for withdrawing into his secret self. Even in the harvest season, when there was more to be done than a younger person could have accomplished and Oliver begrudged every moment that he wasn't working outdoors, he still set this half hour aside, sitting quietly by the window in his study. It was the time to suspend preoccupation with those mundane matters the old Quakers used to refer to as "creaturely activity," the time to center down.

When Daphne was alive, they had had their morning silence by the living room fire in winter, while the dogs lay on the hearth rug. In summer, they sat on the back porch in the old glider, holding hands. Sharing the silence in love had made it a joy. Oliver continued the practice by himself, sitting in his study, which held fewer associations. Yet, more than any activity in his routine, this solitary silence revealed the depth of his loneliness.

Nevertheless, he still welcomed the opportunity to relax and measure his life, face its inadequacies, fan the divine spark within him so that he might more nearly approximate the person he wished to be. But today he was restless, incapable of detaching himself from the thought of all he had to do.

The orchard — it was getting beyond him. Everything ripened at once. The pears. And the Eatons — those large, purple grapes on the vine by the south porch, which Grandmother

Serenity planted sixty years ago. And the Rhode Island Greenings.

The present-day Serenity had been doing the preserving these past few seasons, keeping up with Oliver as he brought in bushel basket after bushel basket from the orchard and garden. But, this year, she was so busy with her studies that she didn't start till late at night and she never quite finished. There was always some leftover produce waiting to be canned or frozen and the kitchen had fruit flies. Preserving was a big job. Serenity ought not to be doing it. With a small child to care for, a husband, her courses — to say nothing of all she did for Oliver — she had far too much on her shoulders.

Oliver tried to forget the orchard for a few minutes, to harvest what William Penn called the "fruits of solitude." But it was useless.

More pressing than anything else this morning was his weekly letter to Heather. Unless he wrote immediately and took it down to the Firbank box at the end of the lane, it wouldn't be picked up till Monday. That letter weighed on Oliver. He couldn't center down.

Might as well cut my meditation short, he decided finally. Attend to the matter that's nagging me.

So he switched to the chair by the typewriter table. Carefully spelling out Heather's name and London address on an aerogram, he added the long string of ciphers that Her Majesty's Postal Service required these days. On the inside of the form, he got as far as *Dear Heather*. Then his thoughts wandered back to the Hollands.

If he were to confide in them — admit to the state of his heart — mightn't his equanimity return?

Right now, he resolved. *Quickly*, before they leave for the University — I'll go and tell them. Right now!

He glanced at the door, up and down the wide planks, painted white, at the antique thumb-latch — the kindly door that always stood between him and the hubbub of the household, when he wanted to write or enter the silence of his soul. He'd get up now and press the latch, pull the door open, walk to the kitchen, tell Serenity and Peter. Now —

But Oliver just sat in his chair, unable to stir.

A southerly breeze, fresh off the ocean, came in through the open window and rippled past his cheek.

In love! Applied to himself, the condition sounded positively amusing — it was so preposterous. That *he* — Suddenly, it struck him so funny that he laughed out loud.

What would Heather say, though, if she knew? *She* wouldn't find it so amusing. Oliver loved his daughter dearly and he knew she loved him, but they seldom saw eye to eye.

His consternation returned as he faced the typewriter again, trying to think of what to tell her. Under no circumstances would he mention the lady who had unaccountably invaded his heart.

Eggplant's enormous now, he wrote instead, choosing a safe subject. *Thee knows how beautiful it is. Mother used to paint mounds, stacked along the side of the barn. Against that weathered red, the lustrous amethyst, highlighted in silver —*

Oliver had plenty of interesting items to report without mentioning the most significant — his new friend's visits. But he felt guilty. Until she came, his letters to London had carried a full account of what was happening at Firbank. Now he was holding out.

If I tell Heather, he argued with himself, even the three thousand miles of ocean between us won't temper the force of her reaction when it breaks on this shore.

What *ever* has got *into* you, Father? she surely would demand to know, shooting off her indignation by return mail, underlining words to give them double strength. You can't possibly be thinking of *marrying*? You were always so *reasonable.*

Marrying? he'd write back. *Me?* Why, I'd never dreamed of such a thing. Till thee suggested it — Heather, how could thee suppose that a younger woman — she's only slightly over seventy — seventy-two, to be exact, how could thee think that a woman like that, a former college dean — vivacious, independent — would want to marry *me?* It's simply that I'm — well — drawn to her. Maybe — yes, Oliver would have to admit — maybe I *am* a trifle moony.

That would send Heather into a panic. Posting her letter without delay, she'd ask plaintively, You haven't *declared* yourself to her, have you, Father? Does this — what *is* her name, anyhow? — does *she* know your intentions?

Before Oliver could protest, before he could reply that he didn't have intentions, Heather would *telephone.* Transatlantic!

I'm flying over *at once.* This is a most inconvenient time, with Stephen away on business and the children home on holiday, but it can't be helped. *I'm coming!*

Heather wouldn't, of course, do anything of the sort. She might be a bit too solicitous sometimes, but she never criticized or said anything unkind. Heather wasn't like that. Oliver's imagination simply invented this correspondence, echoing his daughter's inflections, but imputing words to her that she never would have written. He hated himself for making this up.

It was what Heather *wouldn't* write that Oliver really dreaded. Her pointed silence was bound to intensify his self-reproach. In her usual way, she'd merely respond obliquely, inquiring, perhaps, about the Hollands, the implication being that, with them to look after him and her own annual visits, short though these were — what more did Oliver need? Not a wife, surely.

Are the Hollands being as good to you as ever? she would write. Not letting you overwork?

Indeed they were good to him — if anything (but Oliver

didn't tell Heather this), a little more considerate, sensing that he was troubled.

Their little boy was one subject Oliver could write to Heather about without the fear that it would backfire. Having exhausted the eggplant, he went on: *I wish thee could see how fast Ross is growing. Catching on about the bathroom, too. FINALLY!*

Rereading what he had typed so far, Oliver wondered whether even this was wise. In her last letter, Heather had expressed anxiety concerning what she called her father's "babysitting."

Aren't Rennie and Peter imposing on your good nature? At your age, one can scarcely be expected to —

Oliver had quickly assured Heather that the little he did for Ross couldn't possibly be classified as babysitting. Serenity got him up in the morning and took him to nursery school. Oliver simply called for him at noon, gave him his lunch and put him down for his nap. Later, they went out and gardened till Peter came home and took over. Really, it was nothing. Ross was such a companionable child.

Oliver hadn't found it necessary to add that his own nap was postponed because Ross wanted to hold on to a knobby forefinger until sleep overtook him. Sometimes, Oliver was so tired that, before the child's grip relaxed, he had fallen asleep himself, sitting upright beside the bed.

Heather would not have approved. "Babyspoiling" is what she would have called it. She had brought up four children and considered herself an educationist. Oliver preferred not to argue with her. Ross needed this security. When a little boy's mother is gone all day, *someone* has to —

This letter was becoming more and more difficult. Despairing, Oliver gazed out of the window for inspiration. A cardinal was perched in the hemlock at the edge of the Firbank woods.

Pleading with the bird not to fly away, so he could watch

him instead of writing, Oliver thought of the Hollands again.

Why couldn't he bring himself to talk to these two? He trusted them as if they were his children. Indeed, he felt as close to them as he did to Heather, whom he only saw once a year. The Hollands were here all the time, discussing over supper each evening the day's events, its difficulties and satisfactions.

The dazzling plumage of the cardinal mesmerized Oliver. If the bird would just stay there, holding his attention, this troublesome letter could be put off a little longer.

Didn't Oliver have every reason to confide in Serenity and Peter? When they first came to Firbank five years ago, perplexed lovers themselves, they had confided in him. He and Daphne had been able to help them — Daphne, especially. If only she might have lived to see them happily married a year later!

Now it was Oliver's turn to be perplexed, though the situation was very different. In his case, there was no thought of marriage. That was out of the question for a man who so loved his wife that when she died he felt as if he had suffered an amputation. Nor was Oliver exactly a teenager, at the mercy of inexorable sexual pressures, as Serenity and Peter had been when they first came to Firbank. Still, in his way, wasn't he in need of help, too?

The cardinal had a mind of his own. Indifferent to pleading, he took off. Oliver's attention, unwilling to return to that aerogram, fixed itself on the white curtain that was ballooning like a sail in the breeze.

What was it that drew him to this stranger who, unannounced, had suddenly appeared at Firbank?

No one could be more unlike Daphne. She'd never tried to manage anybody, whereas this woman betrayed, in a well-bred yet overpowering way, how important it had been to her to wield authority in that little college of hers. Still, there was that in her eyes, in her manner, which seemed to contradict this; to mourn for an aspect of living she'd missed; crying out for a different fulfillment. This hunger touched Oliver. He longed to still it, to share the vision he thought she glimpsed here, even as he craved the unaccountable joy and comfort it gave him to be in her presence.

An explosion in the driveway shattered the silence. It was only Peter's van, uncertain — as it was every morning — whether it wished to start. When it consented, Peter drove off for a day of teaching introductory astronomy, after having spent half the night in the Observatory, collecting data for his doctoral dissertation. The heavy workload was telling on him. At breakfast, he had lost his temper with Ross, for whom he usually had unlimited patience.

The van was still audible in the distance when Serenity came out, pulling Ross with gentle firmness. The child was literally dragging his feet. Serenity had to take him to nursery school before going to her classes at the University. If she stopped to cajole him, waiting until he came willingly, she'd be late. There was a howl as she picked Ross up and buckled him into his car seat.

Sighing, Oliver turned back to the room. This letter to Heather — he simply couldn't write it now. It had to be postponed. Tomorrow —

He covered the typewriter and pushed back his chair. As he opened the door and started down the hall toward the kitchen, he remembered how, less than an hour ago, he had urged himself to tell the Hollands — Now it was too late. They'd left.

2.

ALTHOUGH THE DISHES had been washed today and piled in the drainer, the kitchen had its usual morning air of hurried departure. An eggy bib decorated the back of Ross's chair. A stream of orange juice ran down the side of the tablecloth.

On the counter, lying directly in the sun, was the pile of lima beans and peppers that Oliver brought in days ago. They should have been put up by now. But Serenity hadn't got to them yet.

There was an eggplant, too — probably the one Oliver picked last week, the same one he'd written to Heather about. Its green cap, so jaunty when he cut it, was shriveling.

The eggplant reminded Oliver of the unfinished letter. He ought to go back to his study and continue writing. But, surely, Heather wouldn't be expecting a letter from her father this week! She'd realize how rushed he was with the harvest, even though he had been forced since his illness to curtail the planting drastically. Of course, in England, there was less fear of an early frost.

Perhaps Heather didn't remember the frenzy of harvest time at Firbank. How could she have forgotten? As a child, she'd done her part, climbing the apple ladders, shaking the branches, swinging from them, full of fun —

In the middle of the kitchen floor, Peter's work shoes were lying like faithful dogs, waiting for their master to return.

The real dogs, Lion and Duffy, also waited — beyond the screen door. They weren't so patient as the shoes. Vociferously they requested the pleasure of Oliver's company.

"Just a minute," he called to them. "I'll be out in a minute. There's a job to be done in here first."

Carefully stepping around the scattered toys — these days,

he was in constant fear of tripping on a marble or a tiny car and breaking his hip — Oliver pushed in the chairs and wiped the plastic tablecloth that Serenity went in for nowadays. It was easier to keep clean than the bare wood, which he and Daphne loved. Polishing the walnut grain till it shone had given him a pleasure which was reflected in Daphne's eyes when he set the straw mats and indigo-rimmed plates on the gleaming wood. He missed the pewter teapot, too, with its century-old nicks. The Hollands simply dragged a teabag through a cup of water, leaving the bag to stain the saucer and dry up.

How different the house was now from the way he and Daphne had kept it — everything in place, scrubbed and shining, conveying a sense of homely beauty, of order and repose. Still, Oliver thought as he went over to the hutch to straighten the cookbooks, which were falling in a heap onto the family Bible, it's a warm room. The people have left, but some of their aura remains.

It was the aura of young people devoted to each other, to their child, and to him, mixed with an atmosphere of breathless haste, of overburdened lives. They belonged to an age that expected every young man and woman to perform the duties of several persons simultaneously and with perfection.

Serenity had given Ross her wholehearted attention until his third birthday. Then he was supposed to be out of his babyhood, old enough to get along without his mother for the greater part of the day. She and Peter had decided that this was the year for her to enroll in graduate school.

Oliver observed that, when she came home, tired, with mountains of books to be studied before morning and dinner to prepare, she scarcely had time and energy left for playing with her child. She was as devoted to him as before, but she had another commitment and she couldn't afford to slight it.

Not my business, he told himself. Ross is their child. They

must bring him up as they see fit. I had my chance with Heather.

But, more and more, Ross was becoming Oliver's child, looking to him for security and comfort, a bulwark against those sitters who kept turning up.

Oliver felt even more sorry for the parents, caught as they were in this dilemma, than he did for Ross, who was a sturdy little fellow and would grow up somehow. But Serenity and Peter, warm-hearted, generous, conscientious, pressured beyond endurance — what was going to become of them?

He regretted not having followed his impulse to tell them his secret before they left. Tonight — he'd definitely tell them tonight. During supper, he'd confide the cause of his preoccupation these past few weeks. He'd be careful not to worry them, not to give them the impression that they'd have to leave Firbank. At the very beginning, he'd assure them that he wasn't thinking of getting married — that was out of the question. He was simply — well — in love.

But would they understand?

To youngsters in their middle twenties, mightn't it be inconceivable that a man of seventy-eight should fall in love — practically at first sight! — with a woman of seventy-two? This might well strike them as such a ludicrous idea that they would have difficulty in concealing their amusement. Oliver had laughed at himself, but he didn't think he could bear it if these two were to laugh at him. Would they understand?

He'd be forced to point out that people in their seventies were indeed capable of loving, though he'd also have to admit that, before this happened, he himself wouldn't have been able to imagine what it was like; how all-engrossing it could be, or how profoundly it could move one.

He'd never had much sympathy for men who remarried late in life. They generally chose younger wives and he had always suspected that their chief motivation was to be made comfortable in old age, to be guaranteed lifetime care. Only now did Oliver realize that those men might actually have been deeply in love. Rather than just looking out for themselves, they might simply have been moved by the desire to cherish and protect someone. How could it have taken Oliver so long to discover that it was quite possible for a man to become as devoted to a woman in old age as he was in youth?

To think, he would say to Serenity and Peter, that, all this time, I've been so callous and obtuse!

As for the woman being younger — Oliver would assure them that, in this case, the discrepancy was negligible.

If two people love each other, he would exclaim, how can six short years make any difference?

If they loved each other — that was the real impediment.

Scrubbing the sink, he told himself sadly that what drove him to the verge of despair was the conviction that his feeling wasn't reciprocated, not the least bit.

How could it be?

With her interests! he thought. They're entirely outside my range of knowledge. Those composers she's always talking about as if they were still living, as if she actually knew them: the Mozarts, the Haydns, the Strausses — I love music, but with my background — She must find me very dull.

When the kitchen looked a little more shipshape, Oliver stood in the middle of the floor, wondering which of his many jobs to tackle first. Before he knew it, twelve o'clock would be here. It would be time to call for Ross. Oliver must get to the nursery school punctually. The day he was held up for ten minutes because of an accident on the Post Road, Ross was terrified, convinced that he'd been permanently abandoned. The teacher hadn't been able to console him. So Oliver must keep an eye on his watch.

Lion and Duffy were becoming more insistent.

"Just a minute," Oliver repeated. "I'll be right out."

Which job should he tackle first?

The sweet corn had been picked, grated and put in the freezer. It would be good for fritters till Christmas. Blanched, the whole kernels would keep much longer. Austin Young had promised to come over this afternoon and help shock the field corn. When it was dry, Oliver'd put it in the corn crib. After New Year, he'd run it through the sheller and take it to the mill over in Perrytown to be stone-ground. That way, Firbank could enjoy johnnycake all winter.

Corn knife needs sharpening, Oliver reminded himself. Better attend to that first.

He went to the back hall for his floppy white hat.

In the corner, under the row of pegs that held the snow-shoes, the Shaker basket overflowed with pears.

The woodshed opened off the back hall and Oliver stood at the door a minute, looking in. This had been Daphne's studio. Here she painted those masterpieces which were now hanging in museums around the country. And here Oliver found her that day, four and a half years ago, when he brought in her tea. Her heart had stopped, but she was still holding her brush.

The big potbellied stove in the corner, which had made the woodshed such a cozy place, was cold now with the ashes of the last fire Oliver built for her. No one used the room.

Those ashes ought to be cleaned out, he told himself. I keep meaning to —

Standing at the door a moment, Oliver drew solace from looking in.

Daphne spoke to him. Her canvases, stacked against the un-plastered walls, spoke with her voice: portraits of people they'd known; scenes of places they'd visited together, and hundreds of vignettes of Firbank. There was the maple tree outside the woodshed window, painted at every season of the year — in the scarlet, gold and crimson glory of early autumn, shot through with vestiges of summer green; in the tracery of bare branches thrusting into the winter sky; in the first, delicate leafing-out of springtime, with the promise of later fullness. There were the wildflowers — lady's-slippers, blue flag, marsh marigold and violets. There was one little water color, painted on the beach, of sea rocket with its bizarre-looking seedpods sprawling over the dunes. There was even a sketch of the kitchen table as they kept it in those days. A shaft of sunlight streaming in through the back door overlay the polished surface, bringing out the grain of the walnut.

Glancing into the woodshed, Oliver suddenly felt more peace than he'd known in weeks.

Daphne would have understood.

3.

OUTDOORS, the sun felt as warm as in midsummer. This was a rare morning — far too good to be spending on chores. There might not be another day as beautiful as this till next summer.

Oliver started for the barn. When Austin arrived to help him shock the corn, he must have everything in shape. He counted the equipment out on his fingers: the knife, the pole that went into the center of the shock, the corn horse — that contraption they used to stack the sheaves. It would take half the morning to get ready for shocking.

Then, as Oliver stepped out of the warm sunshine into the chilly barn, it came over him like a God-given leading that it was a sin not to be celebrating this superb day. That's how it happened that he did such an unheard-of thing: he turned on his heel and walked out of the barn again, heading for Salt Pond! He, who was so conscientious, who cared for his land as if it were a member of his family — indeed, it was the chief provider — he, Oliver Otis, ran away to sea!

His truancy appalled him. How could he do such a thing?

Yet, even as he asked himself the question, he kept on walking through the field of goldenrod and joe-pye weed, recalling how, at this time of year, Daphne would collect wildflowers and dry them on wire mesh for winter arrangements.

The dogs were ecstatic. Young Lion loped ahead on his long legs. Poor little Duffy, thirteen and ailing, could barely keep up as she trotted beside Oliver. By the time they reached the pond, Lion was already in the dory, preempting most of the space. Duffy hesitated, looking over the edge of the dock. Formerly, she had jumped bravely, too. Now, that seemed risky. Her short body might easily slip between the dock and the boat. She knew Oliver would fish her out. She also knew from sad experience that he might have a good deal of trouble. So she stood there, anguished, lurching forward tentatively, then pulling back in fear.

Her days were numbered. But she so obviously enjoyed her life still, even in infirmity, that Oliver couldn't bear to terminate it. He picked up the affectionate little thing and held her tightly tucked under his arm as he stepped into the dory, not quite so springily himself as in earlier days, but ably enough.

Untying the painter, he cast off, rowing slowly, leaving his cares ashore.

The pond was still, but Oliver could hear the surf crashing beyond the dunes that separated it from the ocean. At the water's edge, the reeds were as green as they'd been all summer. Soon, they'd turn brown; they'd look lifeless. That would be misleading. Deep in the earth, they'd be gathering strength for coming up another year.

The dogs were curled up cozily in the stern.

Exhilarated by the clear air, gliding effortlessly over the glassy pond, Oliver felt as soul-satisfied as the dogs appeared to be.

Enchantment always overtook him out here. Ashore, he had to keep his mind on things. Afloat, he was free to dream. Drifting lazily, he gave himself to the delight of reliving the events of recent weeks.

That afternoon when Serenity brought home an unexpected guest —

He'd been lying on the floor, playing with Ross, when this tall, handsome woman walked in. Soft creases in her face, deepening as she smiled, made no secret of her age. Neither did the white hair, cut short and combed without artful arrangement. But she moved easily. Her open, unaffected manner, the simplicity of her dress, gave the impression that she was younger than her years.

Oliver relived that memory of her first coming to Firbank the way, she'd once told him, she played recordings of *The Magic Flute* and her favorite Mozart concerto — over and over. Repetition didn't detract from the pleasure.

Perhaps things hadn't happened exactly as he recalled. These days, he couldn't quite trust his memory. In his prime, it had been extraordinarily retentive. Now — Perhaps, too, his attachment colored the way he looked back on those events. But this was how they seemed to have occurred that afternoon in early August, when she first came. Starting inauspiciously, without any prefiguration of what was to come, her visit ended leaving Oliver feeling that he had been hit by some unseen force, dislodged from his comfortable security, yet blissful, floating off into a previously unimagined world.

She had caught him in a most undignified position — lying on the floor of the living room, propped on one elbow, his long legs outstretched. Peter and Serenity were late getting home, so Oliver was amusing Ross by building a garage of blocks for the toy trucks. Ordinarily, when the dogs barked, Oliver went to the window to see who was there, but at that moment, he was in the middle of a delicate operation — putting the top row of blocks in place. He thought he heard Peter's van arriving along with Serenity's bug. There were definitely two cars. He didn't bother to get up.

Yes, it was Serenity. She called to him from the entrance hall, just as he was getting the last block into position. Then she walked in, followed, not by Peter but by a woman — a stranger.

They came over to Oliver and stood there, smiling down on him. As he struggled to sit up, his jerky movements caused the garage to collapse with a crash, scattering the blocks across the room.

He felt like a fool.

Ross was hilarious. "Thee busted it, 'cle Oliver!" he shouted gleefully. "Thee busted it!" He dropped an armful of trucks on the ruins and ran to his mother.

But she was bending over Oliver, holding out a helping hand, as she introduced the stranger. "This is Mrs. Mead." She pulled Oliver up, talking all the while.

"I happened to be in the library when this visitor came in. I overheard her telling the new cataloguer that her ancestors were Southern Rhode Island Quakers and she wanted to find out about them."

Ross was tugging at Serenity's skirt, begging to be noticed.

She glanced down at him and placed her free hand on his head lovingly as she went on introducing the stranger. "No one in that library knows as much about Quakers as thee does, Oliver. So I asked Mrs. Mead to come home with me for supper. We haven't had a chance to talk because she followed me in her car. I don't know exactly what she's looking for. She'll have to tell thee herself."

Serenity bent to kiss Ross. "Sorry I'm late, darling. It couldn't be helped." Then, turning to the guest, she asked, "By the way, what's your first name?"

"Loveday."

It was enunciated slowly, distinctly, as if the owner were accustomed to having her name misheard or considered strange, as if there had been frequent necessity for repeating it.

Oliver caught his breath. *Loveday* — how absolutely beautiful! He'd heard it before — where, he couldn't recall. It wasn't a name one could forget.

"Quakers don't like titles," Serenity was explaining, probably fearing that the visitor might think it rudeness on a much younger woman's part to be demanding the given name on such short acquaintance. "When Oliver uses a person's whole name, he isn't being familiar. For him, that's a mark of respect, just as it would be for someone else to say, 'Mrs. Mead.' "

"Loveday," Oliver murmured under his breath, enchanted. Beautiful! Where had he heard it before? He couldn't have known anyone by that name or he'd surely remember. Some woman in history or literature? Loveday — Loveday Hamilton? No. Loveday Ham — It eluded him. "Ancient, isn't it?" he guessed, hoping for a clue.

The face of the Loveday standing before him lit up. "You're the first person I ever met who knew that! Most people think, just because they've never heard it" — she suddenly looked embarrassed — "that it's a joke, corny. They're even rude enough to tell me so. My first name's been a trial all my life. I nearly changed it."

"I think it's beautiful," Oliver assured her and she looked radiant.

But he still couldn't place the Loveday whose name he'd heard earlier.

"I know what you mean about people being rude because your name isn't common," Serenity exclaimed. "I have the same problem. Well, anyway," she added, giggling as she turned from one to the other with mock formality, impersonating a distinguished Quaker hostess, "Loveday Mead, meet Oliver Otis."

He shook the woman's outstretched hand.

She smiled at him. She smiled as anyone would have done on being introduced. And yet, to Oliver, distraught though he was, that smile conveyed more than politeness. It was an intimation.

4.

WATCHING FIRBANK recede as he rowed across the pond, Oliver noticed the sea lavender. Masses of tiny, pale blue flowers covered the marsh like an azure haze. But he didn't focus on it very long. His mind was turned inward, conjuring up the smile with which Loveday Mead acknowledged Serenity's introduction.

She thanked Oliver in advance for his assistance. "It was disappointing," she admitted, referring to her experience at the University library. "I'd driven all the way down from Boston. I'm spending the summer there and I thought, before returning to the Middle West, I'd go to Rhode Island and hunt up what I could find out there concerning my ancestors. But it was late and the reference librarian had left. The person I spoke to didn't seem to know her way around. Luckily, I was," — she laughed — "rescued."

The Historical Society in Providence, Oliver informed her, was the repository for the New England Quaker records.

"Oh! If I'd only known! I drove right through Providence. But then," she added graciously, "if I *had* known, I wouldn't have the unexpected pleasure of coming here."

"I knew thee'd help!" Serenity said to Oliver in that encouraging tone she always used when she was trying to get Ross to make friends with another child.

Then she took the little boy's hand and led him off to the kitchen.

Oliver was still flustered. "I'll be glad to assist thee — I mean, you — in any way I can, Loveday Mead," he murmured. "Do sit down."

Without surveying the possibilities, she settled into the nearest chair, letting her head rest against the upholstered back. Her elbows reposed on the arms of the chair; her hands lay in her lap. She looked at ease, happy to be relaxing at the end of a long, hot drive.

But Oliver was shaken. The visitor had chosen Daphne's chair, the one she'd always sat in. No one who came to Firbank these days, remembering Daphne sitting there by the fire with the dogs at her feet, ever chose it. Not that Oliver wished it to be preserved inviolate, sacred to Daphne's memory — he abhorred sentimental rubbish like that. The furniture was there to be used. But old friends unconsciously avoided the chair. Recalling how, after her first stroke, Daphne came downstairs painfully, leaning on Oliver's arm; recalling the difficulty with which she let herself into the chair, remembering her twisted features and the large eyes with which she tried to speak, old friends would have felt uneasy, taking her place. The stranger sitting there today knew nothing about Daphne. She'd simply dropped into the nearest chair.

This was perfectly evident to Oliver and yet, as he settled himself on the other side of the fireplace in the Harvard chair, he felt so shaken that he couldn't think of anything to say. He just stared at the woman opposite.

She didn't seem to be expecting immediate conversation, for she was looking around the room, observing the shelves of books stacked clear to the ceiling; studying Daphne's portrait of Grandmother Serenity, which hung over the mantel, and the paintings on the walls.

"What a lovely room!" she exclaimed. "That sampler — it must be at least a century old."

"Older. My grandmother made it at the age of eight. All those little stitches — If you look closely, you'll see the date in the lower left-hand corner — eighteen forty-two. Aren't the colors amazingly fresh? In all this time they've scarcely faded."

Loveday got up and went over to the wall where the sampler hung in a narrow gilt frame. Backing off a little, she read aloud: *"Walk cheerfully over the world, answering that of God in every one."*

The words of George Fox, so familiar to Quakers, were evidently new to her, for she read the text twice. Turning to Oliver, she observed, "Sounds like you."

Oliver laughed. She didn't know him. Hadn't they only just met? She couldn't guess what a charge those words laid on a person; how pitifully deficient he was.

He watched her graceful movements as she sat down again; the visible delight with which she noted the cushion of marigolds, dotted with pearly everlasting, in the blue bowl on the coffee table. She seemed in no hurry to talk about her ancestors.

Oliver was in no hurry, either. Who was this woman? Where did she come from? What was she doing in Boston in the *summertime*? And that name! It teased his memory.

Her inspection of the room gave him an opportunity to recover his composure; to take in her appearance, from the sleeveless, white blouse, open at the throat, to the tan skirt, which fell just over her knees. Even if she'd spent the past months in the city, she had reveled in the sun. Her arms and legs were tanned.

She was wearing a wedding ring. Was her husband waiting for her in Boston?

Oliver was frankly curious. She, it appeared, was curious,

also. Was this his house? she inquired. Did the Hollands live with him? Or was it the other way around?

"I don't mean to be nosy," she murmured apologetically. "But nowadays, intergenerational households are rather unusual."

Oliver explained that Firbank Farm had come down to him from his Grandmother Serenity Otis, the one who made that sampler in her childhood and whose portrait, painted in the last year of her life, hung over the fireplace.

"Actually," he explained, "she left Firbank to all her descendants, but I was the only one who was willing to farm. So it came to me, along with her red hair."

Loveday laughed.

"That is," Oliver amended quickly, so she wouldn't think he had illusions about his appearance, "the color my hair used to be before I grew old and lost most of it. The present Serenity and Ross and my daughter Heather all got the Otis hair. Serenity is my cousin Edmund Ross's daughter."

"She's lovely looking."

"Yes. Beautiful, not just in appearance but in spirit. Daphne and I were so surprised when she turned up five years ago. We'd been out of touch with Edmund — you know how these things happen in families. Serenity came here because she and Peter thought they might like to have a Quaker wedding and they wanted to find out how to go about it. A year later, they were married in Kendal Meeting. Peter had a fellowship for graduate study and Serenity had a grant from the Museum of Contemporary Art to assist me with the book I was writing. As they had no place to live, it seemed natural to invite them — "

"*You* wrote a book?" Loveday broke in. "Was it published?"

He ignored the questions. Did she think, because he was a farmer, that he couldn't write?

"Who published it?"

"The Museum."

"You mean, the *Museum of Contemporary Art in New York?*"

"It seemed natural," Oliver repeated, "to invite them to make their home with me, since Serenity was working here and Peter could commute to the University. For their part, they offered to take over the housekeeping and some of the chores. We only expected to do this till my book was finished. After that, Serenity was going back to school. But then, Ross surprised them and they stayed. They've made this a place of friendliness, refreshment and peace. It's four years now. I've had care and loving companionship. They've had a home they enjoy."

"And a built-in sitter."

"Oh no! The little I do can't be classified that way. It's simply that one of the girls Serenity engaged to come in when she went back to school frightened Ross so badly that I begged to be allowed to take over."

"Well, whatever you call it, do continue," Loveday urged. "It's so important for a young mother to get out. I still remember how frustrated I was when the kids were small. I pined all day for adult conversation."

But Ross, Oliver thought, what about Ross? Still, he didn't intend to discuss this with a perfect stranger.

"It wasn't till my husband died," she was saying, crossing her legs, "and I entered graduate school, preparing to support my family, that I really felt fulfilled."

Oliver was shocked. "Fulfilled?" The word escaped him. He wanted to bite his tongue. But how could a woman feel fulfilled by her husband's death?

So, after all, there might not be anyone waiting for her, in Boston or anywhere else.

"Yes," she said calmly, not perceiving his reaction. "I'd always wanted to teach. At the ripe age of forty, I got my Ph.D. in European history."

"If Serenity keeps going," Oliver remarked, "when she gets her doctor's degree, she'll still be in her twenties."

"So much the better. It's harder later, I can tell you. But I worked. And eventually I became Dean of Studies at William Allen White College in Emporia, Kansas." She said it modestly, not to impress, merely to support her contention. "I always used to tell our women students to fight for their careers. Sounds disgustingly aggressive," she acknowledged, "but how else will they ever overcome masculine domination?"

Oliver had no answer. She almost made him feel guilty for being a man. And yet, hadn't Quakers always upheld the equality of the sexes?

"I do hope," she told him, "that the Hollands can stay with you till your — your niece, is it?"

"Cousin. First cousin once removed, to be exact."

"Till she finishes her education."

"As far as I'm concerned, it would be ideal if they stayed forever," Oliver exclaimed. "Some day — maybe quite soon — I'll have to give up farming. Who'll care for Firbank then? My only child lives in England. By the terms of my grandmother's will, Serenity would be entitled to the place. But she wants to be an art historian and Peter's an astronomer. His future's in the heavens. Farming's not for them."

"Naturally," Loveday said, uncrossing her legs again.

They were the color of that honey from Mount Hymettus.

Oliver thought of himself as a gentleman of the old school, though not stuffy — he hoped he wasn't stuffy! — seldom critical of others, only demanding of *himself* the behavior that had been drilled into his generation. Why, he had never even been permitted to see his mother's legs!

And now, thoroughly fascinated, he was unashamedly studying a strange woman's!

How could he help it? One smooth calf was partly turned toward him and the slender feet, resting on flat Oriental sandals, were completely exposed, save for thongs that came up between the big toes and their neighbors, extending to either side of the sole.

Staring at those feet, scrutinizing the long, shapely toes in turn, Oliver suddenly looked up with a start. For the feet had changed position. Their owner must have been aware of his interest.

Yes, she was watching him.

He felt miserably embarrassed. "About those ancestors," he said quickly.

She seemed to have forgotten that she ever had any. Leaning forward a little, she asked, appearing a trifle shy, "Why did you change?"

"Change?"

"You started to say 'thee' to me and then —"

He had explained that only a few old-fashioned Friends still used what they called "plain language" — the singular form in addressing one person, which they considered more in accordance with truth than the modern custom of using the plural.

"You see," he spelled out, "these days, it's merely a language of intimacy. We only use it among ourselves."

As she leaned back again, she looked downright disappointed. How could she be? A total stranger!

"About those ancestors," he repeated. "What were their names?"

"Austell — Thomas, his son Isaac and his *twelve* children. Can't remember all their names," she confessed, laughing. "I have them written down somewhere. I don't know which of them settled in Rhode Island, which were Quakers. Someone 'married out,' as they called it. That was the end."

Fishing in her purse, Loveday pulled out a notebook and put on reading glasses.

"David Austell migrated to Kansas in the eighteen fifties, when the anti-slavery faction moved in to keep it free," she announced, glancing at a page, then looking back at Oliver. "Mother used to tell about the covered wagon. I never paid much attention when she repeated those frontier stories that were handed down to her. It's strange, since I eventually became an historian. But I was just a kid. Even now, I'm not so fascinated by genealogy as by the history of nations or the life story of individuals. It's my daughter-in-law who wants to know. She's making a family tree for the grandchildren but she isn't satisfied with just writing in names. She says where the ancestors lived and what they did should be part of the record."

Oliver thought, Grandchildren! She scarcely looks old enough, though I know she must be. Could have great-grandchildren, probably.

She was giggling. "All Michael and Jed care about is baseball and television. I can't believe they'll ever want to look at that family tree, even if it's completed back to the Missing Link! But I don't want to ignore my daughter-in-law's wishes. Sara Ann's a good wife. Terribly conventional, though."

She was decidedly handsome — not pretty; her features were much too expressive of character, though a certain softness around the mouth seemed to contradict the firmness of her chin. There was grace in the way she sat — something few women seemed to achieve — and she wasn't too thin. Heather was always dieting. Oliver thought she was much more attractive when she let herself go a bit.

Yes, this was a handsome woman and she ought not to be driving all the way back to Boston alone at night. It wasn't safe. By the time supper was over, it would be quite late. But what business was this of Oliver's? She didn't want his protection, only information about her forebears.

"Austell," he murmured, shaking his head. "No, I can't place them."

"Thomas emigrated from the south of England. Somerset, I believe he came from."

"My wife," Oliver said slowly, "came from Yorkshire. She was a painter."

"Do you mean — you don't mean *Daphne* Otis?"

"Yes."

"She was *your wife*? I've heard of her, of course. But I don't know very much about modern art."

"These," Oliver said, waving his hand around the room, "were all done by her."

He hoped she would ask more about Daphne. But she didn't. Reluctantly, he returned to the ancestors.

"With a little patience, you might track them down. For that period we have no membership lists. Friends didn't keep them till later. They figured, anybody could spot a Quaker by his or her speech and dress and testimonies. But they did keep careful records of their Meetings for Business. If your forebears were active in Kendal Meeting, they probably would be mentioned in one of the old Minute Books."

"And they're in Providence?"

"The microfilm is. The original books are preserved at the Meetinghouse in Kendal."

"Is that far from here?"

"Eight miles. If you'd like to run through those old Minutes, I'd be glad to take you there some day."

She looked at him eagerly. "*Would* you take me?"

5.

ROWING LAZILY, lost in recollection, Oliver was carried to the south shore of Salt Pond by the current. When the oars hit bottom, he shipped them.

Lion didn't wait for the boat to be beached. He jumped

out and splashed up the bank. His legs were so long that his belly never even hit the water. But Duffy gazed apprehensively over the side.

"Soon as I get my sneakers off," Oliver promised, "I'll take thee ashore."

These days, getting shod and unshod proved increasingly difficult. First, Oliver's hairline had receded, then his vision, and when people spoke, they sounded oddly remote. Now his feet seemed to be getting farther from his arms.

At last, he stood up, barefoot, and stepped into the warm water with Duffy on his hip. The mud of the flats squished between his toes till he reached dry sand. Taking care not to crush the clumps of dusty miller that lay on the dune in silver mats, he climbed to the top and stood, watching a well-ordered flock of least sandpipers swoop by.

Before him spread a wide expanse of ocean. Yellowlegs moved swiftly through the shallows.

The face of the deep, he quoted to himself, awed.

There wasn't another soul in sight. As the waves rolled in from the horizon and broke along the sunny beach, almost at high water, the world seemed brand new, just coming into being. This was how it must have looked on the morning of creation.

In the beginning, God created the heaven and earth. And the earth was without form and void; and darkness was upon the face of the deep. And the Spirit of God moved upon the face of the waters. And God said, Let the waters under the heaven be gathered together unto one place, and let the dry land appear. And it was so.

Reminded of those words, Oliver thought, The Big Bang!

To Peter, an astronomer who was trying to explain the emergence of the universe twenty billion years ago, the language of Genesis sounded naive. But wasn't it simply describing in primitive terms what present-day scientists called The Big Bang? How similar to the poetic interpretation of the Bible some of their conclusions turned out to be!

The beauty of the pond, of the dunes and the ever-changing ocean had nourished Oliver all his life. Yet now, thinking of Loveday, he found the world even more beautiful. He'd never noticed before how the shadows, cast by swiftly moving clouds, skipped merrily over the sand. When the wind bent the long grasses on the dunes, light rippled like trills of music. The salt spray had a new tang.

Exuberant, Oliver wanted to shout Loveday's name from the top of the dune, shout it with such fervor that the sound would be carried over the seven seas.

Actually, he wasn't capable of uttering so much as a whisper. The exertion of rowing and climbing, coupled with the force of the wind blowing off the ocean, had taken his breath away. His heart pounded. He might have fallen, if the breeze hadn't been so strong that it made an ethereal wall for him to lean against.

How Loveday had enjoyed standing here, when he rowed her over — she who came from landlocked Kansas! Of course, she'd seen the ocean before, in other parts of the world. She had traveled widely.

On that first visit, when she was telling Oliver about her ancestors, she'd said, "For the children's sake, I've tried to find out all I could. Last year I even went to Austria to see where my father's people came from in the eighteenth century. It's a village south of Salzburg. They were Protestants and during the Counter Reformation they were severely persecuted. Finally, in seventeen thirty-three, the Bishop of Salzburg expelled every last Protestant. Twenty thousand had to flee, leaving their farms and cattle untended. Most of them went to Germany, but a little band made its way to the New World.

Johann and Katherl Klaus, my ancestors, were among the refugees who found a haven in Georgia. Have you ever heard of Ebenezer?"

Oliver shook his head.

"That's where they settled first. It's twenty-five miles from Savannah. Oglethorpe gave them the land. The Salzburgers, as the English called them, built a church, The Jerusalem Church, with a swan on the steeple in memory of Martin Luther, and a school, so their children would learn German. I stopped there once on my way south."

"Do you still have relations there?"

"No. I just wanted to see the place. There's nothing left of that settlement. Many of the refugees didn't survive the first winter. The rest secured more fertile land elsewhere. When the West opened up, Johann and Katherl's descendants moved to Ohio. The next generation went as far as Kansas. The family stayed in and around Emporia."

Oliver wasn't so interested in Loveday's ancestors as in her. He could no longer restrain his curiosity. "And your husband's family?" he asked. "You must include them in your family tree."

"Of course. As much as I know — " Her face lost its animation. "We never discussed genealogy and there's no one left to ask about it now. Well, as I was saying, I went to Austria to see where the Klauses came from originally. It's the most beautiful country — snowcapped mountains and lakes with tiny steamers, like toy boats. And the food! All that pastry and whipped cream — " She laughed. "I gained five pounds. The best way to get around was on one of those sightseeing tours. We were taken down into a salt mine, which was scary — like being trapped in the depths of the earth. And the ice caves — You haven't been there, have you?"

"No."

"It's fantastic. The rocks are so cold that, in the spring, when the snow melts, the water streaming down the mountain freezes inside the caves, making the most incredible sculpture, mounds and lacy curtains of icicles. You're in fairyland, in an old German folktale, a world so beautiful and also eerie, I'll never forget it." She smiled at the memory, yet her shoulder twitched, as if she felt shivery.

Oliver said nothing. He felt shivery, himself.

"The bus stopped at St. Gilgen, right on a lake. We were taken to see the birthplace of Mozart's mother. That interested me because I'd just been to the Festival in Salzburg — such glorious concerts! It was a surprise to me to be told by the guide that Mozart's sister lived in the same house after she married the local mayor."

Loveday seemed to assume that Oliver was familiar with the history of these people. He, however, was out of his depth. Like many of the older Quakers, his parents hadn't given their children a musical education. Later, he'd tried to make up for the deficiency by listening to records. In spite of that, he was still ignorant. He enjoyed Mozart's music, but he knew nothing about the composer's relations.

"You see," Loveday was saying, "when I was a little girl, taking piano lessons, I was fascinated by those stories about Mozart and his sister Nannerl playing together as children — he on a tiny violin and she the spinet — going from court to court, dressed in those gaudy clothes, performing for the Empress Maria Theresa in Vienna, Louis XV in Versailles, George the Third in London. It had never occurred to me to wonder what became of Nannerl after she grew up. One never heard any more about her, only about Wolfgang. Then, when I was in Salzburg and went to the Mozart Museum, I saw portraits of her. It was the first time I realized that she had a life of her own after that colorful childhood and I began to wonder what it was like. In the Museum, I pieced together a few facts. Talk about masculine domination! Nannerl was one of the worst victims."

Oliver felt guilty again.

"So," Loveday continued, "when the bus stopped and I stood before the house where she'd lived, studying a bas-relief on the wall with heads of the mother and daughter, both looking so wistful — " Loveday paused. "I don't know how to describe what I felt."

Suddenly she leaned forward, looking at Oliver earnestly, even, he thought, self-consciously, as though she were about to make a confession. "Something happened to me there," she said, almost in a whisper. "You'll think it queer — " She hesitated. "It was as if Nannerl reached down from that bas-relief and touched me on the shoulder, begging me to tell the world that *she* was somebody, too — not only as a prodigy, but later. I've learned a lot about her since, about the whole family. That's why I'm East — to do research at Harvard."

She stopped, studying Oliver, as if to determine whether he was taking her seriously.

His recollection of Loveday's first visit was momentarily suspended, as a group of blackbellied plovers ran swiftly along the shore. He scanned them, hoping to spot a golden plover, rarely seen in these parts. There was none. All the while, Loveday never left his mind. Even as he watched the birds foraging, Oliver's memory of her, studying him to determine whether he was taking her seriously, remained vivid.

He was taking her very seriously.

She must have sensed it, for she blurted out, "It's changed my whole life — that one short stop on a sightseeing tour. All the plans I had for my retirement, the things I'd been looking forward to doing — Nannerl crowded out everything."

Now it was Oliver who leaned forward. "And you're doing

it? You're telling the world that this — what did you call her? — that she was *somebody*?"

"Her name was Nannerl. It's a nickname. The l on the end's a diminutive. She was baptized Maria Anna Walburga Ignatia Mozart." The long, imposing name was intoned with amusement. "And when she married, she became" — downright laughter — "the Baroness Berchtold zu Sonnenburg born Mozart. But all her life, she was just known as Nannerl. How she must have suffered! A gifted artist, pushed into domesticity, merely because of her sex — You realize — don't you? — that it's a hundred and fifty years since she died. In all that time, no woman has ever been inspired to tell her story. I keep wondering, Why did she ask me? I'm not a musician."

There was something both touching and grand, Oliver thought, about Loveday's readiness to respond to a cry for recognition. Her desire to right past wrongs had the authentic ring that Quakers spoke of as a "leading." At first, he had simply been attracted by her charm. Now he felt drawn to something in her character. He wanted her to succeed.

"The research you're doing — most of the material must be in German. Can you read it easily?"

"Yes, I took it in college. My doctoral dissertation was on the social scene during the Congress of Vienna in eighteen fifteen. The sources were in German, sometimes in French. That was a fascinating topic."

"Tell me about it. I know the map of Europe was carved up there. But the social scene — what was that?"

"The social scene," she explained, "interested the emperors, kings and princes more than the political. With their courtiers, cooks and favorite ladies, they numbered a hundred thousand visitors, all converging on Vienna to celebrate Napoleon's overthrow and exile to Elba. Even those whose countries were bankrupt splurged on parades, balls and banquets. The stately minuet was replaced by the waltz. Everyone whirled madly. Suddenly, during a ball in Metternich's palace, news came that Napoleon had escaped. The spree was over."

Oliver listened, enthralled.

"Beethoven's Seventh Symphony was performed for the sovereigns. It was so innovative, everyone thought the composer must be mad. Schubert, a boy of eighteen, was writing the *Erlkönig* and Nannerl Mozart was giving piano lessons." The excitement that had animated Loveday's face disappeared. "I don't know why I'm telling you this," she murmured. "Nobody cares. My children are sweet. We get along fine. But when I start talking this way, they just look bored. Nobody's really interested."

Before Oliver could insist that *he* was, Ross came running in.

Hurling himself against Oliver's knee, he eyed the stranger warily.

"What is it?" Oliver asked. "Is supper ready? Thy Daddy isn't home yet. Was thee sent to call us in?"

"No."

Sensing the child's anxiety, Oliver took him on his lap.

Ross, assured that he wasn't about to be abandoned to the mercy of yet another sitter, regained his usual cheerfulness. The radiance of early childhood — such a joy to behold! — overspread his face.

Trailing clouds of glory, Oliver quoted to himself, setting the child down on his feet. Aloud he said, "Thee ask thy mother how long till supper."

Ross ran out of the room.

Oliver hoped his guest would continue her narrative.

But she showed no inclination to go on. Instead she said, "Toby, my younger son, was the same way, at that age. Scared of strangers. During my husband's illness, neighbors sometimes took the children off my hands. The other two didn't mind, but Toby got upset."

What happened to him when you went back to school? Oliver wanted to ask, only it seemed obtrusive. Had Toby outgrown his anxiety by then?

"You'd like Toby," Loveday remarked. "I wish he'd get married. He's living with a girl he's crazy about — I haven't met her — but he doesn't seem to have the faith to make a commitment." She paused, apparently thoughtful.

What she said reminded Oliver of the Hollands. Their relationship started like Toby's and his girl's, not because they didn't have the faith to make a commitment; they were simply too young. To regularize the relationship, Serenity's parents tried to rush them into a wedding under religious auspices which were merely a formality. At this point, Serenity was led to come to Firbank. Oliver recalled that she'd been unable to conceive of marriage as anything more than an understanding between two people. He'd had to explain that it affects everyone, the unborn children, the whole of civilization. He'd been very blunt.

"If it's only yourselves you're concerned with, why bother with a religious ceremony?" he remembered asking Serenity. "You could disregard these responsibilities and simply live together." She looked horrified. She hadn't expected this from him!

But, a year later, when she and Peter were married in Kendal Meeting, it was with a mature grasp of their commitment, which was to become a blessing to him and to all who knew them.

Of course, Oliver would never have discussed the Hollands' personal history with an unknown visitor, but her candor made him long to reciprocate. Hearing their story, she might have felt encouraged about Toby.

"It's charming, your plain language," she said after a while.

Oliver confided how happy he was that Serenity and Peter used it with their child. Before they came to Firbank, he explained, they'd never heard it spoken. Then they began using it with each other.

"You see," he said, "it's the language in which they made their marriage promises. And when they came to live here, they slipped naturally into responding in the way I spoke to them."

"A mark of their affection for you."

"I think so. It's all the more gratifying because my daughter revolted against the peculiar practice as soon as she went to school. The children laughed when they heard her speaking to her mother and me. Even as a grown-up, she never overcame the aversion."

"How contrary life is," Loveday murmured, laughing. "Your daughter has the right to say 'thee' and 'thy,' but doesn't care to, while I — it makes me wish that ancestor of mine hadn't married out!"

Standing on the dune, facing the ocean, all Oliver really saw was Loveday's expression as he recollected her saying this. The words were no doubt intended to convey amusement, for she laughed, but there was a hint of wistfulness in her eyes and in the tone of her voice that went straight to his heart and lingered.

He turned and started down through the steep sand, so absorbed in remembering Loveday that he neglected to pick his way carefully between the clumps of eel grass till they stung his feet.

Then he noticed the dowitchers, drilling in the mud with their long beaks. An osprey was flying overhead.

At the water's edge, Oliver lifted Duffy tenderly into the dinghy beside Lion, who was already reclining on the thwart. He pushed the boat clear of the beach and climbed in.

"Make room for me, both of you," he demanded.

Like the wake from the dip of his oars, the recollection of that wistfulness in Loveday's eyes trailed him all the way across the pond.

6.

DREAMING of Loveday's first visit, of the touching way in which she had shared her secret, Oliver was scarcely conscious of reaching shore. He tied up the dory mechanically and followed the dogs along the path without noticing where he was going, still recalling Loveday as she sat in Daphne's chair.

"Would you like to see a bit of Firbank?" he had asked her, when Ross came back with the news that supper wouldn't be ready for half an hour. "There seems to be just time for a short walk."

"Yes, indeed!"

"Me, too," Ross begged.

Oliver took the little boy's hand and stood up, telling him to wait and let the lady go first.

Those sandals, Oliver thought anxiously, as she moved toward the door. They're not made for walking in the woods.

But he didn't like to comment on her attire and he had nothing better to offer. Serenity's shoes would never fit her.

At the door, she stopped. Turning to him, she asked, smiling the way she did when they were introduced, "Won't you call me Loveday?"

Something went queer in Oliver's chest. He had the sensation he used to have in swimming, when he'd been under water for what seemed like hours and he surfaced at last.

"If you think it too obnoxious —" she added quickly, "most people do — maybe you'd rather use my nickname — Lowdy."

"No!" Oliver declared vehemently. "I think your given name's beautiful."

"You're the only one who's ever said that to me. When I became Dean, I was afraid the students would make fun of it behind my back. I almost decided to call myself L. Austell

Mead, which would have sounded pretty impressive, don't you think? But, somehow, dropping the Loveday seemed unworthy — out of character for an historian."

"I'm glad you didn't do anything like that! The name just suits you."

"It's really old, you know."

"Yes, I've heard it somewhere. Can't recall — It'll come to me."

"I looked it up once and found that it goes back to the Middle Ages. When serfs quarreled, the lord of the manor appointed a day on which they had to settle their dispute amicably — a 'day of love,' they called it: *dies amoris*."

"All the more reason for you to treasure what was conferred on you."

"In the beginning, it seems, the name was given to girls who were born on that day. Then the origin was forgotten and girls were named Loveday who were born any time. The nickname's ancient, too."

Was she hoping he'd use it? He couldn't.

"I don't like nicknames," he informed her. "Rennie, for instance. How can anyone call her that, when one might be saying, 'Serenity'? I'll be happy to use your beautiful name, Loveday. You must call me Oliver."

He held the screen door open for her, but she lingered on the threshold.

Casting her eyes down, she murmured, "I don't know why I told you so much about the Mozarts, Oliver. I don't usually talk like that. But something in the way you welcomed me, the way you looked when I started speaking — so interested — seemed to *invite* it."

Rowing back across the pond, Oliver savored the delight he had experienced that afternoon, when, foreshadowing the friendship that was to come, she stood at the door and asked him to call her Loveday.

But *Lowdy* — no! He could never call her that. It would be a desecration.

He walked back to the house along the path on which he had taken her that summer day when the sun was starting to go down. Oliver thought he remembered everything he told her as they walked together while Ross skipped ahead with the dogs: how much bigger his garden used to be — Daphne had raised herbs, too; how he had grown Christmas trees for their cash crop. Then he pointed to the acres in the distance which he called the Vietnamese Forest, telling her about the experiment he had conducted in wartime for revitalizing ravaged soil.

"Those defoliation bombs!" he'd exclaimed. "Imagine killing the leaves on a tree. It's almost as sinful as killing a person. Moreover, we know now that those bombs *would* eventually kill or harm persons irreparably — not alone the innocent civilians on whom they were dropped. We're constantly hearing that some of the men who were required to inflict the damage are themselves suffering from exposure to those chemicals."

"I know," Loveday said sadly.

"Even before this became established, I was so distressed that I had to do something. At the time I thought, While there may not be anything I can do to stop the damage, if I can just find a method for restoring life to contaminated soil, then, when the war is over, we'll be able to bring back those defoliated mangrove trees along the coast and the other vegetation our chemicals have destroyed. So the survivors will be able to live there. We'll go to Vietnam and make the land bloom again."

"Go to Vietnam? You were *going* there?"

"Why not? In nineteen eighteen, Daphne and I went to France. She nursed the sick and I helped farmers rebuild their homes and restore their land. That's where we met."

He had paused, hoping she would want to hear more about Daphne, but she was silent.

"I assumed," he went on, "that after the Vietnam War, large numbers of us would be sent over to repair as much as we could, just as Friends did after the other wars. So I took those acres you can see from here and tried to simulate conditions in Vietnam —"

"Here, in New England!" she cried. "The climate's so different. Vietnam's tropical."

She laughed at him. Well, she didn't exactly laugh. She was too polite. But her tone betrayed how ridiculous she thought he was. When the project began, Oliver had often encountered this reaction. Some Kendal folks allowed as how they thought he was crazy. Then, when he actually succeeded —

From Loveday, though, he had hoped for immediate understanding. Instead, she laughed — almost.

At the time, it had hurt him. In retrospect, he found he could defend her. She was an historian, an academic. What would she know about farming? No more than he did about those musicians of hers.

Loveday Mead and Oliver Otis simply weren't on the same wavelength. This was all too apparent. For some strange reason, he was irresistibly attracted to a woman with whom he had very little in common. He knew that now. But on her first visit, he'd hoped that *she* —

"New England's where I happen to live," he remembered telling her. "This is all the land I had to experiment with. I did what I could."

Patiently, he had explained to her how, after killing the vegetation in those acres, he tried various formulae, till he found one that revitalized the soil so that the seedlings he subsequently planted in it did grow. It had taken years of labor and failure, building smudge fires on winter nights, treating the soil over and over, but, in the end, he triumphed.

"Then," he concluded sadly, "after the war was over, I never had a chance to go to Vietnam and apply what I'd learned. None of us were allowed into the country."

Loveday looked as if his experience were as disappointing to her as it had been to him.

"I still worry about those trees," he confided, grateful for her sympathy. "Do you suppose they were ever saved?"

Now, six weeks later, the warmth of that sympathy filled Oliver with such joy that he forgot where he was until he reached the barn. Then he resolved to make up for having run away by working extra hard and getting all those chores done.

Maybe he ought to start by cleaning the ashes out of the stove in the woodshed. If there should be an unusually damp spell, the sulfuric acid in the ash would pit the lining of the stove. He'd been meaning to do this ever since Daphne died. But something had always held him back — the foolish desire to keep her studio the way she'd left it. Now he really must do it. Yet, when he glanced at his watch he found there was no time to do anything. Eleven-thirty! He must start for Kendal at once. Otherwise, Ross would be waiting for him at nursery school, feeling abandoned and inconsolable.

Well, Oliver reflected, no harm in leaving the stove as it is. I've let it go this long. If anyone should ever want to warm the woodshed again, those ashes will make a good bed to build a fire on.

Out on the highway, he caught himself thinking of Loveday. Driving an ancient pickup truck on the Post Road is no time to be moony, he admonished himself.

But he found it hard to concentrate. The traffic whizzed past an old man who was so ensconced in a dream that he took no notice of oncoming cars. He was recalling the morning when he first took Loveday to Kendal in this same truck. He had apologized for not being able to give her a more comfortable ride. She didn't seem to mind.

This was, he'd explained, his only vehicle. He went on to describe how he'd taken Daphne to meeting in it after her stroke. Leaning on him, she had mounted his grandmother's old horse block and climbed into the cab. At the Meetinghouse, two men always met them with a wicker armchair. They lifted Daphne out of the cab into the chair and carried her between them up the steps of the Meetinghouse with a flourish.

"Ceremonially, gaily," Oliver remembered telling Loveday, "as if she'd been a queen making a royal progress, instead of a helpless invalid going to meeting."

The first time Oliver took Loveday to the Meetinghouse, he stopped the truck in front of the building a second before parking in the yard. He wanted to gauge her reaction. How would she take the plainness — the dove-gray clapboards, the clear windows? Would she love the simplicity, as he did?

"It's beautiful!" she'd exclaimed and he was pleased.

They'd climbed up into the gallery, where the old books and records were stored in a seachest, and he had spread the huge, leather volumes out on a bench. Sitting side by side on the chest, they had leafed through the old Minute Books, starting with the ones that were written in the early eighteen hundreds, hoping to find some reference to Loveday's ancestors.

Deciphering the archaic handwriting was slow work. It required two more visits, but they had found nothing — no record of early Friends named Austell. So she would have to come again!

The weeks between her visits seemed endless.

Still, they were bearable, compared to Oliver's fear that Loveday might some time discover what she was looking for. They would be sitting on the seachest together, running their fingers down the pages of those Minute Books and suddenly, they'd see it — a Minute recording William or David Austell's concern, appointment to a committee, or removal to the West, or a reference to one of Isaac's twelve children. If they did — if they found what she was looking for, she'd have no reason for coming back to Firbank. And if she never returned —

The thought was so devastating that Oliver failed to see an oncoming car until it was almost upon him and he just missed landing in a ditch as he swerved to avoid it.

Realizing how narrowly he had escaped disaster, Oliver was mortified. That he should nearly have an accident simply because he was dreaming about a woman — not Daphne; another woman, one so unlike his wife that it was almost as if Oliver had become another person.

But I *feel* just the same! I *am* the same. Only, he thought wryly, only — I'm in love.

Did every woman bring out a different side of a man's character? The one who was working this change in Oliver sometimes seemed to be at war with herself, divided in will, in mind, in heart, though she spoke with such assurance that she probably wasn't aware of that part of herself which was totally different, which Oliver believed he discerned more clearly than she did, which drew him so inexorably to her.

Daphne hadn't had to fight for equanimity, except after the stroke, when, for a relatively short period, she lost the will to paint because her right hand was paralyzed and she succumbed to the frustration, the terrible frustration of not being able to speak. But in the last year of her life, Daphne came to terms with her situation. She attained a tranquillity of mind that drew young Serenity to her and it was Daphne who guided the girl out of her youthful distress.

Loveday seemed to be at odds with herself. And yet, surprisingly, when Oliver was with her, the part of him that death had fractured seemed almost whole again.

Was it to reconcile the opposing forces in her nature that

he longed to take Loveday in his arms and hold her fast? Not altogether, he was forced to admit.

She's not my wife! How can I feel that way about someone I scarcely know?

If only he could free himself from this terrifying obsession! It was driving him to destruction. The truck was careening madly all over the road, across the yellow line, then back onto the soft shoulder.

I'll land in the ditch, Oliver cried aloud, clutching the steering wheel with all his might, not sure he could right the truck again.

But he was saved — miraculously. What saved him was Heather — a sudden vision of her horror-stricken face, were she to find out what was happening to her father. Heather —

She must never know, he told himself, when his attention was once more fixed on the road and he moved straight along. I mustn't hurt Heather.

His heart was thumping.

When he reached the school and stuck his head inside the door of Ross's classroom, relief and joy sprang into the child's eyes.

And Oliver, bending down to put his arm around the tiny waist, also felt relief and joy. The terror on the highway, the outrageous thoughts — surely these were just caused by some momentary aberration that might never come again. Maybe his digestion —

On the way home, they stopped at the cove, the way they did every noon, to talk to the swans and the egret. Then they had lunch and Oliver put Ross down for his nap, settling himself beside the bed. Instantly, a little hand grabbed his forefinger and held it fast.

He felt blessedly calm now. He hadn't, after all, lost control on that perilous ride in to Kendal. He was all right. And the truck wasn't damaged. It might easily have been *totaled*, as they say these days. That would have grieved him as much as if he'd been hurt himself.

Heather was always advising him to turn in the truck for a compact.

You don't need that monster any more, she wrote in one letter. *Now that you aren't cultivating the acres, just the garden— A small car will be more comfortable for you, much easier to handle. At your age—*

To her, the truck is only a vehicle, Oliver thought. But it's a lot more than that. It's as dear to me as Grandmother's horse was to her. I feed and water it, have its little ailments attended to. I understand its moods, know how to coax it along on a cold morning, when it would rather sleep. And it responds to my touch. How can I forsake this faithful companion, leave it standing in some dealer's lot and drive off with a cute little upstart?

The captive forefinger was growing numb. Flexing it slightly, Oliver thought with amusement that life would have been a great deal simpler, if, as his joints aged, his feelings hadn't remained those of a much younger man. He still craved the companionship of a charming woman. He longed for intimacy in keeping with his age—what that might constitute, he didn't know. Until Loveday appeared at Firbank, his future seemed predictable—a continuation (at best) of the present, with his powers slowly diminishing. But now, anything might happen. The possibility filled Oliver with alarm.

And yet, it was invigorating, too. Disparate though they were, he and Loveday shared an essential quality. Recognizing this, Oliver, who'd felt stunted and desiccated since Daphne's death, had the surprising sense of resurgent life. They were both what Friends called seekers—open to leadings of the spirit.

Even at her age, Loveday was questioning and growing. Unlike many contemporaries, who considered themselves completed and polished, clinging to opinions formed earlier and never reexamined, she betrayed a pathetic hunger for a different outlook, almost a different self.

Oliver thought of himself as a seeker, too — one who looked on religion as a never-ending quest, rather than assent to prescribed doctrine. Whither the quest might lead was a mystery, but if it truly appeared to be heading in the direction of God's will, it must be faithfully followed.

The squirming forefinger was clutched with a tighter grip. Nearly asleep, Ross seemed to be afraid of being abandoned.

Oliver was drowsy himself, yet he felt more lively in spirit than he'd been this morning, when he was trying so hard to center down. He was closer to the source of his strength, transcending all understanding. He hoped that something of what he was feeling was being passed on to the child through the hand that gripped his finger — less the security of a trusted person's presence than the inner assurance of divine care.

Or perhaps it was the other way around. Perhaps the child was communicating this to Oliver with the hand that held the knobby finger. For, Oliver's habitual reserve was melting away, demolishing his defenses, overcoming the fear of exposing his heart. He couldn't even wait now till the Hollands came home. The desire to speak of Loveday, which he had resisted for weeks, became irrepressible.

"Ross," he asked in a low voice, "does thee remember Loveday Mead, who came to see us?" He so wanted Ross to remember! "Does thee?" he pleaded.

Ross nodded sleepily. He was still holding the finger.

"Thee sees," Oliver whispered, hoping the child was awake enough to hear, "I love her."

7.

THEY OVERSLEPT.

By the time they emerged at the back door, Austin Young was already in the barn. They could tell because Kelly, his setter, rushed out to greet them, provoking the Firbank dogs to declare their territorial rights with deafening barks.

Austin was pulling the corn horse out from its place against the south wall of the barn. The knife had been sharpened.

There was something about Austin's shy smile that Oliver found touching. It belonged to a man who wished to be more outgoing than he was capable of. He hardly talked. Oliver understood him. As a boy, Austin had worked at Firbank. He and Judy were active in the Friends Meeting. When Daphne died, it was Austin who had quietly attended to the little things. He had gone to the airport to meet Serenity and Peter. He had brought extra benches up from the Meetinghouse basement so that the many people who converged on Kendal to honor Daphne could be seated at the meeting of thanksgiving for her life.

Getting the corn horse out to the field was slow work, especially as Ross, who was determined to help, was constantly in the way.

"I planted less this year than ever before," Oliver told Austin. "Only a few rows. Beginning to know my limitations."

Even so, shocking was a big job. They went about it in a unison born of having often worked together, gathering the stalks and tying them up without talking at all.

The cry of Canada geese made Ross stand still. He pointed to the sky. The birds were flying swiftly, bound for Long Island, their long necks outstretched.

"Winter's coming," Austin told the child. These were almost the first words he'd spoken.

Oliver watched the geese, marveling at their sense — so often wanting in humans — of where they came from and whither they were going. Their purposeful movement reminded him of Loveday, who had known just what she wanted to do when she retired. Yet she had "sat loose," as the old Friends used to say, so that when a leading suddenly came to her, she put aside her former plans and gave it her whole attention.

Oliver turned back to the field of green shocks standing in rows, symmetrical, straight, yet each with a tilt and shape of its own. These bundles of corn were a link between him and all the husbandmen who worked their land through the ages, back to Biblical times. They were beautiful. He wished Loveday were here to enjoy the sight. As for the johnnycake into which this corn would be transformed next winter — she'd never taste it, for she'd be back home.

On her second visit, she had confided to Oliver that her research at Harvard was progressing. She had discovered some fascinating facts about Nannerl Mozart.

"She was in love with Franz D'Yppold, the tutor to the Archbishop's pages," Loveday reported, "only," she added, incensed, "that domineering father, Leopold, wouldn't let her marry him. Franz's prospects of advancement were too modest. But, Oliver, Nannerl *loved* him! And he loved her. Shouldn't that have been enough?"

Loveday's sympathy for the thwarted couple was contagious. Oliver felt for them himself.

"Wolfgang cared deeply for his sister," she assured Oliver. "He urged her to leave Salzburg with Franz and come to Vienna, where Wolfgang had established himself as a composer, far from their father's domination. In Vienna, he wrote Nannerl, Franz would certainly find work and they could marry. But instead of going, the obedient daughter meekly renounced Franz. At least — well, I wish I knew what really happened. Later, she married a horrible man, much older, with a raft of unmusical children. This Berchtold zu Sonnenburg suited Leopold because he was the mayor of St. Gilgen and possessed a petty title. You know how Austrians worshipped aristocracy. But the title didn't make Nannerl happy in her marriage."

Just recalling Loveday's outrage caused Oliver, standing in his corn field, to ache for those star-crossed lovers who lived two centuries ago.

Or was it actually Loveday who caused this ache? For he had a hunch that her own marriage had been anything but happy.

On later visits, she had easily been prevailed upon to spend the night in Heather's old room overlooking the pond, where Serenity stayed when she came here as a girl. Oliver enjoyed the enthusiasm with which Loveday threw herself into the ongoing life at Firbank, naturally, as if she were a member of the family. She had helped Serenity with the preserving till the pile of produce on the kitchen counter disappeared.

As they shelled limas and canned tomatoes, Loveday and Serenity chatted, but not the way Kendal women did. These two discussed academic matters, Serenity's courses, her long-term aspirations, the prospects for her career.

Loveday didn't hesitate to point out that, just at present, the job market was particularly bad for art historians. Museums and colleges had to cut back. Some of their most important projects weren't being funded.

"I don't mean to discourage you," Loveday told Serenity, "only to explain that you may have to be very patient about getting a job, even when you have your Ph.D."

Listening to their conversation, Oliver realized that this was just what Serenity had been needing — someone to talk to who understood the problems of young people.

Tonight, Oliver told himself as he and Austin prepared to take the corn horse back to the barn, tonight he would tell Serenity and Peter of his indescribable joy in possessing such a friend.

Wrapped in his reverie of Loveday, already picturing, even foretasting the happiness with which, he was sure, the Hollands would greet his news, Oliver realized that he was ignoring Austin. They were almost at the barn, caught up in a whirl of dogs. With a twinge of conscience, Oliver tried to make amends for neglecting Austin, who'd been kind enough to help him at a time of year when a potato farmer had more to do himself than he could manage.

"How's thy crop?" Oliver asked. "Good?"

"Yup."

There was a long pause.

Oliver hit on another topic of conversation, regretting that he hadn't been polite enough to think of it first. "How's Judy?"

Austin looked away. "Okay," he muttered after a spell, adding, "I guess."

Oliver turned to him quickly, but Austin avoided his eyes. What did that mean — he *guessed?* Was there trouble? Serenity had hinted something once.

Without facing him, Austin cried in a tone more desperate than Oliver had ever heard him use before, "What do they want, anyway?"

"Who?"

"The women. I don't understand them. Seems everything I was brought up to think a good man's supposed to do is wrong now." Austin swung around and faced Oliver. His usual taciturnity was breaking down. "That hymn Mom used to like, I sing it in the shower sometimes. 'Dear Lord and Father of mankind' — you know? Judy used to like it, too. Then, suddenly, real angry, she says she don't want to hear it no more. That word — 'mankind' — should be 'persons.' I thought all along that's what mankind means — men and women, both."

"It does."

"Judy says no. But 'persons' don't fit the tune and the rhyme don't come out right. Can you change the words of a hymn? We've sung it so long."

Oliver found it hard not to laugh. If Whittier's poem, written over a hundred years ago, was to be revised, then all the other Quaker writings, which were genuinely not sexist — not even those that dated back to the seventeenth century — would have to be rewritten.

Austin had become so talkative that Oliver realized he was upset.

"The trouble all started," he explained, "because I called Judy my girl — always had called her that — you know — loving-like. Twenty years! I thought she enjoyed it. Then, one day, it makes her mad. 'I'm not a girl,' she yells at me. 'I'm a woman, forty-eight years old. How'd you like for me to call you a boy?' I couldn't see what she was driving at. I hadn't done nothing mean or said hurtful things. Sure, I'm not a boy. Nobody'd think of calling me that. But I wouldn't want to call Judy my woman, like she was loose or something."

They entered the barn. Pulling the corn horse back into its place, Austin clammed up again.

Serenity's little car came puffing up the drive. Ross dashed over to meet his mother.

Standing ankle-deep in hay, Oliver tried to think of an answer to the question, What do they want? Loveday would know. He didn't. The women of his acquaintance varied in their aspirations. How could he lump the whole sex the way Loveday once labeled men as oppressors? Maybe she'd enlighten Austin, who was pitifully begging for guidance.

The corn horse was back in its place against the wall. Austin had finished the work he came to do. He turned to Oliver and, looking at him squarely now, said slowly, "Judy's left. Walked out."

"No!" Oliver exclaimed. He couldn't believe it.

"Yup. Gone to New York to find a job. Says she don't want to be nothing but a farmer's wife all her days. Now the children are out from under — "

Oliver thought of Loveday, how she had felt fulfilled for the first time when her husband died and she had a chance to prepare for a career. Loveday would understand Judy's impulse. But leaving Austin! Going to New York! Would Loveday approve of *that?*

All Oliver could think of to say was, "It's a hard life, thee knows, being a farmer's wife."

Austin waved this aside. "Never complained before," he argued bitterly. "Not even when she was taking care of Mom in her last illness. Always sweet and good-natured. What started it all was this group she was going to in Providence. Assertiveness, that's the word she learned there. Kept saying she had to exercise assertiveness. But I was always good to her, Oliver. Anything she wanted, if I could give it to her — What am I supposed to do?" he implored. "Can't just sell out because she wants the city."

Oliver saw the logic of this.

"What would I do in New York?" Austin demanded. "Born on the farm. Worked here all my life. Couldn't get a job in New York and the kids still need the money I send them regular. What am I supposed to do?" he repeated, begging for help.

Oliver's heart reached out to Austin but he said nothing. He was not going to speak until he had something really helpful to say. This was not a time for banal expressions of comfort, or for making judgments, but only for joining with Austin as he sought Truth.

"Give her time, Austin," he begged then. "She's entitled to

her life, just as thee is to thine. But she does love thee. I'm sure of that. Daphne was a member of the Committee on Clearness that met with Judy before your marriage. Maybe, when Judy has had time to consider her feeling for thee, when the excitement of the city wears off, she'll come home. Thee mustn't reproach her then. Just rejoice and enfold her in thy love."

Austin shook his head. "No," he said. "Judy won't come back. She's proud."

Oliver moved a step closer to Austin and looked at him earnestly, hoping that, in the companionship of silence, Austin would turn to his Inward Teacher for understanding.

"Stay and have supper with us," Oliver urged after this quiet interval.

Austin shook his head again. "Got chores," he said. Unable to control his emotions any longer, he turned away and left without a backward look, climbing into his truck after Kelly, turning on the ignition.

But then he leaned out of the cab. "Reason I told you," he said, "is, Judy's on that Yearly Meeting committee. She used to go to Cambridge for it. With her not going, there won't be no representative from Kendal."

"Bring it up at Monthly Meeting. We might appoint an alternate until Judy makes her intentions known."

Austin drove off and Oliver stood at the back door, watching the truck turn into the lane. Only then did he feel the full weight of the Youngs' difficulty.

He'd known them both since they were children. He and Daphne were Overseers at their wedding. With continuing concern, Oliver unobtrusively (he hoped) communicated his readiness to be of assistance to them in any eventuality. And yet, when the Youngs were in trouble, they hadn't told him.

What could he have done? Once people who've loved each other cease to enjoy being together, what can anyone do? Only grieve.

There was that in Oliver's nature which refused to accept the inevitability of decay in sacred relationships. He knew he couldn't have prevented the breakdown of their marriage, but perhaps if Austin and Judy had come to him and had felt his prayerful concern, they would have recalled their wedding, the wholeheartedness with which, in the presence of God and their friends, they promised each other to be loving and faithful *as long as they both should live.* Just recalling that might have rekindled their desire to be together. They'd certainly been loving and faithful for many years.

But what one promises with all one's heart in one's twenties, Oliver reflected sadly, doesn't necessarily obtain in one's fifties.

Was it wrong of a religious body to bestow its blessing on promises that might not be kept to term; that, judging by statistics, very likely wouldn't be?

Austin and Judy fell between two generations whose views on intimate relationships were poles apart. Their parents had been solid Quaker farm folk, who needed each other in order to survive. Their children, on the other hand, experimented with what they called alternative lifestyles, which were not necessarily based on the expectation of permanence. Caught between these two extremes, was it any wonder if Austin and Judy were in a muddle?

Oliver took care not to blame either one, even in his secret heart.

Love is a living being, he reminded himself. When it sickens and dies, we mourn. What was the cause of the disease, which party contracted it first, is immaterial. Autopsy won't bring love back to life.

Oliver only wondered wistfully why Judy should choose to leave her spouse when he, who wanted nothing more than to be with his, should be deprived. Judy still might come back. Daphne never would.

Standing there in the dooryard amidst the bronze and gold chrysanthemums — that charming little rock garden his grandmother had planted and Daphne painted year after year — Oliver reflected that a love characterized by lifelong constancy survives the bodies that contained it. No one mourns for love such as he and Daphne had been blessed with because it's immortal.

But what of this new awakening in him, the overpowering attraction of a woman with whom he couldn't hope to share such unity? And suppose — suppose by some miracle she were to reciprocate his feeling, would this new love, flowering in the autumn of life, survive the winter?

It suddenly struck Oliver that he'd never searched his heart for answers to these questions. He had been *playing* at being in love, concealing his feelings, the way he composed those letters to Heather, which he never put on paper.

Letters!

Serenity must be home by this time. She would have stopped at the bottom of the lane to pick up the mail. There might be a letter from Loveday — just a word to tell Oliver how she was getting on with her research. She'd never written to him, but maybe —

He entered the house and, without stopping to hang up his hat, rushed to his study. Yes, Serenity had put a big pile of letters on the desk. A quick glance told Oliver that they were all either bills or appeals.

He heaved a sigh.

But, he reasoned with himself, unless Loveday were planning another visit, what was there to communicate about? Their lives were so separate! For all Oliver knew, she might not even be in Boston any more.

She wouldn't have gone back to Kansas without finding out something to add to the family tree, would she? Without telling Oliver, without saying goodbye, at least?

Serenity was upstairs, giving Ross his bath. When she heard Oliver crossing the front hall on his way to the living room, she came rushing to the head of the stairs.

"Oliver," she cried, waving a sheet of paper, "look what I've got!"

He saw at once that something momentous had happened. Serenity hadn't been this ebullient since she went back to school. Now she was running down, leaving Ross, naked and plaintive, watching her from the landing.

Even before she reached Oliver, he recognized the letterhead of the Museum of Contemporary Art.

"It must be from Aquila Chase," he said.

"Yes," Serenity exclaimed, bubbling over with happiness. "Here, read it."

Oliver fished in his breast pocket for his glasses. He could feel the impatience this slight delay caused Serenity. So he passed over the salutation and read to himself as rapidly as he could:

You will recall that, at the time of Daphne Otis's death, a fund was established in her memory by various art lovers. This has been augmented by the proceeds from the sale of Oliver Otis's biography, which has enjoyed great success. The Museum Trustees voted on Wednesday to earmark this money for the appointment of a curator who would have charge of our Daphne Otis Collection.

Since you knew Daphne Otis well and contributed so greatly to the biography, it seems appropriate to offer this post to you before anyone else is considered. In view of your special competence, the Trustees are waiving the academic qualifications they would ordinarily require.

Oliver reached for the newel post to steady himself. Glancing briefly at Serenity, he saw his own joy reflected in her face. Then he read the last paragraph:

Could you come down to New York as soon as possible and

discuss this? If you need a place to stay, I can put you up.

All his life, Oliver had tried to accept adversity with grace. But good news undid him. And this letter overflowed with good news — the esteem in which Daphne was still being held; the success of his book; Serenity's incredibly wonderful opportunity.

"Isn't that something?" she exclaimed. "Me, a first-year graduate student — they want *me* in that museum!"

At the top of the stairs, Ross was howling.

Suddenly, Oliver saw beyond the splendor that had dazzled him when he read the Museum's offer.

"Peter," he murmured, looking from Ross to Serenity, whose face still glowed. "Won't he mind giving up his job? He was so happy to get it. Won't he mind?"

"For a chance like this?" Serenity cried. Then she turned gravely thoughtful, but only fleetingly. The elation returned to her face. "I can't wait to tell him. He'll be so excited. Thee knows how Peter loves me."

8.

SITTING at the round table in the cozy kitchen with Serenity and Peter on either side and Ross opposite, Oliver bent his head over the plastic cloth and silently gave thanks. His hunger for food was second to his hunger for loving companionship and the Hollands satisfied both. Gratitude overwhelmed him.

Serenity was holding his right hand and Peter his left in their habitual clasp before breaking bread — the reassuring touch of fellow pilgrims traveling through life along a road that is sometimes obscure and invariably hazardous.

Still bowing his head, he wondered what had happened while he was out in the chickenhouse collecting the eggs. Peter had come home. Serenity must have showed him the letter from the Museum. How did he react? It posed a threat to his future. For so young a man, Peter had attained a remarkable position in the University. If Serenity accepted the New York offer, Peter —

With an affectionate squeeze, they let Oliver's hands go.

He sent an appreciative smile across the table to Ross for observing the reverent silence. Ross ignored him. When Peter was home, he had eyes for no one else.

Little wonder, Oliver thought. There couldn't be a better father. I just wish he weren't so overworked.

These days, Peter's nice, friendly face constantly looked preoccupied and his bright yellow hair, which was a length Oliver found pleasing — not too short, not too long — always seemed to be parted in several places, as though Peter had just run his fingers through it in perplexity. Recalling how easygoing Peter had seemed when he first came to Firbank, Oliver asked himself, not for the first time, why young people should be so overburdened these days.

Then he remembered how troubled he and Daphne had been at that age, just after the First World War, when they were having difficulty coming to terms with a world that could tolerate the suffering they had witnessed in Europe.

Probably every generation has had to cope with some crisis, he concluded.

And, even with the pressures exerted on it, this was a rarely happy family. The parents were pursuing or preparing for the careers of their choice. The child was a joy — affectionate, alert, content.

That is, Oliver was obliged to add to his unspoken observations, he's content as long as one of us is with him. That sitter Serenity left him with early on did something so frightening, he's never got over his fear of strangers. He can't even tell us what happened.

It was a constant source of wonder and gratitude to Oliver that he should be included in the loving circle at this table. Instinctively he must have known when to be present and when to retire.

As he started eating, he thought with emotion that this was the time he'd been looking forward to all day — the opportune moment when he would confide his love. But before he could think of a way to lead up to the delicate subject, Peter announced that he was in a hurry to get back to the Observatory and Serenity fretted over her imminent exam. It hardly seemed timely for an old man to burden them with the state of his heart.

Savoring the delicious casserole Serenity had made, Oliver thought of Austin, alone at Periwinkle Farm, probably eating a can of hash in front of the television.

Serenity and Peter would have to be told about Judy. They'd take it hard. The Youngs had been Overseers at their wedding.

Overseers ought to maintain stable marriages themselves, Oliver reflected. If they are going to separate, what can we expect from others? When Daphne and I were married, older Friends could be relied on. They were formidable sometimes, but they practiced what they preached. They didn't ask us to make a promise they weren't going to keep themselves.

Peter had turned to Oliver. He was excited. "Thee saw the letter Rennie got from the Museum? Isn't that *something?* Even before she's finished school — Rennie has it made!"

His joy in her good fortune seemed to indicate that he was prepared to give up his own job so she could accept the offer. Just like Peter!

"It's not only what Miss Chase wrote about *me*," Serenity admonished him. "But about Oliver, too — the success of his book."

"*Our* book," Oliver corrected, beaming. "Without thee, I'd still be struggling. And to think that the Museum sees fit to appoint a special curator for the Otis Collection — what a tribute! If only Daphne could have known, when she was paralyzed and so discouraged, that some day her work would be appreciated to this extent."

He was tempted to tell Serenity how much it would please him to have the Collection entrusted to her but he kept still. She didn't appear to be taking the offer seriously and he didn't want to encourage her to do something that would endanger the unity of the family. It was unthinkable, but if Serenity were to go to New York and Peter hung on to his job here — why wouldn't he? — mightn't they end up like the Youngs?

The very supposition sent what felt like a chill through Oliver's heart. It reminded him of his disagreeable duty. He put down his fork and, in a low voice, reported that Judy had left home.

Far from being the shock he had anticipated, the news didn't make a ripple. It elicited no comment at all.

"I'm sure," Oliver said — someone had to say something — "she'll return soon."

Serenity shook her head. "No. She's taken a year's lease on an apartment."

So Serenity and Peter knew! They'd known all along. They hadn't told Oliver because they figured it would upset him. A year's lease! He really was upset.

"By the way," he managed to say, "Judy's been going to Cambridge to represent Kendal Friends on the Committee for Reviewing the Queries. We'll have to appoint someone else."

Peter scratched his head. "Alice Hill would be very good, or Clara Ludlow, or Lucas Lang."

But Oliver was still thinking of the Youngs' tragedy. "Austin seemed so surprised. I must say, *I* never dreamed Judy'd do anything like this. I knew she was unhappy. Austin's a good man, but his own mother told me before she died that he wasn't sensitive enough to Judy's needs. You remember how good she was to Mary Young, nursing her through that long illness. I never dreamed —"

"Judy!" Serenity exclaimed, as if hit by an idea. "That's where I'll stay when I go to New York — at her apartment. She'll take me in."

"Thee's *going?*" Peter asked incredulously.

"Of course! Thee doesn't think I'd turn down a chance like that?"

"It's terrific. But I didn't suppose thee'd really go. What for? Thee isn't seriously thinking of taking the job; is thee?"

Oliver waited breathlessly for Serenity's reply.

"How can I tell till I go to New York and find out more about it — exactly what they want me to do and how much they'll pay? Then we can talk it over — weigh your job against mine, decide which one to choose. I'll go right after my exams, the first day thee's free to take care of Ross. When can thee?"

"Not till vacation. I'm teaching every day."

"Vacation? I can't wait that long. They want me right away. Never mind. I'll take him with me, stop off in Neville and leave him with Mother and Daddy. They'll love it."

"Ross won't."

"No," Serenity admitted, "he won't." She frowned. "Wasn't for him, I guess I'd stay with Miss Chase. The Director of the Museum! A very successful woman. Who knows? Maybe some day I'll —"

"She doesn't have a child to look after," Peter pointed out, adding ruefully, "and a husband."

Ross was banging his empty bowl with a spoon.

"Does thee think," Serenity demanded, removing the bowl, "I can't look after my husband and child in New York as well as here?"

Whether she was angry or just bantering, Oliver couldn't make out. She certainly had her heart set on going.

Deprived of his percussion instrument, Ross started to howl.

"Look, Rennie," Peter said, trying to make himself heard above the racket. "I'm not going to stand in thy way. But I can't throw up my job." He leaned across the table and stretched out his arm to take Rennie's hand, pleading with his eyes for understanding. "It's the first security we've had. Besides, Professor Evans counts on me. How can I just walk out? New York — all that smog — one can't even see the stars. What would I do in New York?"

To Oliver, this last had a familiar ring. Barely an hour ago, Austin had asked the same question.

Letting Serenity's hand go, Peter got up and lifted Ross off his chair.

"Thee could take care of Ross," Serenity suggested, laughing. "Be the househusband."

Peter let this pass. He sat down again with a contented son curled in the crook of his arm.

Serenity seemed to be on the verge of tears. "I've waited so long," she complained. "Four years just to start grad school and now I have this chance — "

"Now thee wants to quit."

"Oh no."

"Rennie! How's thee going to combine going to school in Rhode Island with working in New York?"

"Maybe I could transfer."

Oliver tried to think of some excuse for leaving the table. The discussion was tearing him apart. The Hollands' dilemma might be more readily resolved without his presence. But they hadn't had dessert and he didn't want to make matters worse by interjecting his own discomfort.

This was a real impasse. Neither Peter nor Serenity was making an unreasonable demand, yet one of them would have to sacrifice a great opportunity. Could the strongest of marriages withstand such a tug of war?

I must have trust, Oliver said to himself with the fervor of prayer, trust that, when they meditate on this together, they'll have a leading.

Although Ross was quiet now, Peter still raised his voice. "Suppose, after a few months or even a year, thee decides thee doesn't like that setup — what then? We'll have nothing to live on."

"Not like working at the Museum of Contemporary Art? Why it's the most — "

"What will we do then?" Peter reiterated, disregarding her. "And Ross — what about him? He's used to the country, running around in safety everywhere."

"Kids grow up in the city, too," Serenity argued.

Then she faltered. Evidently, she hadn't considered any of the negative aspects attached to the offer. She'd been too dazzled. Now it was she who reached across the table, seeking Peter's hand.

Instead of giving it to her, Peter pushed back his chair and walked around the table with Ross in his arms. He plunked the child on Serenity's lap and, squatting beside her chair, put his arms around them both. "Thee's right," he said, his voice calm again. "It would be a mistake not to look into the offer. Thee go to New York. I'm sure Clara or Alice would help Oliver with Ross for a day or two. I'll be here at night."

Suddenly aware of Oliver, of what their leaving Firbank would mean to him, Serenity turned and said in a soft voice, "Thee — if we go, thee'll be alone again." Her eyes filled with tears.

Oliver reached out and gave her shoulder a pat. "I'll manage," he said, "same as before. My life has no bearing on thy decision. When you came here four years ago, we only expected the arrangement to last a few months. I've had so much more. I'm very grateful. But now, thee must do what's best for the three of you. Think it over."

Loveday, he thought, if she only returned my affection, we might — Then these dear children wouldn't feel responsible for me. But Loveday —

For all he knew, she was a thousand miles away. He'd never see her again.

Peter was clearing the table.

Putting Ross down on the floor, Serenity got up to fetch the dessert. On her way to the refrigerator, she stopped behind Oliver's chair and leaned over to kiss his bald spot.

"*Be still and cool,*" he murmured, looking up at her fondly. "*Be still and cool in thy own mind and spirit from thy own thoughts.*"

"Say!" Peter exclaimed, standing there with a plate in each hand. "That's beautiful. Did thee make it up or is it a quote?"

Oliver went to the shelf above the hutch where the devotional books from which they read after breakfast on First Days were ranged higgledy-piggledy amongst the cookbooks and took down George Fox's *Journal.*

He went back to his chair and hunted for the page from which he'd quoted. Peter and Serenity sat down, too, leaving the stewed pears she had dished out untouched, waiting for Oliver to read.

Just a few years ago, he'd have been able to locate the page at once. Every First Day, he and Daphne read a portion of the *Journal* aloud. The worn book often opened of its own accord at their favorite places. He used to be able to quote whole pages from memory. But now, Oliver couldn't seem to find Fox's letter to Lady Claypole.

Slowly thumbing through the book, he came to the page from which the phrase on the sampler was taken — that stirring exhortation Fox addressed to Friends from a Cornwall prison. It was one of Daphne's favorites. Today it seemed to clamor for Oliver's attention. He glanced up, hoping Serenity and Peter wouldn't mind if he read this to them first. It would take a little longer. No, he mustn't dally. They looked patiently, politely hurried. Later, when he was alone, he'd reread this passage. Putting his napkin between the leaves to mark the place, he moved on.

"Here it is," he announced, "the letter Fox wrote to Lady Claypole, Oliver Cromwell's daughter, because he'd heard she was troubled. *Be still and cool in thy own mind and spirit from thy own thoughts. Then thou wilt feel the principle of God to turn thy mind to*" — remembering how he had repeated these words over and over to comfort himself after Daphne's death, Oliver was so overcome with emotion that he had difficulty seeing — "*whereby thou wilt receive his strength and power from whence life comes, to allay all tempests —*"

The ring of the telephone interrupted the reading.

9.

SERENITY hurried to the front hall to answer the telephone. She stayed a long time.

Judging by Peter's expression and by the inclination of his head, Oliver concluded that he was trying unsuccessfully to determine with whom she was speaking. Did he fear it was Aquila Chase, following up her letter, urging Serenity to come?

"Can't be a toll call," Oliver assured him, as the conversation continued. "It's much too long."

Peter relaxed. "Must be one of her Kendal friends."

He's always cheerful and secure, Oliver reflected. Suddenly, a little piece of paper arriving in the mail makes him so nervous that some gossipy call frightens him. And why wouldn't it?

I'm going to tell them, Oliver decided. Soon as Serenity returns to the table, I'll tell them of my love, even if they're preoccupied.

He'd confide how profoundly this stirred him. Listening, they might become more conscious of their own love — its value and the danger of putting its strength to the test.

Peter seemed to have forgotten that he was in a hurry to leave. He lingered at the table, playing with the salt shaker. "Can't understand Judy," he was saying. "Always so concerned about people, the rights of minorities, so full of compassion for people she didn't even know. How could she treat her own husband like that? Wouldn't blame Austin if" — there was a trace of uneasiness in Peter's expression, as if he was afraid of shocking Oliver — "if he took up with someone else. What's a man to do when his wife up and leaves? I mean, Austin's still young enough. Maybe at thy age — "

"*Even* at my age," Oliver assured him. "I sympathize with Austin. One never outgrows the wish to be loved."

Certainly not in his own case, Oliver thought. But Peter had no way of knowing. More than ever, Oliver regretted not having confided his secret earlier. He'd do it as soon as Serenity returned.

"How could she treat her own husband like that?" Peter asked him again.

Envisaging the effect of the announcement he would make — if Serenity ever got through talking — Oliver couldn't think of a suitable answer. He simply repeated what he'd said to Austin: "Thee knows, it's hard, being a farmer's wife."

The commonplace remark called up a picture in Oliver's mind of a woman so overworked that she had lost all her charm and initiative. To his intense surprise, the picture wasn't of

Judy Young, who clearly had plenty of initiative left. It was of Loveday.

How, he asked himself, could I expect *her* —

The connection startled him. What did Loveday have to do with this? A *farmer's* wife?

Peter was recalling the summer he worked for Austin, before he and Serenity were married.

Oliver barely heard him. He had just had a revelation and it was staggering.

All along, he told himself, aghast, I've been denying that I wish to marry Loveday. Tonight, for the first time — *Do I wish to? Do I really?* Have my denials been a gross deception? I shouldn't have written those misleading letters to Heather, not even in thought.

"Funny," Peter observed now, "the way things happen. That summer, when I was driving Austin's tractor, learning what it's like to be a potato farmer, he kept telling me thee ought to sell out."

This brought Oliver's attention back fast.

"*I* ought to? Sell *Firbank?*"

"He said the farm was getting too much for thee. And now, five years later, thee's still here, doing fine, but Austin's the one who may have to sell out. If Judy insists on staying in New York, what else can he do?"

Trust Peter, steadfast Peter, to believe that love would endure, whatever sacrifices it might require!

"The farm *was* a bit much for me," Oliver conceded, "till thee and Serenity came here to live. With the help you've given me, things have gone very well. It wouldn't have been so difficult if, while I was still recovering from the shock of Daphne's death, I hadn't been given the chance to write. All my life, I'd been wanting to, but when I was asked to write two things at once — an article for a scientific journal and a full-length book — I was out of my depth."

"Lucky thing for us both," Peter put in, "that Professor Anselm offered me the fellowship. Just the same, it was too much. Thee got sick."

"Yes. But I never would have sold out. How could I allow these acres, which have been in our family for generations, to be broken up into building lots or covered with concrete for a shopping mall? Peter, imagine our generous garden being bulldozed, the orchard and the Firbank woods cut down!"

Serenity was still on the telephone. But Peter looked less tense.

Unwittingly, Oliver had given him comfort by declaring that, whatever happened, Firbank would remain in the family, a place of refreshment and peace, a place one could always return to if one was obliged to leave.

Oliver's own anxiety eased. Peter and Serenity's devotion to each other and their sense of belonging somewhere would bring them through this crisis, somehow.

"And the Vietnamese Forest," he exclaimed, "where thee and I worked so hard — if I sold Firbank, all our labor would have been in vain. We can't apply the formula we discovered, as I had hoped, but — who knows? — it may still be of use somewhere, if," he added bitterly, "men keep on killing other men's vegetation."

His mind jumped from the agony of that war, now thankfully a thing of the past, to the soul-searching of the young Quakers who were presently facing registration for another military draft. What was he doing to support those whose consciences prevented them from complying? Old though he was, didn't he, who had suffered in the same cause, have a duty to stand beside them? But this wasn't the moment to face that question.

Peter was looking at him intently. "I remember," he said, speaking softly because Ross was beginning to stir, "after Rennie'd been here the first time, she came back to college starry-eyed about thee and Daphne. Thee had secretly put thy grand-mother's beautiful, leather-bound copy of Woolman's *Journal* in her book bag for a present. She didn't discover it till she unpacked. Does thee remember that?"

Oliver remembered Serenity's first visit to Firbank very well. The Woolman passages he'd quoted to her at the time had contrasted sharply with the artificial world from which she came. The experience had shaken her. She wanted to bring Peter. They longed to live at Firbank. When Ross was born, the two of them had only one desire: to stay here and rear him in the harmony, simplicity and devotion to Truth that the place had evoked for them.

"We were both gung ho about the *Journal*," Peter recalled, "always reading bits aloud to each other at college. Thee'd told Rennie how thee and Daphne discovered it when you were first married, how you made a pilgrimage — that's what we wanted to do, too. You were coming back from that pilgrimage to take a job thee didn't like, just to make money so thee could write in thy spare time. You were eating sandwiches near the lighthouse at the mouth of the Connecticut River when Daphne asked why you couldn't stay at Firbank and run the farm."

Oliver laughed. "Yes, and I exclaimed, '*Me?* Farm?' I didn't say, 'Me, a Harvard man,' but farming was the last thing I'd ever thought of doing."

They were both chuckling over this when Serenity returned from the telephone.

"It's for thee," she told Oliver. "Loveday."

Like that she told him, after chatting so long. "It's for thee — Loveday," as if it were just anybody calling him. Shouldn't she have shouted to him to come, the minute she heard that melodious voice?

Oliver jumped up with the alacrity of a young man. "Calling from *Kansas*?"

"Boston."

10.

WHEN HE REACHED the telephone, Oliver felt speechless.

It didn't matter. A hundred miles away — only a hundred, not a thousand — Loveday's greeting vibrated with excitement.

"Rennie told me the news."

"About the Youngs?"

"No, she didn't say anything about the Youngs. She told me she's been offered a terrific job in New York."

"Oh, that."

"It's marvelous. To think, Oliver — she doesn't even have a Master's! And in the present job market — You must be delighted."

"Well, it's taken us all by surprise."

There was a pause.

"I see," Loveday said more slowly. "It didn't occur to me till now. I should have thought of it — your life will be greatly altered by their leaving Firbank."

"I'll manage," Oliver tried to say with assurance, though it didn't come out sounding quite that way, "same as before. But Peter and Ross — they're the ones who're going to suffer."

"It's Rennie's turn, Oliver. High time she had a chance." Then Loveday changed the subject. Her tone changed, too. She sounded absolutely jubilant. "Reason I called — I just had to tell you — something's happened to me. Something wonderful."

Oliver's heart plummeted. She wasn't announcing her engagement, was she? Why had he been so slow?

"It's what I secretly wished for all these years, never thinking it would really happen some day. Now, it's going to!"

Why was I so slow? Oliver reproached himself bitterly.

"I'm going to write a book!" Loveday declared with such exuberant anticipation that Oliver, greatly relieved, thought she couldn't begin to know what travail lay before her. "Tomorrow I'm going to write the first chapter. I had to tell you."

She had to tell *him!*

Weak with relief, he somehow found it possible to voice his confidence in her literary ability, about which he actually knew nothing. She'd never even written him a letter.

"The way it came about," she continued, "I had lunch with one of my former students who works in a publishing house here. When I told her about the research I was doing, she said Nannerl's story ought to be written up. How else will the world ever know that Nannerl was somebody in her own right, not just the great Mozart's colorless sister? Of course, we can't be sure anyone will publish it. I have to write the book to find out."

While Oliver was felicitating Loveday on her enterprise, she changed the subject again. He was having trouble keeping up with her.

"I don't know if Rennie told you — she's going to New York for an interview and she's worried about Ross. She doesn't want you doing more for him than you already do and Peter isn't cooperating."

"He can't stay home, Loveday. He's teaching. As a former dean, thee — I mean, you — should understand."

"Yes, I know. That's why I offered to come. *I'm* going to be the babysitter."

"Oh!" That was all Oliver was capable of saying. She was coming!

"Do you mind? It's just to help Rennie out."

Mind? He was in heaven! But, just to help Serenity —
wasn't she coming for his sake, too?

"Mind?" he repeated stupidly. "It'll be first-rate. I'll be delighted." In honesty he felt obliged to add, "Ross is the one
who'll mind."

This didn't discourage Loveday. "That's all right. He may
be a little sticky at first but we'll get along."

Overcome with joy, Oliver had a boyish impulse to declare
to the faceless telephone what he didn't believe he could ever
acknowledge in Loveday's presence — the full state of his heart.
Only, Loveday was ringing off.

She's coming, she's coming! he sang to himself as he hurried back to tell the Hollands, tell them everything.

The kitchen was empty.

Peter must have left for the Observatory. Overhead, footsteps told Oliver that Serenity was tucking Ross in. The kitchen
he loved looked desolate and uninviting. It was nothing but a
repository for dirty dishes, a dump for the debris of a meal
from which satiated diners had withdrawn.

No one was there to share his joy. But at the west window,
the setting sun shed tinges of splendor on the ruffled curtains, drawing Oliver outside to witness the ball of fire sinking
into Little Narragansett Bay.

He walked down the path for a last glimpse of the pond.

How close he'd come to declaring the state of his heart
over the telephone! Had Loveday not begun to ring off at that
moment, what would he have said? That he loved her — yes.
Would she have inferred that he was proposing marriage? Nothing was further from his intention. For a moment, at dinner,
he'd speculated that Serenity and Peter wouldn't have to feel
responsible for him any more if Loveday returned his affection.
But Loveday didn't. And anyway, as he'd assured Heather in

those imaginary letters, he was simply being moony, nothing more. *Marriage? At his age?* Out of the question!

In the gathering dusk, only the outline of the dunes appeared, silhouetted against the red sky. Out at sea, the lighthouses were already at work. Oliver visualized them, one by one: Fisher's Island, Little Gull, Montauk in the west; Block Island to the south; Point Judith in the east.

All his life, he'd looked to those lighthouses for comfort and direction. They had piloted him into harbor when he sailed home after dark. Their very constancy had communicated itself to him. They could be counted on in fair weather or foul, in blizzards and haze, even in the fogs that often blanketed this coast, when the doleful signals gave sailors their bearings. One might not be able to see the lights, but they were there.

No one to share his joy? How could he have thought that for an instant? Loveday was still in New England! Northeastward, beyond Point Judith, she was there, getting ready to come to Firbank!

What more could he possibly wish for?

He didn't stay to watch the twilight deepen, for he suddenly remembered the passage that he hadn't had time to reread at supper — the exhortation to Friends, which Fox wrote when he and his companions were imprisoned in Cornwall for refusing to take off their hats in the presence of a magistrate — an honor they reserved for God.

Oliver turned and, whistling to the dogs, who were reconnoitering among the reeds, walked up the path again. From time to time, he stood still, so little Duffy could catch up.

Back in the kitchen, Oliver switched on the light. The book, with the napkin inserted in the place he wanted to reread, was still lying on the table, surrounded by dirty dishes. Serenity no doubt planned to clean up later, after she'd finished studying. But with an exam tomorrow, she needed sleep. Rolling up his sleeves, Oliver went to the sink, ran the hot water awhile, then happily dabbled his fingers in the soapsuds.

Shaking them dry, he went over to the table to collect the dessert plates. But he couldn't resist picking up the *Journal* first, pulling out the napkin and putting on his glasses. The book opened to the place from which the words on the sampler were taken.

Standing there, scanning the page — just for a second! — Oliver suddenly felt his heart soar. For his eye had lit on the name he'd been trying to remember — *Hambly*. Loveday Hambly! That's where he'd heard the name Loveday before — it belonged to one of Fox's earliest followers. The news of the Quakers' persecution had spread across Cornwall. Instead of acting as a deterrent, it drew to the prison those men and women who were longing for a religion they could truly believe in. They wanted to hear Fox speak. Among them was Loveday Hambly.

Forgetting the dishes, Oliver read, *And hearing the sound of Truth, she and her sister came afterwards to visit us in prison and were convinced. They have gone through great sufferings and spoiling of goods for Truth's sake.*

The whole story of Loveday Hambly came back to Oliver now — how her cows were taken away because she refused to pay tithes for the support of a clergy that did not speak to her condition; how she herself was imprisoned. Her home became the center of Quakerism in that part of England.

About this time, Fox continued in his *Journal, I was moved to give forth the following exhortation: be patterns, be examples in all countries, places, islands, nations, wherever you come, that your carriage and life may preach among all sorts of people, and to them. Then you will come to walk cheerfully over the world, answering that of God in every one; whereby in them ye may be a blessing, and make the witness of God in them to bless you.*

Still holding the book, Oliver stood there a long time, gazing out beyond the curtains into the darkness, watching the Fisher's Island light flash across the water.

To walk cheerfully over the world — This is no frolic, he thought, freshly aware of the sobering words. It's no light-hearted stroll through life but the ultimate demand on one's humanity. To speak, not with words but with one's character; to uncover beneath their ego-needs that divine spark which ignites *all sorts* of people — the unlovable as well as the lovely. And *answering* — uncovering the spark in one's self. To bless and thus be blessed.

It's no frolic, he repeated to himself. But in those rare instances when one finds strength to walk erect that way — what good cheer!

The magnificent prose reverberating through his being, the discovery of that other Loveday — the "Quaker saint of Cornwall," as she was called — and, above all, the foretaste of the living Loveday's coming raised his spirits to heights they hadn't attained in years.

She's coming! he sang to himself.

He couldn't wait to tell her about her namesake. Wouldn't she be pleased!

But his elation was not unspoiled. His conscience took care of that. The letter to Heather — he should have finished it this morning.

As he worked his way through the dishes, it suddenly struck him that now he had something of importance to put in that letter. Heather would be very much interested in Serenity's job offer and all the changes it portended for Firbank.

The moment he finished cleaning up, he went to his study and turned on the light. This morning, he hadn't been able to think of anything to say. Now his thoughts came faster than his fingers could type.

She plans to spend two days in New York next week being

interviewed, he wrote. *Peter has classes, so he can't take care of Ross, but a new friend of the family has generously offered to come and help. I hope Ross won't prove difficult. Thee knows how he hates being cared for by strangers. Anyhow, thee needn't worry about my doing too much.*

Our friend has been here a few times this summer. She is a widow, the retired dean of a college in Emporia, Kansas, who has been doing research at Harvard for a book she plans to write.

The aerogram was pretty well filled up by now. Oliver sent his love to Stephen and the children and signed off, neatly creasing the form.

He would have liked to think that it was his conscience, which all along had been troubled because he was holding out on Heather, that made him add a postscript, just as he was on the point of licking the gummed flap. But devotion to truth made him admit, even as he wrote, that what prompted him was the pleasure he took in writing about Loveday.

She's a charming woman, good company. When she's here, I feel whole, as I haven't felt since Mother went. Nothing to worry about, dear. Thee knows thy father isn't a foolish old man.

PART TWO

Loveday

1.

BETWEEN PERRYTOWN and Kendal, a double row of maples lines the Post Road for six-tenths of a mile. Just beyond the maples, on the left, a side road branches off, zig-zagging till it nears the upper end of Salt Pond. Little more than a sandy trail covered with broken scallop shells, it peters out in front of a rural mailbox marked Firbank Farm. From there, a narrow lane leads up to the house.

Loveday had no trouble locating the side road. This was her fourth trip to Firbank.

The place had beckoned her back ever since she left it. Impatient to get there, she began watching for the maples as soon as she drove through Perrytown, though she knew they were still miles off. She was only at the old grist mill, where Oliver took his corn to be ground between stones for the johnnycake Loveday liked so much.

When the maples finally appeared and she started to drive under the leafy arch, she caught her breath. The arch was a portal through which, on previous visits, she had passed into a world of unsuspected enchantment.

The first time she came, it was midsummer. She found herself proceeding under a thick, green canopy without a chink of sky. Now, sunlight filtered through leaves that were scarlet, gold and lemon-yellow. Where the foliage had begun to thin, patches of cloudless blue pierced the canopy and shimmered like a Madonna's robe. Just so had the radiance of stained glass in Chartres Cathedral taken Loveday's breath away.

She had had the same feeling of transcendence last year in Salzburg, when, after climbing three flights of stone stairs, she stood in the room where Mozart was born. There was his spinet, his baby violin. There in that room, it all began — the glorious music that irradiated Loveday's life.

Only, in Salzburg, she knew the outcome of the story — the events that unfolded so dramatically, from the birth in that very room to the end in a pauper's grave — whereas, passing under the arch of maples between Perrytown and Kendal, she was entering a world in which everything that happened came as a surprise.

Jewels of leaves fell carelessly onto the hood of the car. Leaning out of the window, Loveday laughed as whirls of color, blowing past, almost touched her cheek. Then she reproached herself for letting her tires mash the red carpet, flecked with gold, that had been rolled out in welcome.

Oliver once told her that the Highway Department had intended to cut down those trees and widen the road so cars could whiz by two abreast.

"The most magnificent maples in the State of Rhode Island!" he'd declared indignantly. "Local inhabitants protested, but the authorities paid no attention. On the drawing board, the project looked perfect to those city planners. All that nice macadam instead of some useless old trees!"

With relish, Oliver had described what happened early one morning when the authorities assumed the protesters would still be asleep. Climbers arrived in trucks with bucket saws, only to be greeted by a crowd of neighbors who'd kept watch half the night. They were embracing the trunks of the trees so resolutely that the Department was forced to conclude that if it wished to accommodate speeders, it would have to commit mass murder.

Oliver didn't say that he was among those who had risked their own limbs to save the trees. But, impatient though she was, Loveday slowed up a little and scanned each trunk, wondering which one he had thrown his arms around in protective devotion.

The world she was entering, she thought happily, as she felt the scallop shells crunch beneath the car — this world was unlike any she'd ever known, one she'd supposed existed only in romantic novels — the kind nobody read any more — a world in which goodness took precedence over success and gentleness prevailed.

At Firbank, there was an almost palpable beauty. There was calm, not inactivity — the place was a beehive — but an awareness of unfailing security, though the doors were never locked. And yet, the man who communicated all this was completely human, chock-full of idiosyncrasies — plenty of those in Oliver! — brimming over with humor and, at the same time, possessed of a self-knowledge that awed Loveday. Firbank was a revelation, the antithesis of the world she'd frantically pushed through during all her working life.

Returning had become almost an obsession. Loveday had difficulty understanding why. She only knew that the desire was so strong that she would have done almost anything to realize it.

After the first five minutes there, she was always "snowed," as the youngsters at college used to say. (What was the current term? Now that she was retired, her slang vocabulary was out of date.)

Would Firbank be the same for her this time? How long can enchantment last?

She'd been sitting in her furnished apartment on Beacon Hill in Boston, trying to think of some excuse for inviting herself again, wondering whether it would be impertinent to call Oliver on the pretext of sharing some news. The interest that Mary Day, her former student, had shown in Nannerl's story seemed sufficient. Actually, Mary, who was now an editor, had had reservations. Although she listened, fascinated, when Loveday recounted a few of the incidents in Nannerl's life, she observed that Loveday was an historian and she doubted whether a scholar could write biography in a style that would entertain the general reader. But Loveday didn't have to go into all this when she telephoned to Oliver. During the conversation, he might, in his cordial way, take the occasion to invite her.

Things had turned out far better than Loveday expected. To use Oliver's quaint phrase, "way opened" for her. Rennie answered the phone. Before Loveday had a chance to present her flimsy excuse for calling, Rennie poured out the details of *her* situation — her great job offer and the difficulties it had raised. Rennie's predicament gave Loveday a perfect opening and she grabbed it. She'd go to Firbank and babysit!

Not only did this provide just the opportunity Loveday had been wishing for; it also gave her a chance to back Rennie in the struggle with those two men, who couldn't seem to grasp how much a young woman needs a life of her own. Over the telephone, Loveday could hear the gratitude in Rennie's voice when way opened for her, too. Ross would be in good hands.

But, Loveday wondered, now that she was nearly there, would she be up to it? People were always commenting on how young she looked. As a matter of fact, she was unusually well and energetic for her age. Still, there were times when those aches and pains that come with age unexpectedly gripped her — nothing major, just enough to make her aware that no matter how young she might seem, in actuality —

Was she up to taking care of a small boy?

Her grandmotherly experience — that phase that demanded physical strength — went back several years now. Michael and

Jed, the youngest of the grandchildren, were almost teenagers and didn't need anyone's assistance, except with their homework.

What would Ross be like? On her previous visits, he had still feared her. Would he take to her this time? Oliver adored him and if Loveday failed to win over the child, she'd lose Oliver's esteem.

Well, how much was there to lose? He was gracious, listening to Loveday with that extraordinary interest, as if what she were saying mattered wholly to him. But he listened that way to everyone. She'd observed, when neighbors dropped in, how well he remembered events in everyone's life, how he inquired about those who were ill, how touchingly he spoke to the children. Although he always looked at her with a warmth that, in another man, might have signified special affection, Loveday Mead really meant no more to Oliver Otis than anyone else. And she knew it.

So how much of his esteem was there to lose? And why did she care?

It wasn't, she assured herself, Oliver but the whole ambience of Firbank that attracted her — the old white farmhouse that seemed to be part of the surrounding countryside rather than dumped on it, the silo in back, the red barn. Her discovery of the place had been altogether an accident, so unlikely that it seemed almost to have been preordained, except that Loveday didn't believe in things like that.

No, I didn't discover Firbank, she thought. It discovered me. I didn't even know what I was getting into when it suddenly reached out and took hold of me, just the way Nannerl did when I stepped out of the bus in St. Gilgen and saw her in bas-relief on that house.

As she followed the winding road, feeling the crunch of the shells beneath her wheels, she remembered how reluctantly she had driven down to Rhode Island on that hot afternoon in August to look up her ancestors in the University library. Sara Ann had been asking about this in every letter.

No one else in the family had ever expressed any interest. It was curious that an in-law should be the person who wished to reconstruct the family history rather than one of her own children. They were such here-and-now people, untouched by that fascination with the past which motivated their mother.

No wonder they look bored when I ramble on about Nannerl! But I wish they took more interest.

Arriving at the library, Loveday found she'd picked the wrong afternoon. The reference librarian was out and the one who listened to her request was either new or incompetent.

After thumbing through the card catalog for a few minutes, the librarian gave up. "Sorry I can't be of more assistance. Quaker genealogy — well, we seldom have any call for that nowadays. I wouldn't know where — Our reference librarian had to leave early — a family emergency. If you'll come in to-morrow, maybe she can help. I'm a cataloguer and don't know."

"Tomorrow! I'm just here for the afternoon. Drove all the way down from Boston especially." At college, Loveday hadn't been in the habit of accounting for her actions to members of the staff, only to the president and trustees. So it surprised her when she heard herself practically apologizing to this little librarian for being late. "There was a traffic jam coming out of Boston or I would have been here sooner."

"Oh, Route One Twenty-eight!" the cataloguer had exclaimed, rolling her eyes. Here was a subject she did know something about. "Isn't it *awful?*"

At that point, something very like a miracle occurred. A young redhead came over and offered to help.

"This is Mrs. Mead," the cataloguer told her, repeating what she'd just been told herself. "From — " But the woman had already forgotten the name of the college Loveday had mentioned in the hope of getting attention in a university where she wasn't known. This maneuver had opened doors at Harvard. Surely here —

The cataloguer had already forgotten. "From — "

"William Allen White College in Emporia, Kansas," Loveday said with dignity.

"That's it! I knew it was somewhere out west."

"I was the Dean of Studies."

"Oh."

The woman began to look impressed.

Loveday didn't enjoy acting this way, but life had taught her that if you want things, you have to pull rank.

The cataloguer covered up her embarrassment by trying to make a joke when she introduced the redhead as Rennie Holland, a graduate student. Giggling, she added, "I should have said *Serenity* Holland, but we never call her that."

Just because the woman wasn't familiar with the name, she seemed to think it funny.

Loveday immediately felt for the redhead. They had a bond. Her own name sometimes amused people. Going around with a name like that, they implied, one must be queer. And so Loveday said quickly, "What a beautiful name! We all could do with a little serenity."

She thought this Serenity — or would she prefer to be called Rennie? — unusually attractive, with that head of red curls and blue eyes that seemed maturely thoughtful. It would have been unfortunate if the name hadn't fitted, but she did look more serene than most of her contemporaries.

"Excuse me for eavesdropping," she was saying, "but I couldn't help overhearing what you asked Miss Mustard and I think my cousin might know. He's a Quaker and he's lived in South County most of his life. Chances are, he knows about your family. Anyhow, if he doesn't have it himself, he probably can tell you where to get the information. Why don't you come home with me for dinner?"

A total stranger! Inviting Loveday!

If she had had anything better to do that evening, she would have refused the invitation out of hand. But that dreary apartment didn't draw her back to Boston.

While Loveday was considering whether she should accept, the librarian gushed, "Yes! Mr. Otis is the person to tell you." She sounded relieved. Hunting for stuff she knew nothing about would have held her up. "I know Mr. Otis," she assured Loveday. "He comes in here all the time. Charming old gentleman."

Loveday wasn't interested in old gentlemen, charming or otherwise. She was after historical data and she knew that eighteenth-century records were preserved in libraries. It was unlikely that what she wanted would be in private hands.

"Is he an historian?" she asked this Rennie.

"No, he farms."

That didn't sound very promising. Refusing to commit herself, playing for time, Loveday had asked, "Where does he live?"

"At Firbank, about forty miles from here. It really isn't anywhere. I mean, not near any town, just Kendal. That's so small, you probably never heard of it."

"No. But then, I'm not a New Englander."

"Would you mind leaving now? I was about to go home. Oliver's taking care of my little boy and I want to relieve him. Do you have a car?"

"Yes."

But Loveday hadn't yet agreed to go, had she?

"You'd better follow my bug. It's rather tricky finding the way after you turn off the Post Road."

If Loveday had had anything better to do that evening, she

certainly wouldn't have gone deep into the country with a perfect stranger in order to consult an old farmer about her ancestors.

And if she hadn't gone, if she had missed that chance, if because of a theater ticket or some trifling social engagement she had refused the invitation and had driven back to Boston —

My whole life, she told herself solemnly as she passed the mailbox and chugged up the lane, my whole life would have been different.

2.

ON THIS, her fourth visit to Firbank, Loveday hadn't even set foot in the place before she was snowed. The enchantment already overtook her when she drove up to the old house. Touched softly with the rose of the setting sun, it looked slightly mysterious, as though almost anything might happen inside. There were maples here, too, huge ones at each corner of the house, framing it in clouds of color. And there, standing in the doorway, was Oliver.

The dogs came rushing down the porch steps to give Loveday a wild reception.

As she drew up beside the old horse block and stopped the motor, it dawned on her that, with all its beauty, Firbank wasn't what drew her back so forcefully. Reaching for the ignition, she felt this amazing discovery burst upon her: it wasn't Firbank; it was Oliver.

Tall and erect, he ran down the steps and hurried toward her.

She noticed at once the uncommon aliveness in his face, which had struck her the first time she saw him. This vitality, the outward expression of his inward life, was unlike anything in Loveday's experience.

The realization that it was Oliver and not the place she was drawn to proved so upsetting that Loveday lost her poise. Instead of returning his greeting, she blurted out, "Where's Ross?"

Those were Loveday's first words on her fourth visit to Firbank. What a betrayal of anxiety!

Opening the car door, Oliver answered, smiling down on her reassuringly, "He's upstairs with Serenity."

"Oh, hasn't she left? I thought — "

"She's going tomorrow morning." Then, as he always did when Loveday arrived, Oliver said cordially, "Welcome to Firbank. I hope you had a good trip." He lifted her bag out of the car.

She found herself standing in the driveway, taking his outstretched hand, meeting his eyes, which were unmistakably joyful. She'd forgotten how blue they were — vivid, like a much younger man's. But then she looked down stupidly at the weeds growing between the sandy ruts of the driveway, as if nothing mattered so much as crabgrass.

Loveday wanted to tell Oliver about the splendor of the maples on the Post Road, about the red carpet flecked with gold. Had he, she thought of asking playfully in order to hide her embarrassment, rolled it out for her? Yet no words came.

As he stood aside to let her pass through the door, she wondered, What's the matter with me? Am I getting the flu or something? I've always been comfortable here, self-possessed. Suddenly I act like a teenager. Me — Dean Mead — shy and ill at ease!

Then the gracious entrance hall enfolded her and she felt better.

Rennie was coming down the stairs, followed by Ross, humming happily. As they rounded the curve at the top, Loveday could see his red curls bobbing above the banister. Then she glimpsed his face and caught her breath.

Ethereal, she thought, remembering her own children at three.

Ross didn't see her, perhaps because his mother was coming down ahead of him, perhaps because some inner vision pre-occupied him. As he reached the bottom, Loveday stepped forward and bent down to kiss him.

Sudden fear stiffened the little body. It wriggled away and hid behind Rennie.

"Oh," Loveday murmured. "I shouldn't have rushed him."

"Are you the babysitter?" Ross asked tremulously, barely peeking out.

Loveday laughed. "The babysitter? *Me?* I'm just —"

But hadn't she told Oliver on the telephone that she was coming to be the babysitter? With Oliver standing right there beside her, how could she deny it now? He had told her frankly that Ross would mind her coming so it really didn't surprise her.

What did shock her was Rennie's greeting.

"Hi," she murmured coldly.

Even Lion and Duffy had expressed greater enthusiasm, receiving Loveday as though she were the friend of the family she felt she had come to be.

Rennie's greeting was more like a rebuff. It sounded as if she wished Loveday hadn't come. Ordinarily, she was happy to see her. Didn't she want to go to New York, after all? On the telephone, she'd been dying to.

Usually, she carried Loveday's bag upstairs, but this afternoon Rennie excused herself, saying she had to go down to Four Corners for gas. The station wouldn't be open yet when she left in the morning.

While she spoke to Loveday, Ross kept pulling at her jeans

Time he stopped being such a baby, Loveday thought, an
noyed.

Oliver patted Rennie's shoulder and told her to take her
time. He would see Loveday to her room.

"By the way," he added, "if thee should speak to Judy
when thee's in New York, ask her whether she wishes to be
replaced on the Committee to Review the Queries. It convenes in Cambridge tomorrow evening and Kendal Meeting
won't be represented. Once the Meeting knows that Judy
definitely isn't going to serve any more, it can appoint someone else."

"Okay."

Rennie moved toward the door but Oliver seemed to be
detaining her with his eyes, as if he had more on his mind.

"Is Judy in touch with her children?" he asked hesitantly.

"Yes. They want her to go back to Austin. I don't think she
will."

Rennie took Ross resolutely by the hand and started out
the door again.

"Oh, and, Serenity," Oliver called after her, "ask Judy
whether she'd like me to come and see her."

This stopped Rennie. "Thee means — thee means thee'd
go all the way to New York?"

"Why not? I can take the train. But I don't want to go
unless she'd like to see me. I keep thinking about her — how
she must miss Friends."

Rennie looked touched by the offer. "I've been thinking
that, too."

Carrying the bag, Oliver led the way upstairs and across
the landing to the ell, explaining a bit breathlessly about the
Youngs' situation.

"Doesn't surprise me too much," he admitted as he ushered
Loveday into the little room she had occupied before. "Mary

Young, Austin's mother, worried a good deal about Judy. Just before Mary died, she told me how lovingly this daughter-in-law took care of her. Judy said nursing gave her a feeling of doing something for someone in need, while much of what she did on the farm might just as well be done by a machine. So now she's left."

Instinctively, Loveday sided with this Judy, whom she didn't even know. Why should anyone do meaningless work?

But Oliver seemed baffled. "What," he asked, looking a little embarrassed, "what do you think she really wants? Her husband asked me. I thought you might know. I confess, to me, the marriage would have seemed more important than anything else."

"You men just can't understand how a woman feels."

It was clear from his expression that indeed Oliver couldn't understand that particular woman. Loveday saw no point in prolonging the discussion. She smiled at him to indicate that, while they didn't agree, they were still friends.

The room was exactly the way she remembered it back in Boston, when she sat by the telephone, trying to think of some excuse for calling Oliver in the hope that he'd invite her.

The ell was the oldest part of the house. Some of the beams had settled so that the floor sloped disconcertingly. But once she got her balance, Loveday found this delightfully familiar. The brass bedstead, the diminutive fireplace, the sketches that covered the walls — portraits of a little girl at six months, at a year, at three or four — all were precisely as she remembered.

Oliver laid the bag on the luggage rack and started to leave.

"Is this your daughter?" Loveday inquired, pointing to the sketches.

He stood still on the threshold and turned. "Yes. Daphne did those more than fifty years ago. Since then, the grandchildren have slept in this room, when Heather brought them over. Now those children are grown." Backing into the hall, he added, "Heather paid us a lovely visit in July. I must be patient now till next summer."

Loveday was curious about Heather. "Does she resemble you?"

"Who? Heather? Oh, no! She's good-looking."

So are you, Loveday almost exclaimed. But he might think it fresh.

He already seemed uneasy. Was it because they were conversing in the bedroom? Maybe it was improper of her to be holding him up. But she didn't want him to go.

"Well," Oliver conceded, "she's tall, like me, and has the Otis hair — red and curly, like Serenity's. That is, Heather's *was* red. It's silver now. Gracious! The window's still open. I'd better shut it for you. It sticks."

He came in again.

Loveday stood in the middle of the room, watching him struggle with the antique sash.

From the back, she thought, one never would guess his age, he carries himself so beautifully.

But it was more than his carriage that distinguished him. It was his bearing, the combination of dignity and humility. To Loveday, these had always seemed mutually exclusive. In Oliver they were clearly intertwined. The sense of personal worth that gave him such striking dignity actually seemed to spring from his humility of spirit.

Turning from the window he suddenly looked at Loveday with a light in his eyes that she'd never seen before. Her heart lurched. It was almost as if he had the impulse to come toward her and take her in his arms.

Of course, Oliver did no such thing. It was just Loveday's crazy imagination. In reality, he walked right past her to the door.

Her heart kept jumping. Was it because she had imagined — Or was something wrong? Last time she was here, her heart had done the same thing. She ought to see about it. With her family history, she shouldn't disregard these symptoms.

About to close the door behind him, Oliver popped his head in again.

Loveday felt better.

"I forgot —" Oliver said apologetically without coming in. "In the excitement of seeing you again, I forgot to ask about your book. Ever since you telephoned, I've been thinking about it, wondering how it's progressing."

Loveday looked at the sloping floor. "Well, you see, it isn't a book — not yet. I'm only just collecting material. I don't quite know when to stop going to the library. Sometimes I wish Nannerl hadn't laid this on me. Some day, I'll have to settle down and start writing. It's a temptation just to go on and on with the research."

Oliver nodded knowingly. "And never write a word," he added, opening the door wide. "At some point one has to discipline oneself to begin." Sounding reluctant to leave, he murmured, "Any time you're ready, come down. I'll be in the living room. But don't hurry. Dinner isn't till six-thirty."

"Can I help?"

"I think Serenity has everything under control."

He started to go a second time, but now Loveday detained him.

"She doesn't seem pleased to see me. Has she changed her mind?"

"No. But she's faced with a difficult decision. I'm sure Serenity's grateful for your coming, just that she's troubled. Till now, she hasn't had a clear leading. Maybe, after the interview at the Museum, she'll understand better what her choice should be."

"I'll talk to her tonight," Loveday promised. "Give her a little push."

Here was something she was eminently qualified to do.

Babysitting was out of her line these days, but career counseling —

Oliver didn't seem to appreciate the offer. He changed the subject. "I've been thinking about your ancestors. Last time you came, we tried to locate them in the Minute Books of the eighteen hundreds. But maybe they were around here before the Revolution. Would you like to have another look at those Minute Books? We could go to the Meetinghouse tomorrow while Ross is at nursery school. It's just possible," Oliver added, frowning — Loveday wondered why — "that we may turn up something in the seventeen seventies."

Loveday didn't want to turn up anything. That would remove the excuse for another visit. She changed the subject, too.

"Oliver," she pleaded, taking a step closer in her earnestness, "don't let Rennie miss this marvelous opportunity just because Peter wants to stay here. A husband's job isn't more important than a wife's."

She expected him to dispute this, but, to her surprise, he answered calmly, "Only Serenity can be the judge of what's right in this case. We who love her can best support her, not by taking sides or offering advice, but with our prayers, leaving her free to seek divine guidance."

Suppose she doesn't find it? Loveday thought. But before she had a chance to challenge Oliver, he left again.

And this time, he didn't return.

3.

STILL STANDING in the middle of the sloping floor, Loveday felt rejected. Why should Oliver restrain her from helping Rennie?

Hadn't he himself offered to go all the way to New York to see this Judy, who seemed to have run away from home? What right did he have to do that, while preventing Loveday from counseling a friend of hers?

If Rennie didn't find that divine guidance he wanted her to seek, someone would certainly have to step in. And who was better fitted than Loveday?

If a woman with her experience didn't help a younger one to become more than just someone's wife and some child's mother, wasn't she failing the younger woman?

At William Allen White, she had counseled hundreds of girls — thousands, possibly — awakening them to a concept of their potentialities which the culture tried to suppress. If she could do this for women she didn't know personally, why shouldn't she advise Rennie, for whom she had developed a great liking? How could Loveday be expected to keep still? With all his courtesy, Oliver didn't seem to value Loveday when it came to having an input into the Hollands' affairs.

Adjusting her balance to the crazy slope of the floor, she noticed a yellow rose standing in a slender vase on the dressing table. Oliver had placed it there. She knew because he always did that when he was expecting her. Sniffing the delicate scent, she thought, How can I feel rejected?

She could forgive everything when she was so happy to be in this room, with all the familiar objects — those terra cotta figurines of a woman playing with her child — Oliver's wife made those, too. Serenity had told Loveday about them on an earlier visit.

"For Heather to play with," she'd explained. "Daphne was convinced that a small child will take care of the most fragile toy, if it's really beautiful."

Loveday, the experienced grandmother, had refused to believe this.

But Serenity offered proof. She took up one of the figurines and ran her hand tenderly over the surface. "You see," she had said, grinning triumphantly, "they've survived."

Looking around the room now, Loveday was pleased to find that the pale blue bedspread, sprinkled with irises and daffodils, was still there. Though it was faded and worn, it had a charm one seldom saw in modern designs.

Rennie had apologized for the shabby spread when she took Loveday to the room for the first time. She had explained that when she and Peter came to live at Firbank, Oliver had wanted to replace it, but she wouldn't let him.

"Don't take that away," Rennie recalled having begged him. "I love it. I remember, when I came here the first time, that was one of the things I fell for. It's part of my Firbank. Don't take it away."

Rennie had observed ruefully that, in the intervening years, the spread had grown even shabbier. "But I still love it," she'd added.

Loveday had come to feel a similar affection for those faded irises and daffodils. They belonged on the antique bed.

In a way, she thought, delighting in her recognition of the familiar furnishings, this is more like home to me than the apartment on Beacon Hill, even — but how could this be? — more than my house in Emporia.

Each time she came here, she found a new selection of books on the bedside table. Did Oliver hope she'd read all his favorites during her visit? She'd have to stay weeks.

This time, there was *The Journal of John Woolman.* So he wanted to introduce her to his eighteenth-century hero, a contemporary of Mozart, but, she gathered, a man of quite different views! Beside this *Journal* was a history — *Quakers in Boston.* That, Loveday decided, she must read when she went to bed. Curious, she took it up for a moment to glance at the blue dust jacket.

On it was a photograph of a statue — some woman in

Quaker dress, sitting on a bench, probably in some Meeting-house, lost in contemplation. Her expression held Loveday's attention. The statue was arresting because it conveyed so much feeling. The woman looked solitary, threatened, yet courageous and at peace. Who was she?

Yes, this was the book Loveday would read tonight. Putting it back for the present, she caught sight of a fine binding and ran her forefinger over the smooth leather spine. She didn't have time to look at the book now — Oliver was waiting for her — but, with a start, she noticed the title, tooled between bands, *Daphne Otis, Her Life and Art.* Under this was the author's name, Otis.

That's Oliver's book! Loveday exclaimed to herself. The one he wrote! He disciplined himself to begin. And to see it through.

He'd never shown it to her. But then, she'd never asked to see it and he would have been too modest to foist it on her. By placing it here unobtrusively along with the others, he made the book available, in case Loveday should be interested in reading it.

Part of her was eager to; very curious. Part of her didn't want to.

When Oliver spoke about his wife, Loveday felt uncom-fortable and she didn't encourage him to go on. She guessed this was because of the unusual tenderness and pride in his voice. They made her a little jealous. Her husband had never spoken about her that way. He'd cared for her as much as he did for anybody — she knew that. But Bill wasn't capable of caring, not, at least, the way Oliver cared about his wife, even about a stranger who happened to come to his house.

And Loveday had so wanted to be cherished! When she was young, affection and passion bubbled over in her. She had put everything into the marriage. She tried to make some-thing of herself so Bill would be proud of her. But all her efforts were wasted. He didn't even notice. When he knew he was dying, he showed less sorrow over becoming separated from Loveday than about forsaking his dog.

She had resolved at once never to risk surrendering her life again.

From the first she had been aware of this one flaw at Firbank: the tenderness and pride in Oliver's voice when he spoke of his wife. It hurt her. She always defended herself by changing the subject.

Maybe, too, Daphne's professional success roused some envy in Loveday. To be both cherished and famous — that was too much.

It wasn't only Oliver who rubbed Loveday the wrong way in speaking of Daphne. Rennie and Peter did, too. Their admiration and affection for her constantly came out in little remarks.

"The most liberated woman I ever knew," Rennie said once. "Even after she was paralyzed, when she was unable to speak and completely dependent physically, she had this — well — " Rennie laughed as she used the only word that seemed appropriate, "serenity."

Remembering her unresponsiveness at the time, Loveday hated herself. How could she have been envious of a dead woman, one who'd spent her last years in utter helplessness?

Sighing, she went to the window and gazed out at the pond. The ocean wasn't visible. She knew it was there, though, back of the dunes. Sea gulls were circling over it, disappearing toward the horizon. The sun was beginning to set. It was beautiful.

It's not really that I'm jealous, Loveday said to herself. I'm glad Daphne had the love. What hurts is only that Bill couldn't have given me something like that. If he had, I would have been more content.

Her students respected, admired her, even. Yet few communicated real affection. Was it her name that put people off? But Oliver thought it beautiful.

He must be terribly lonely. Had he really been thinking of taking Loveday in his arms? His old-fashioned code would never have permitted such a gesture, but had he been *thinking* of it?

Men were attracted to Loveday. Several had tested her resolve not to marry again, but she hadn't fallen for anyone. Two or three had made less enticing advances. In both cases, she was determined to preserve her independence. Still, she liked being friends with men and, maybe just because they knew she had no designs on them, most of those she encountered seemed to feel comfortable with her.

But what good was her previous experience now? Oliver was altogether different from any man she'd ever known — more perceptive, fearlessly confronting the truth, free of sentimental illusions. At the same time, Loveday found him touchingly innocent, free of guile.

Innocence like his makes a man vulnerable, she thought, unpacking her bag. If he had embraced me, it would have been nothing more than innocence. At his age, passion is certainly a thing of the past. That liveliness of his fools one. He seems so much younger.

Carrying her comb and brush to the dressing table, she noticed the rose again. Oliver had chosen a bud whose opening would coincide precisely with her arrival. She could visualize him bending over the bush earlier in the day, cutting it in anticipation of her coming.

On her earlier visits, he had always taken her out to see the garden after the supper dishes were washed. They had strolled around the house in the twilight while he commented on the health of every plant in the flowerbed. It had been such a dry summer, he explained, that only the hardiest perennials had flourished. Each time they made these rounds, Oliver would stop before a rose bush. Taking out his jackknife, bending stiffly, he would cut the most perfect bud for Loveday, extending it with a solemnity — almost homage — that made it seem like a sacred offering.

Loveday was already looking forward to going out with Oliver this evening. It would be chilly now; she'd have to wear her coat. But the sky was clear. The stroll would be a lovely prelude to the talk they'd have by the fire, when they came indoors, as the stars were beginning to appear.

She ran the comb through her hair and started to leave the room. On second thought, she decided to put on the dress she'd brought. It wasn't necessary here. Nobody cared. The wraparound skirt and knit top she had on were okay. But she'd brought the dress, her favorite, a soft blue-and-rose paisley print on a creamy ground. She might as well wear it.

Combing her hair again, she frowned at her reflection. Her hair was falling like those autumn leaves. Before long, she'd be as bald as Oliver. Ought she to look into buying a wig? The very idea made her shudder.

Turning from the mirror, cleaning her comb with distaste, she suddenly asked her reflection, What did I mean, back there in the lane? What was I getting at when I thought, If I hadn't come here, my whole life would have been different? Something wonderful certainly has opened for me at Firbank. But my *whole life* — What did I mean?

It was ridiculous. And yet, as Loveday left the room and crossed the landing, she knew that, in her heart, she believed it.

Oliver must have been listening for her footsteps because, as Loveday came down the curving staircase in her paisley print, he was waiting for her, standing at the bottom, his shining face uplifted.

And now there was no mistaking his impulse. His arms were stretched wide to receive her.

She would have gone to him. Why not? What more did it imply than simple friendship?

But before she reached the bottom step, he caught himself. His arms fell to his sides.

4.

THINGS were not the same at Firbank this time, even though dinner was served as usual at the round table in the kitchen, preceded by the customary silence and ring of hands. The old blue-and-white plates, which Loveday admired so much, were heaped as usual with johnnycake and vegetables from Oliver's garden. Nevertheless, in some subtle way, things were different. The underlying unity which set Firbank apart seemed to be missing.

As they began to eat, Rennie briefed Loveday, running through Ross's schedule. She appeared tense. Peter, who was ordinarily a listener, talked all through the meal about variable stars and intergalactic space, in the self-conscious tone of the young instructor trying out tomorrow's lecture on his long-suffering family. Oliver's expression was set at attention but his eyes kept wandering. And Ross whimpered in a monotone that irritated Loveday.

She fixed her gaze on Peter to assure him that *she*, at least, was spellbound by his lecture. Actually, she didn't understand a word. Relaxing for a second, she turned away.

Oliver was staring at her!

Had a sliver of red beet escaped from the fork and landed on her chin? Was her hair rumpled? One of her buttons undone? She wiped her mouth nervously, put her hands up to feel her hair and glanced down at her dress. Reassured, she raised her head again.

Oliver was still staring at her. Their eyes met. He quickly turned and concentrated on Peter.

With equal haste, Loveday spun in the opposite direction, facing Rennie. How troubled she looked! Loveday's heart went out to the girl — woman. She must help her, never mind Oliver's admonition to keep hands off. After the evening stroll, she'd ask him to excuse her and she'd have a talk with Rennie. She'd do what she could to stiffen that young backbone. A wonderful opportunity mustn't be allowed to slip by, just because here, in the country, woman's place was still supposed to be in the home. With a little encouragement, Rennie'd fight for her rights.

But Loveday wasn't sure how she should phrase her counsel so it wouldn't provoke a negative response. She really didn't know Rennie very well. A certain reserve on the younger woman's part baffled Loveday. She'd done everything she could to break it down, calling Rennie by her nickname instead of the formal one Oliver preferred. She had also assured Rennie and Peter that it would be quite proper for them to use *her* nickname — Lowdy — but, like Oliver, they never did. They seemed to think of her as still a dean. This slight but apparently irreducible distance made strategy difficult.

Maybe, while Loveday toured the garden with Oliver in the cool of the evening, she'd think of an effective plan.

When the meal was finished, Rennie went to the old-fashioned sink and filled the dishpan. Oliver cleared the table. Loveday, impatient to go out with him, followed, carrying a couple of plates. Ross climbed onto Peter's back for the journey to bed, which was preceded by the good-night ritual.

Horse and rider circled the kitchen, stopping first so Ross could shower his mother with kisses. Next, he was carried to

Oliver. He snuggled against the old man. But when it came Loveday's turn, Ross drew away.

"Don't you love me?" she asked with mock chagrin.

Ross's eyes, level with Loveday's, looked straight into hers as he answered unequivocally, "No."

Peter hurried him off. At the door, Ross twisted his neck and shook his head vigorously so Loveday wouldn't be left in any doubt.

She laughed. Her feelings weren't hurt. Just a child —

She was still laughing when Oliver startled her by announcing that he had to leave for Kendal at once.

"A meeting," he explained, adding anxiously that he was already late.

It had never occurred to Loveday that Oliver might run out on her. What could be so important? Now she did feel hurt.

Rennie turned around. "Oh," she exclaimed, "the Called Meeting. I forgot about that. It's tonight; isn't it? Peter's on duty at the Observatory. I'll have to stay home with Ross."

Why didn't Oliver volunteer to stay home instead — with Loveday? They'd sit by the fire and chat. Well, the unexpected turn of events did provide an opportunity for that talk with Rennie.

"I'm sorry," Oliver was saying to Loveday. "It's unfortunate that this meeting coincides with your visit. I do have to attend." His tone was apologetic; his expression was pleading. "Would you come? May be a bit boring. If you don't mind that —" He sounded eager but not insistent.

Loveday considered the invitation. If she went, there'd be no time to speak to Rennie, who was leaving for New York at dawn. She, Loveday, would be running out on a floundering younger sister, just as Oliver was prepared to run out on her.

He had gone over to Rennie. " 'Be still and cool,' " he said, putting his arms around her and smiling down affectionately.

"Give my love to thy parents. And don't forget to tell Judy Young that I'll come, if she wants me."

Rennie brightened instantly. There was a bond between those two that Loveday was only just beginning to appreciate. And judging by Rennie's response, "Be still and cool" must be household words which had been invoked in so many previous crises that they'd acquired the power of a charm. At any rate, Rennie returned the smile and patted Oliver's sleeve.

But Loveday was annoyed.

Still and cool! she thought scornfully. The worst possible advice. What Rennie needs is to be assertive and on fire, not still and cool.

Clearly, Loveday must stay here and counteract Oliver's well-meant but misguided efforts. This, then, was her decision — to stay.

So when she found herself climbing into Oliver's pickup truck under a starlit sky, breathing the tangy salt air, she wondered how it had come about. Her determination to do her duty had been canceled out by her desire to be with Oliver. The most vital of all her attributes — her will — had run out on her. She hated herself.

"What's this you're taking me to?" she asked, as he turned on the ignition.

"A Friends Meeting ordinarily convenes for the transaction of business once a month. But occasionally there are urgent matters. Then we meet at the call of the clerk, as we're doing tonight. I'm afraid you'll think our deliberations maddeningly slow. That's because, just as we seek guidance in our meetings for worship, we wait for it in our meetings for business."

"Meetings for business?" Loveday repeated, astonished. "What does business have to do with religion?"

"What else is religion but the business of our lives?" he countered almost sharply. "It's not a Sunday pastime. No one," he added more calmly, "ever put this so beautifully as John

Woolman. 'To turn all the treasures we possess into — ' " Oliver hesitated, obviously groping for the rest of the quotation, " 'into the channel of universal love' " — he paused again — " 'becomes the business of our lives.' "

In the dark cab, his voice sounded surprisingly youthful.

The channel of universal love — The business of our lives — Poetic phrases, lilting like music. Noble, Mozartean cadences. But what, exactly, did they mean?

At the bottom of the lane, Oliver turned onto the Kendal road. It ran close to the shore. Far out at sea, lighthouses sent powerful beams across the water. Oliver named them for Loveday: "Fisher's Island, Little Gull, Montauk, and, on this shore, Watch Hill."

As the truck headed inland, she recalled how, the first time she came over this road, Oliver had said that Kendal, Rhode Island, was settled in the seventeenth century by weavers from Kendal in Westmorland. The earliest Friends went out from the north of England to bring men and women everywhere the good news of God's love, traveling even to the New World.

"In the Massachusetts Bay Colony, they had a rude reception," Oliver had told Loveday sadly. "Simply because they were Quakers, they were imprisoned and whipped at the cart's tail. A woman and three men were hanged on Boston Common. The only colony to offer sanctuary was Rhode Island."

The historian in Loveday didn't forget facts like these, but what impressed her most was the deep emotion with which Oliver had referred to them — how poignantly he seemed to identify with the suffering of people who lived over three centuries ago.

This evening, his mind was on the meeting they were about to attend. "The main item for consideration," he said, as street lights began to appear on the outskirts of town, "is the disposition of a bequest. A beloved Friend, Melissa Gray, has left her home and the residue of her estate to the Meeting. We are to use them for whatever purpose seems best. There have been many proposals, but so far none has met with general approval. We can't act without that."

Loveday was intrigued. "Think of all you'll be able to do with the money," she cried.

But Oliver sounded far from jubilant. "Most of our members have very moderate incomes. We operate on a small budget. Suddenly the Meeting's affluent. It makes us uncomfortable."

To be uncomfortable because of *having* money struck Loveday as downright amusing. She knew only too well the importance of a bequest. Many a kid's college education depended on some rich person's dying.

The truck's headlights picked up a road sign, *Entering Kendal.*

They drove on through the darkness till the high beam of an oncoming car blinded them. Loveday blinked. Though the car passed in an instant, she kept her eyes closed. The words of the sign, now a long way back, still danced brightly behind her lids, flashing a promise — or was it a warning? — *Entering Kendal.*

5.

ONLY GLIMMERS of light shone through the tall windows of the Friends Meetinghouse as they mounted the steps. Once inside, Loveday saw why — there was no electricity. Flickering oil lamps hung in brackets between the windows. The antique lamps were charming, but, even augmented by reflectors, they gave barely enough illumination.

How old-fashioned can one be? Loveday thought, amused. That's what the Meeting should do with its troubling wealth

—install electric light. There! I've solved the problem. Now we can go back to Firbank and sit by the fire.

Oliver was running a finger along the shelves of books that lined one entire wall in the vestibule. The finger stopped at a small, deep gray volume. Before Loveday could make out the title, he had removed the book and slipped it into his coat pocket.

At the door of the meeting room, he stood still a moment to explain in a whisper that the chairperson — "Clerk," he called her — was Clara Ludlow. She was a pretty, middle-aged woman.

"The Assistant Clerk," Oliver added, "is Neil Hill. He runs a boatyard on the Kendal River."

This pleased Loveday — a woman had the top post; the man was her assistant.

Oliver led the way on tiptoe to an empty bench. As soon as they were seated, he closed his eyes, draining all expression from his face. He must already be seeking that "leading" he kept harping on.

The meeting was never called to order. No need — the room was intensely quiet. Everyone in it seemed to be meditating.

A feeling of extraordinary intimacy and trust emanated from the silence, as if, in this hush, Oliver and Loveday might tell each other things they normally wouldn't dare say, wouldn't even be able to articulate.

Suddenly he stood up, fished in his pocket for the book and flipped the pages till he found what he was looking for. Raising his head, he said clearly, yet in his usual tone, "As we start to deliberate, let's consider some of our traditional Advices. These weren't laid down as rules of conduct, only as reminders, which all of us need from time to time." He began to read: *"Take heed, dear Friends, to the promptings of love and truth in your hearts, which are the leadings of God."* Oliver paused for a moment, as if to take heed himself, studying the implications.

Loveday was studying him. He really was good-looking, however much his modesty might lead him to deny it.

Turning a page, he continued: "*Use your abilities and possessions not as ends in themselves but as God's gifts entrusted to you. Share them with others.*"

That's what I was trying to do with Rennie, Loveday thought, aggrieved — share my abilities. And he wouldn't let me.

Oliver's next words made her feel less smug.

"*Use them in humility and with courtesy. Guard against the love of power; be considerate of the needs of others and respect their personalities.*"

Love of power! During the demonstrations in the sixties, when college students forgot the respect they owed their faculty, one strident young hothead had accused Dean Mead of loving power. At the time, she'd dismissed the affront as unworthy of notice, or thought she had. But the injury must still be festering, otherwise she wouldn't be recalling it now, after all these years. Was Oliver speaking to her?

He closed the book and returned it to his pocket. As he was settling himself on the bench again, his sleeve accidentally brushed against Loveday's arm. The contact sent a surprising tingle through her. But the recollection of that student's remark, which she'd long tried to forget, arrested the pleasurable sensation.

Love of power! The accusation had hurt the more because Loveday'd been so convinced that only devotion to duty motivated her, not the desire to run people. Perhaps it wasn't always easy to distinguish between the two. Evidently even Friends had to be cautioned.

Had Oliver read that passage because he thought it applied to Loveday? Impossible. He had no way of knowing.

The personalities of her students — it had never occurred to her that she ought to *respect* them; her function was to instruct and mold — to counsel. The demonstrations hadn't made her more considerate of her students' needs. On the contrary, she thought now, she had simply become more determined to show who was in charge.

The sound of the Clerk's voice made her look up.

"At a called meeting of Kendal Meeting of Friends, held at Kendal, Rhode Island, Tenth Month twenty-fifth," the Clerk was saying, standing behind a small table that had been brought in to serve as a desk. "Nineteen members are present." She paused to give the Assistant Clerk a chance to write this down, then said, "At this time we welcome Loveday Mead, a visitor at Firbank Farm."

Hearing her name, Loveday jumped. Friends were turning to her. The pensiveness had left their faces. They smiled, enthusiastically taking this stranger into their midst.

She smiled back and turned to Oliver. He was looking at her with unmistakable *pride*. So he hadn't heard the disturbing recollections that passed through Loveday's mind a few minutes ago!

Unpleasant though these had been, she was glad she'd come. It seemed to make Oliver happy.

But he was right about the proceedings being boring. Well, not boring — exasperating. These people, especially the younger ones, were so impractical. Their whole idea seemed to be to get rid of that money as quickly as possible. Individuals, who looked quite sensible otherwise, made suggestions for selling the house, liquidating the assets and giving the proceeds to disadvantaged people in this country, in Laos, Cambodia, in dozens of other places around the world. Loveday wanted to stand up and tell Friends to look out for themselves first.

The discussion was getting still more unreal when a man near the front of the room rose. He kept quiet till the Clerk recognized his wish to speak by saying his name, "Lucas Lang."

Oliver whispered that Lucas was a teacher in the High School.

"How would we present the money?" he asked. "Quaker service has never been impersonal. We don't just send checks. They're simply part of a much larger testimony — friendship extended by human hands. Which of us is in the position to travel to Indochina or even across the United States? Remember how in seventeen seventy-five, Boston was under siege? The inhabitants had difficulty getting food. Friends in other Colonies, England and Ireland raised large sums for their relief. Well, you know how it is — you help the folks of your faith or on your side, not just anyone, certainly not your enemies. But the Quakers had no enemies; they refused to fight or side with either the Americans or the British. So they sent Moses Brown of Providence and four other Rhode Island Friends to Boston to bring relief 'without distinction of sects or parties.' To enter the town, these Friends had to get permission from General Washington, who'd just taken command of the American Army across the river, in Cambridge."

Loveday was entranced. This was her kind of stuff!

"Washington's headquarters were in Craigie House, Cambridge, later the home of Henry Wadsworth Longfellow, just across the street from where the Friends Meetinghouse stands now. Moses Brown and the other four, whose names I've forgotten, went to Craigie House and asked George Washington to let them pass through the lines with a flag of truce. Washington told them it was impossible; smallpox was raging in Boston. Many of the inhabitants had fled to Marblehead and neighboring towns. So the five Friends caught up with the refugees who lined the roads all the way to Gloucester. They helped almost seven thousand people, speaking to each one, except the war prisoners in Salem, whom they weren't able to visit. The jailer was given money to provide extra rations for them. The Friends wrote down the name, occupation and re-

ligious denomination of each person who received money, along
with the amount. We still have this record. It was compiled by
our dear friend, Henry Cadbury."

Loveday was stirred by the historical account. She was sorry
when the man finished.

"I'll only be comfortable disbursing our bequest where we
can make personal contact like that," he concluded.

After the man sat down, there was a silence. It seemed inter-
minable. Loveday was thinking over what he'd said. How could
this handful of people make contact with all those they wanted
to help? But in the Revolution, five spoke to seven thousand,
so why couldn't nineteen contact a few?

A little old lady had struggled to her feet. She seemed
nervous. Loveday didn't catch the name when she was recognized by the Clerk.

"I remember Daphne Otis telling—"

Loveday glanced at Oliver. His calm expression didn't
change. Evidently, he was used to having Daphne recalled.

"—about her work in France during and after the First
World War," the old lady was saying, breathing hard. "Daphne
was part of a team stationed at the Swiss border to assist the
prisoners of war when they were being repatriated. The workers
carried bowls of soup to those broken people in the trains. She
always said it wasn't the nourishment that heartened the prisoners—most were too sick to eat—so much as the few
friendly words from strangers, who cared enough to come to
them. When Lucas spoke, I was reminded of what Daphne
said. I agree. We should only offer money where we can make
a personal testimony of love."

After yet another silence, the Clerk announced that it was
growing late. She believed it was the sense of the Meeting that
no action be taken until there was another opportunity to consider the question. She asked the Assistant Clerk to read the
Minutes.

Loveday jumped when she heard him read her name. The welcome was recorded, along with the various suggestions for the disposal of the bequest and what was referred to as "the sense of the Meeting."

There was a final period of silence. Then Oliver turned to Loveday and extended his right hand. As she took it in hers, the tingle went through her again.

Along the rows of benches, people were shaking hands with their neighbors.

That welcome turned out to be no mere formality. Friends crowded around Loveday. Their cordiality was touching. They knew nothing about her, where she came from, whether she had status. They welcomed her with an amazing warmth simply, their manner implied, because she was a person. This was unique in her experience.

After all that silence, they chatted like magpies.

Oliver listened to everyone with characteristic attention.

It's more than politeness, Loveday said to herself. It's genuine interest. He cares about people.

The woman who had chaired the meeting came up to her and extended her hand. "I'm Clara Ludlow," she told Loveday. "We were so pleased to have you with us tonight. Will you have dinner with John and me tomorrow?" She turned to Oliver and repeated the invitation. His smile conveyed his pleasure in accepting.

"Thank you," Loveday said. "You're all so cordial."

The intimacy and trust generated by the silence seemed to have knit Friends together so that they were unwilling to part. They lingered, still chatting, in the aisles, in the vestibule, even outside.

As Oliver and Loveday finally broke away, he took her arm companionably and led her toward the truck. The moon had come up, making the Meetinghouse yard almost as bright as the interior.

Opening the door of the cab for Loveday, Oliver looked up at the stars. "That universe Peter sees through the telescope," he observed. "I can't grasp it."

"Neither can I," Loveday confessed.

"But this canopy," he said with emotion, "has spread beauty and poetry over me all my life. Its very mystery is a kind of knowledge. On a clear night, the few constellations I can identify with my naked eye are always in their proper places, waiting to greet me."

6.

LOVEDAY woke early.

It took her a minute to remember where she was. That strange sound under her window — In Boston, the roar of the traffic kept up all night. Here, there was no noise at all, except for this muffled sputtering and what Loveday had recently learned to identify as the cry of sea gulls.

Then she realized that she wasn't in Boston, but actually in the ell at Firbank. What she was hearing was Rennie's bug, warming up for the trip to New York. Rennie wouldn't be back till tomorrow afternoon.

Loveday turned over and tried to doze off again.

When she hadn't had enough sleep, she was inclined to be irritable the next day and this was going to be a trying one, coping with Ross. Suppose her blood pressure went up? She must keep calm.

She'd only had four hours' sleep. Last evening, on the point of turning out the light, she'd foolishly picked up Oliver's book from the bedside table, just to glance at the reproductions of Daphne's paintings. Some of them were scenes of Firbank that Loveday recognized. Completely absorbed, she had no idea how late it was getting till the grandfather clock downstairs struck two. She had read the book from cover to cover!

This morning, bits of the story kept running through her head, preventing her from going back to sleep. Finally, she gave up and reached for the book. Certain passages intrigued her.

Oliver began by describing Daphne's childhood home, a stone cottage in the north of England.

Countersett is a tiny village at the foot of the Buttertubs Pass in the Yorkshire Dales, tucked between the Roman Road and Semmer Water. From the middle of the Seventeenth Century, it was a Quaker stronghold. George Fox is said to have slept at The Hall. John Woolman stopped to worship in the Friends Meetinghouse next door, on his walk across England in 1772. Daphne's earliest memory was of lying in bed and hearing the horn that was regularly sounded each evening to guide any travellers who might be lost in the fog on the surrounding fells.

At sixteen, Daphne entered the Academy of Design in York. Then the First World War came and she joined the Anglo-American Friends Mission — "The Mish," Oliver called it affectionately. She went to France to nurse in a children's hospital in the Marne. Later, transferred to Savoy, she assisted broken war prisoners, who were being repatriated.

Loveday knew about this. The old lady had referred to it last night.

Daphne was so shaken by the suffering she witnessed, Oliver wrote, *that, to preserve her sanity, she sketched every evening, recording the terrified faces she'd seen. Her well-known drawing, entitled* The Repatriates, *was made at that time.*

In the States, meanwhile, Oliver was being court-martialed and imprisoned for refusing to bear arms. In that war, there had been no exemption from military service for conscientious objectors.

Prison! Loveday thought, appalled. *Oliver's been in prison.*

For someone so sensitive, so trusting, to be at the mercy of military guards — Yet he bore no visible scars — bitterness or cynicism.

After his release from prison, Oliver wrote, without going into details about his experience there, he also joined the Mish. He immediately sailed to France, where he helped farmers restore their houses and ravaged fields. While on leave, during an air raid in Paris, he met Daphne.

They were married after he graduated from Harvard. Oliver took Daphne directly to Firbank to visit his grandmother, Serenity Otis. It was while they were there that they made the "pilgrimage," as he called it, which changed their lives.

With great restraint — Loveday thought she knew only too well how proud Oliver actually was — he wrote about Daphne's success, beginning with the portrait of his grandmother, the first Serenity. It established Daphne's reputation. Commissions for portraits began coming in faster than she could work. Together with the Christmas trees Oliver raised, portraits became the Otis cash crop. From that time on, Daphne enjoyed a success matched by few American artists.

She was a mother, too.

That Daphne, Loveday thought. She had everything.

Oliver wrote lovingly of Heather. She began helping on the farm when she was still quite little, feeding the chickens, following her father around. With time, she did a day's work, like a boy. All too soon, Heather went off to school. When she graduated, she married Stephen Thirsk, the son of Daphne's classmate at the Academy of Design, who had come to America to study engineering. Stephen took Heather to England with him, just as Oliver had taken her mother to the States.

Firbank was bleak without Heather. But, every summer, she and Stephen came over to spend their holiday. Those were joyous times! The second year they brought little Oliver Otis Thirsk. Later, Daphne and Gwen and Henry came along.

As the grandchildren grew up, other interests claimed their attention in the holidays and they visited Firbank less frequently.

There was no hint of self-pity in this statement, but Loveday suspected she knew how much Oliver missed his family. What was Heather like now?

All that love she'd been surrounded by in childhood! But isolated in the country, locked into a religion that was a whole different way of life, nonviolent, chiefly concerned with the needs of others. Very noble. Yet wasn't it cruel to send a child into the world with no training in self-preservation? That plain language —

I think it's charming, Loveday said to herself, *but Heather's little friends thought it ridiculous. She felt odd.* How could her parents have maintained their peculiarities at her expense?

Heather seemed to have made motherhood her career. Was this to be different from Daphne, even to outsmart her with four children instead of only one? The daughter of such a successful woman — wouldn't she have tried to do something outstanding, too — perhaps in another field? Instead of just —

Why am I so curious? Heather doesn't have anything to do with me.

Skipping to the end of the book, Loveday reread Oliver's heartbreaking account of Daphne's stroke: how it twisted one side of her face; how it deprived her of the power of speech and paralyzed her right arm so she could no longer paint or, indeed, care for herself.

Slowly, he wrote, *agonizingly, she learned to use her left hand. But the zest for painting was gone. Then, one day, not quite a year before Daphne's death, a young cousin of mine, whom we had never seen, another Serenity, came to Firbank*

She had beautiful features and coloring. Her manner was gracious. But she was troubled, buffeted by adolescent impulses and confused about values. With the artist's perception, Daphne saw something in this young woman that stirred her — a promise. For the first time in three years, she felt moved to paint. This portrait turned out to be more than a likeness of an individual. It proclaimed the dawn of a day Daphne believed that whole confused generation would eventually waken to. It was her last and unquestionably her greatest work. Known as The Second Serenity, *this canvas hangs today in the Museum of Contemporary Art in New York.*

A portrait of Rennie! In that museum! Why hadn't anyone ever told Loveday? Oliver and the Hollands were simply too modest. Maybe they thought she knew. No wonder the Museum wanted Rennie to work there!

This book wasn't just a biography. It was the record of a rare marriage, unlike any Loveday had ever heard about.

Marriage, she'd always assumed, was first of all an arrangement for physical fulfillment and secondly a division of labor. It was an accommodation. Two people carefully staked out their claims and traded off sacrifices.

But Daphne and Oliver seemed — at least, in the book — never to have staked out anything. They'd made no recognizable claims, demanded nothing. They were quite simply each other's servants, motivated by a devotion that transformed service into a glorious privilege.

But I always thought being a servant was demeaning, Loveday said to herself, puzzled. Especially in marriage — Especially for a woman —

Paradoxically, disregard of their own prerogatives appeared to have given Daphne and Oliver freedom, enabling them to live their lives as they wished. Was it their commitment to each other that freed them?

If Loveday hadn't happened to know the author, she would have suspected the story was overdrawn. But she knew Oliver. He wasn't capable of misrepresenting.

Suddenly faint, she dropped the book on the blanket. A wave of regret, almost like nausea, swept over her. If only she'd grasped years ago what she was learning about life at this late date! Here she was, seventy-three next birthday, and only just beginning to understand.

What good does it do me now? she asked herself bitterly. It's too late.

Some coffee — that was what she needed. At home, she always went to the kitchen down the hall and made herself a cup as soon as she opened her eyes. She would take it back to bed and sip, gradually coming to. But here, the kitchen was downstairs, way at the back of the house — someone else's house. Still, she was supposed to be in charge today, wasn't she?

Why not sneak down?

It would mean passing Oliver's room, which was right at the head of the stairs. But these antique doors, made of solid, wide planks, were really soundproof. Anyway, his hearing wasn't acute.

Loveday got up and glanced out at the October morning, surprised to see Peter in the dooryard, walking toward the barn. So he was already out, doing the chores!

Crossing the landing in her housecoat and slippers, stepping gingerly, concentrating on the floorboards to avoid making them squeak, Loveday reached the head of the stairs before she saw with a shock that Oliver's door was open.

Too late to turn back! He was looking straight at her.

7.

PROPPED AGAINST PILLOWS in a big, old-fashioned bed-stead, Oliver had been reading his Bible. When he raised his eyes, he was looking directly at Loveday.

She felt fussed. She hadn't expected to be caught sneaking downstairs, or rather, to be catching Oliver in bed.

But he smiled unselfconsciously and wished her good morning, keeping his finger on the page to mark the place.

"I opened my door so Ross can come in," he explained. "His mother's left and his father's outside. If he can't fly in to me, he'll panic. I hope you rested well."

"Not long enough. I read your book, cover to cover. Just meant to glance through it, but it — well — involved me. You write beautifully."

"For a farmer," Oliver put in with a grin. Serious again, he recalled, "I planned to become a writer. After the First World War, I tried to get a job in publishing so as to make a living, while writing. But because I'd been a conscientious objector, I was turned away."

Loveday interrupted. "This puzzled me. I always thought the men who wouldn't fight were given farm work or something. A friend of my brother — "

"That," Oliver explained, also interrupting, "was in World War Two. By then, Congress recognized a man's right to obey the Biblical command against killing. But in the first one, all men of eighteen were inducted into the Army. If judged sincere, conscientious objectors were assigned to noncombatant duty. Most Quakers felt this still supported violence. So they had no choice but to disobey their officers. That led to courts-martial, even some death sentences."

"You," Loveday cried, horror-stricken, "were you — ?"

Oliver acted as if he hadn't heard. "As I was saying," he broke in, "after the war, all I could get was a job in advertising which I disliked. I had Daphne to support, though, and she had a nasty cough. We thought a trip south might do her good. So, before starting the job, I bundled her into Grandmother's Model T, never dreaming we were going on a pilgrimage — that we'd be overtaken by it. But that's what happened."

"*Overtaken?*"

"Yes. Passing through New Jersey, we spent the night in Mount Holly and stayed in the house John Woolman had built. While we were there, we discovered his *Journal*, in which he describes his trip south to plead with the planters to free their slaves. As Daphne and I read, we were so moved that we decided to follow Woolman's route. By the time we returned to Firbank, the whole concept of our future had changed. I never took that job. We stayed and helped Grandmother run the farm."

"I'm glad you did!"

"Think of it! Fifty years had to elapse before I got the chance to write. But then the Museum commissioned that book and even gave Serenity a grant to help me with it. I loved writing about Daphne. It was like having her back."

Once again, jealousy gripped Loveday. But she also saw how glad Oliver was that she liked his book. She rated with him, too!

"I've been wanting to tell you about her," he said softly, "only you never seemed interested. You see, it's impossible to understand me without knowing Daphne, both her art and her personality." He drew the bedclothes a little higher over his chest.

"I've never heard of anything quite like the relationship you wrote about," Loveday murmured. "You both seemed just to want to *serve* each other. Didn't you mind? In those days, the woman did the serving while the man went out and got recognition. Didn't it ever bother you that she became famous while you just — "

"Farmed?" He turned his head to gaze out of the window. "No, that was important, too, even if it didn't win acclaim. And, after years of struggle, my experiment in the Vietnamese Forest seemed significant to the foresters at the University. No, I didn't resent her success. I rejoiced in it. We weren't running a race to see who could beat." He turned back to Loveday. "Why would a husband and wife do that?"

"We did. At least, I — "

"Besides," Oliver was saying — he evidently hadn't heard her — "Daphne didn't paint for recognition. It came as a surprise. And it never really impressed her, even when the Museum put on the Fiftieth Anniversary Show. She didn't live to see that, but she did have the fun of choosing the pictures that went on exhibition. She always used to say that what she painted never turned out to be as beautiful as the vision she had in her mind. So her work never satisfied her, no matter how much the critics praised it. She painted simply to project that vision, just as I farmed to have what early Friends called 'unity with the creation.' That's getting to be almost impossible nowadays."

"Why?"

"Farming's becoming big business. Little acreages, like mine, are being bought up for more than they can produce. Heavy machinery is brought in that ruins the land — packs down the soil so it doesn't drain properly. It's hard now to farm the way people used to — for their family's sustenance and satisfaction." Oliver closed the Bible and laid it on the little stand beside his bed.

Loveday was holding onto the banister with one hand, clutching her housecoat with the other. There was something dreamlike in this conversation, between a man in blue pajamas and a woman in negligee. It seemed unreal. And yet, the old man propped against the pillows, his bald head defenseless as a baby's, spoke with such genuine feeling that she knew it was not a dream. Quite possibly, it was even more real than what she ordinarily thought of as the real world. She had simply arrived by chance at a place where life was lived on a different plane.

She couldn't restrain herself from blurting out, "I just don't see how the two of you did it."

Oliver looked at her squarely. But his eyes didn't seem to take her in, as he focused on his recollections.

"You see, when we married and I brought Daphne to Firbank, we were both still haunted by the suffering we'd seen. We felt great anger over the willful damage inflicted on people and the earth. Little by little, as we lived here with my grandmother, the first Serenity, we overcame the anger. Her calm understanding healed us. We progressed from destructive anger to joyful creativity."

"Your grandmother must have been a wonderful person."

"She was. Lately, I've been thinking that our present Serenity may turn out to be as wonderful in her way as the one she was named for. Don't you think so? Much depends on how she resolves her present dilemma. It was very good of you, Loveday, to come and free her, so she could go to New York."

That made Loveday uncomfortable. Face to face with Oliver, how could she keep from telling him that she'd been wishing for an excuse to come? She hadn't been quite honest. But if she were to tell him, what would he think?

"There was something else," he added diffidently. "It's not easy to talk about. But I'd like you to know." He looked down at the patchwork quilt and said softly, "Every morning, Daphne and I spent half an hour together, reaffirming what lay in the ground of our being, seeking direction silently, and yet, of one mind. Why this meant so much to us, I can't explain.

But it may have accounted for what you call our desire to serve each other. Every aspect of our love seemed sacred, so our reverence for each other merged imperceptibly into our reverence for God."

Listening more with her heart than her ears, Loveday didn't notice Ross coming up behind her on his little bare feet until he brushed past.

" 'cle Oliver!" He dove into the big bed.

Oliver put an arm around the child, but when he spoke, it was to Loveday, thanking her again for having come.

Afraid she might reveal how desperately she'd hunted for an excuse, she swung around and started down the stairs.

"I'm going to make myself some coffee," she announced over her shoulder.

Before she reached the second step, Oliver called her. When she turned back and looked questioningly at him, she saw the self-consciousness she had expected earlier.

"Would you —" he asked hesitantly.

He'd like me to bring him some coffee, she thought. How ungracious of me not to think of that.

"Don't unless you really want to," he pleaded before she had a chance to offer. "Would you care to join in the silence with me this morning?"

"Me, too!" Ross cried.

Oliver smiled down at the child who was nestled in the crook of his arm. "Thee, too," he promised. Then he looked eagerly toward the door. Disappointment gradually overspread his face.

Loveday knew it was because she hadn't accepted. She pulled at her housecoat.

Reaffirming what lay in the ground of their beings, seeking direction silently, yet of one mind — Last night, in the Meetinghouse, what Oliver read had been deeply troubling. Loveday didn't want to be stirred up again.

"Will it be like last night?" she asked. "Or more like Transcendental Meditation?"

The disappointment in Oliver's expression changed to hope.

"I believe," he said, "Transcendental Meditation is practiced to relax tension. Ours is a time of retiring into our innermost selves, yet seeking divine light together. As the light reveals our shortcomings, tension may mount, but if this drives us to set things right, we eventually find peace."

Loveday was far out of her depth.

His eyes were beseeching her.

She looked down at the landing. Finally she murmured, "I guess I'll join you," adding quickly as she once more glanced up at Oliver, "I was just going down to make coffee. Would you like me to bring you some?"

"No, thank you. Ross and I are about to get up."

Ross jumped out of bed.

Suddenly aware of her responsibilities, Loveday swung around and started back to her room, forgetting the urgency of the coffee. "I'll just get ready," she told Oliver, as she went. "Then I'll come back and dress him."

"No!" Ross shouted after her. "You won't."

8.

ALTHOUGH LOVEDAY was determined to discharge her duties faithfully, it turned out that there was nothing for her to do.

She had taken longer than usual deciding what she should wear, uncertain of the impression she wished to create. Should she pull on her slacks, casting herself in the role of efficient housewife, stressing her preference for the casual? Or should she wear the wraparound skirt and knit top she arrived in yesterday, which would make her look more feminine?

The skirt and top — she finally settled on them. Glancing in the mirror one last time, she approved of the choice. She looked nice. But she had vacillated so long and fussed with her hair so much that by the time she emerged from the ell, prepared for a confrontation with Ross, he had disappeared.

She went down and found him in the kitchen, perched on a pile of telephone directories that were placed on a regular chair. He was pushing a tiny car across the table.

"Stop!" he commanded. "Don't walk! Wait! Walk!"

Oliver was reading the newspaper. He rose stiffly as Loveday entered.

"Sorry I took so long," she murmured. "I was going to dress Ross."

"He dresses himself. Looks it," Oliver added with a chuckle, "doesn't he?" Yet, when Loveday promised to comb out the tousled curls at once, Oliver became unexpectedly severe. "We encourage independence," he declared, as if to say, Keep your hands off him. Can't you see that's what he wants?

Surely, Oliver didn't intend to take the child to nursery school unkempt? That put Loveday in a bad position. She had volunteered to serve as surrogate mother, yet she was forbidden to spruce up her little charge. Instinctively, she looked around for help. "Where's Peter?"

"He's left."

Robbed of her usual self-possession, Loveday wailed, "I was going to fix breakfast, too."

It was ready. The table had been set with care. In the center, a handful of marigolds, orange and russet, standing in a pewter mug, still glistened with dew.

"Come and sit down."

Though gracious, Oliver's invitation betrayed how impatient

he was to begin eating what he'd prepared. His faultless manners wouldn't permit the meal to begin till his guest came down, but he and Ross could hardly wait till she was seated before reaching for her hands.

On earlier visits, the quaint silence which preceded meals at Firbank had made Loveday slightly uneasy, particularly the ring of hands — an embarrassingly sentimental gesture, she thought. But this morning she disregarded it, anxiously eyeing Ross. Without his parents to subdue him, would he keep still?

He did. All the while, though, he peeked at Loveday solemnly and she realized that *he* was checking on *her*.

She looked down quickly, studying the design on the cereal bowl. The pungent marigolds wrinkled her nose.

Somehow, the order of things had got reversed. Instead of Loveday being in charge of Ross, *he* seemed to be in charge of *her*, determining what she might and might not do, reproaching her for not being reverent during grace. No one had ever made Loveday feel so immature as this three-year-old child.

Oliver raised his head and let their hands go, smiling at each in turn.

It wasn't till breakfast was over that Loveday got her first chance to be domestic. She washed up. Oliver dried. Ross dragged a chair to the cupboard, climbed on it and put the dishes away.

Don't drop them, Loveday wanted to warn him. This precious, old china!

Watching nervously, she remembered Daphne's theory that children take care of beautiful things. Ross did. Daphne triumphed again.

When they moved into the living room, the sun was streaming through the bay window, illuminating the portrait of Oliver's grandmother. It was the focal point of the room. *Daphne's painting!* Her presence dominated everything here.

She's dead, but I can't get away from her, Loveday thought bitterly. Gives me the creeps.

And yet, Loveday couldn't take her eyes off the picture, either. What fascinated her was its springtime mood. She knew it had been painted shortly before Serenity died at the age of eighty-three, but it radiated such zest that she could only think of youth. Though the old woman's dress was Quaker gray, it wasn't drab. On the contrary, it shimmered. The fichu around her slender neck was purest white. She carried a bright pink parasol, for it was sunny where she stood, beside a clump of daffodils in the dooryard at Firbank. Overhead, silhouetted against a sky that proclaimed this to be the most serene place on earth, ancient oaks were just beginning to leaf out.

Noticing Loveday's interest in the portrait, Oliver observed, "John Greenleaf Whittier, the Quaker poet, wrote about 'the Indian summer of the heart.' That phrase always makes me think of Grandmother. In old age, she radiated the translucent atmosphere and mellow sunshine that dispel the frosts of autumn."

"What a beautiful phrase!" Loveday exclaimed. "How does it go again?"

> "Years have passed on, and left their trace...
> Yet hath thy spirit left on me
>   An impress Time has worn not out...
>   The shadows melt, and fall apart,
> And, smiling through them, round us lies
>   The warm light of our morning skies, —
>   The Indian Summer of the heart!"

Oliver excused himself for a minute.

The Indian summer of the heart, Loveday repeated to herself, watching him walk toward the door. That applies equally to Oliver!

Ross had disappeared. Alone in the room, Loveday went over to the wall where two long wedding certificates and an old lithograph hung side by side. She had read the certificates on an earlier visit. The left-hand one belonged to the first Serenity and her husband, Edmund Otis; the one on the right was the Hollands'. When they came to live at Firbank, Oliver had explained, he wanted them to regard it as home and urged them to bring any treasures. The older certificate was already hanging here. They thought it would be interesting to put theirs up beside it. Although separated by more than a hundred years, the wording of the two, all but the names and places, was practically identical.

The lithograph portrayed a Quaker wedding in the early nineteenth century. Light from a diamond-paned window in the gable of a Meetinghouse shone on a young couple, standing, hand in hand, evidently making the promises spelled out in the certificates — to be "loving and faithful, as long as we both shall live." Both wore an expression of quiet elation. The bride's long dress had an embroidered bodice, partly covered by a flowing shawl. A Quaker bonnet hid her hair. The groom had on a frock coat and knee breeches with white stockings. There was no minister. Older people sat behind the couple on raised benches. Most of the men wore broad-brimmed hats. All the women had bonnets.

Loveday remembered how nervous she'd been at her wedding, when she stood before the minister and repeated words he coached her to say. Nervousness was what she remembered chiefly. The couple in the picture were speaking for themselves, standing before God and their friends. The picture communicated a joyous solemnity, which moved Loveday more than anything she recalled about her own wedding.

Oliver returned. Seeing Loveday studying the picture, he came over to join her. "Do you like it?"

"I find it very touching."

"So do I. It seems to portend that the occasion will sustain these two all their lives, in fair weather or foul. Don't you think so?"

"We-ell — I don't know about *that*. Maybe. Why are some of the men wearing their hats in the Meetinghouse? I should have thought — "

"It was a testimony against class distinction. Others took off their hats in the presence of their betters. Friends were egalitarian. They only took off their hats to God — when they offered prayer. You can see that the custom was already dying out. The Elders are wearing their hats. The fathers of the couple" — he pointed to them — "have taken theirs off."

"The clothes remind me of the period I wrote about in my dissertation. But except for that top-heavy bonnet, there's nothing about the bride's outfit that's typically Quaker."

"No. This was the period when progressive Friends were beginning to adopt the dress and manners of the World's People, as they called non-Friends. Gradually, nothing in their appearance or speech remained to distinguish them."

"What a pity!"

"I don't think so. If they had stayed apart from the world, Friends might have died out, like other peculiar sects."

"But you still cling to the plain language," Loveday teased, laughing.

He took it good-naturedly. "I'm just an old fogey. This picture originally belonged to Serenity's grandmother, who was the daughter of the first Serenity." Oliver turned for a second and gestured toward the portrait over the mantel. "The daughter married a man of another denomination and left the Society. Her son, Serenity's father, found the picture when he was disposing of his mother's effects. He didn't have the heart to throw it away, yet it didn't fit with the decor in his house, so he put it on the third floor landing, where no one would be likely to notice."

"It deserved better," Loveday asserted. "Just because it was old-fashioned — "

"But something amazing happened. The picture caught our Serenity's fancy. As a little girl, she used to talk to the bride whenever she went up to the attic. It made her curious about her heritage. When she was thinking of getting married, she decided to find out what a Quaker wedding would be like. That's what impelled her to look us up."

"So this picture, which the father rejected, determined the direction of the daughter's life. How fantastic! Sounds like a novel."

"A leading, I would call it."

Ross reappeared. His expression was deadpan, though he looked at Loveday out of the corner of his eye, as if he wished her to notice him. He had combed his hair himself, slicking it down in front so zealously that drops of water trickled onto his forehead. In back, his hair was still tousled.

Oliver and Loveday exchanged glances of amusement.

"You look very nice this morning," Loveday commented.

Ross gave her one of his radiant smiles — the first ever.

"Come and sit down," Oliver urged.

Loveday always chose the same chair, the one she'd taken the first time she came. She thought of it as her chair and she took it now. But the sun shone directly in her eyes and she got up again.

Seeing her walk toward the couch, Oliver went to the window.

"Please sit in your usual place," he begged, drawing the curtain far enough to shade her. "It gives me pleasure. Our friends avoid that chair. They seem to think it's sacred. You see," he explained, almost in a whisper, "it was Daphne's. But I like it to be used. When that chair's empty, I feel as though

I'd suffered an amputation. With you there, I'm whole again."

With *me* there! Loveday thought in wonder, gladly complying. *I* make him whole again! *I!*

9.

OLIVER settled himself on the other side of the hearth, with the dogs at his feet. The liveliness that ordinarily made his expression so engaging left it, as he withdrew to the habitation of his spirit.

Ross climbed onto his lap and rested his head against the old man's chest, playing quietly with the buttons on his shirt.

Peaceful, that's how the two of them look, Loveday decided.

She herself felt apprehensive. Could she call her thoughts home from their wanderings? Could she control her fingers, keep them from drumming out the theme which kept running through her head — the Rondo of the concerto for two pianos which Mozart composed for Nannerl?

In her determination to relax, Loveday clenched her hands. Her eyes, shielded by the curtain, continued their wanderings, involuntarily returning to the portrait, which was still in full sunlight. Its delicate colors glowed.

Tenderness and humor were in the old woman's face, an eagerness to meet the future — one would have said, to *grow up!* She seemed to be poised on the threshold of winter, cheerfully waiting to flower again in a more favorable climate. Loveday thought of the poem.

From time to time, Oliver stroked the curls of the child whose cheek pressed trustingly against him. But his attention was elsewhere, a long way off. He was what he called "centering down."

Even so, Loveday was aware of some inexplicable communication. Not that she could read Oliver's thoughts. It was more elemental than that. The strange silence conveyed meaning never quite defined by words. A mystery.

Ross was watching Loveday again.

She gazed out of the window, pretending not to notice, but she knew now that the unspoken communication wasn't only between herself and Oliver. It was a three-way thing.

She'd never had this communication with her own children. How could she, when she'd only just discovered it herself? Reflection required leisure and there'd been precious little of that in Loveday's busy life, certainly none when the children were small. Even if there'd been time, their constant squabbling would have made reflection impossible. There was still less opportunity when Bill was sick and later, when Loveday was struggling through graduate school and fighting for a foothold in the academic world. The more she advanced, the less time she had to herself. A dean's days are crammed with appointments, staff conferences, social functions.

What with enforcing rules and prescribing courses for students who resisted taking them, Loveday couldn't stop to mull over each person's needs and goals. She couldn't even meditate on her own.

How could I have been so superficial? she asked herself, looking down into her lap. It was wrong, cruel even, not to get to know those students as persons, to consider their needs. And maybe if I had reflected on my own, "waiting on God," as Oliver calls it, "seeking guidance" — how does he know it's *God's* guidance he's getting? — maybe I would have done better.

Too late, she thought sadly. My career's finished.

Even after she retired, would it ever have occurred to Loveday to sit down like this early in the morning and just do *nothing*? With the housework, engagements, babysitting the grandchildren and now the book she planned to write — Everyone knew that people were busier after retirement than they'd been before. No, even at this stage, Loveday would never think of sitting down early in the morning and just doing nothing.

Doing nothing? She was, she discovered, suddenly very occupied, engrossed in watching and listening to a video tape that appeared to be passing through her head, more real than a dream, inexorable as memory. The voice was her own, though different from the way she thought she sounded. The image was of a young, attractive girl who was determined to have a career as well as a husband, the latter not to interfere with the former. But things didn't turn out the way she'd planned.

William, Junior, came ahead of schedule. In the thirties, there was no maternity leave, no day-care. Loveday had to give up her job. It was low grade anyway, with no promise of promotion for a woman. Once she'd dropped out of the labor market, she figured she might as well go ahead and have the rest of the family. Will was still in diapers when Emily was born. By the time Toby arrived, Loveday was stir-crazy.

She always thought she'd borne her frustration heroically. But the video tape was shattering. On it, Loveday's expression and the tone of her voice were chronically dissatisfied. She kept demanding her rights. Even while she did the proper things — cooked, cleaned, looked after the kids, ironed Bill's shirts — she crabbed: Bill was free to go out and advance in his job; she was a captive.

No wonder, she thought, watching and listening to herself in horror, no wonder our marriage held so little joy.

Toby was just starting school and Loveday was seriously studying the want ads — not wistfully, the way she'd done for years, but with real hope — when Bill got sick. Nursing him was like having another baby, a big, irritable, terminally ill baby. Loveday felt cheated, not by him — he couldn't help it — but by life. Why me? she heard herself ask on the tape, as she cleaned up the mess in Bill's bed — more revolting than an infant's. Why me?

Her self-pity, viewed and heard against this penetrating silence, was so shaming that Loveday tried desperately to recall some redeeming aspect of her marriage.

We did have a satisfactory physical relationship. We did have that, at least. For a few years, anyhow. But the joy that still seems to illuminate Oliver — that we never knew.

She couldn't read his thoughts and she certainly hoped he couldn't read hers. For she was wondering what kind of man he was. Behind his controlled exterior, his strict, old-fashioned code, was there conflict? Beneath the openheartedness with which he reached out to a strange midwesterner, what was he really like?

A passionate man? Or had his devotion to tradition, to the discipline imposed upon him by his religion, repressed him?

Maybe, she thought with surprise, the very rigidity of that tradition, which seems so ludicrously puritanical — maybe in some contradictory way, it was actually liberating. That bit about Oliver and Daphne being each other's servants sounds so naive. Yet it seems to have given them greater freedom.

How passionate was he?

Well, Loveday thought, smiling indulgently as she watched him stroke the tangled curls, he's an old man now. No matter how he may have been once, that's past. Still, I'd give anything to know what he was like.

Ross was watching her again and she felt the blood rush to her face. It was as if the child were accusing her of trying to spy on Oliver and his wife as they lay in that big, old-fashioned bed.

What business is this of mine? Loveday asked herself, embarrassed.

But, nowadays, wasn't everybody's love life everybody's business?

Not Oliver's! It doesn't concern me. Anyway, why do I care?

He had invited her to join him on a spiritual journey and what was she thinking about?

Did all that control actually create the nobility she saw in Oliver? How could it? Inhibitions were supposed to warp people. The whole idea behind the current permissiveness was to make people less neurotic, wasn't it? Looking around the quiet room, Loveday felt puzzled. Nothing seemed to add up.

A small sigh made her turn. Ross was sliding down from Oliver's lap onto the rug. Very quietly, he started to play with his trucks.

Oliver paid no attention. His knobby, work-worn hands lay on his knees, motionless, yet they seemed to be reaching out, to be gently drawing Loveday away from her curiosity toward his aspiration. Just as she hadn't discovered Firbank but had been discovered by it, so now she didn't voluntarily participate in his mood: it overtook her.

Yet, this exercise, which he found so rewarding, made her anything but peaceful.

Bill's shadowy image appeared on the tape, very different from the picture she transmitted to the children, who'd been scarcely old enough to remember what he was really like. Their impression of him had been created by her after his death, unconsciously constructed to present herself as a woman victimized by male domination.

The image on the tape denied this completely. It put her in a very poor light. Here was a genial man who hadn't been tough enough to cope with her complaints, who was already seriously ill before he was forced to admit it.

Could the slowly progressing illness have been responsible for what she considered his lack of feeling? Was it she who'd been insensitive?

In agitation, she clutched her left hand with her right, appalled by her confrontation with a self she wasn't willing to own, a petulant woman who nagged her sick husband and deceived her children.

Wasn't she exaggerating? She hadn't been that bad. Just the same, she wanted her children to know the truth.

I must go home, she thought miserably. I must go home and tell them the way it really was.

This was the last thing she'd wanted to do when she was hanging around in the East months longer than she'd intended to stay, lingering in the hope of returning to Firbank.

I must go home.

Suppose the children couldn't understand because what she needed to convey now was so different from what she'd always claimed?

How explain the sudden change? Just sitting quietly with an old farmer and a solemn little boy — how could doing that have made her see things so differently?

Wasn't it a bit overdone, melodramatic?

Not if she could communicate Oliver's approach — uncritical of others, demanding of himself; his eager quest for Truth. It was catching. Even before the video tape made it clear, this realization had been creeping up on Loveday — that she'd failed Bill rather than that he had dominated her.

She looked at Oliver imploringly. Help me, she begged him silently. Then she turned away and shut her eyes, already seeing herself at home.

"I'm not the same person I was when I left here last spring," she would say to Will, Emily and Toby as soon as she got there. "Something happened to me at Firbank. I don't know how to describe it. That man and his wife seemed to have found freedom in serving each other with all their hearts. Discovering it made me see that, in opting for the role of grudging slavey, I let myself become trapped in marriage. It wasn't your father's fault. I did it to myself."

If she said these things to them, how would they react, her sensible, middle-aged children?

"Say, Mom," she could just hear Will drawling, "sounds like you're in love."

And Emily, whose marriage had been a disaster — wouldn't she work on her mother not to get romantically involved? "At your age," she'd most likely warn, "it's even more risky."

"That isn't it!" Loveday would cry, wishing she'd never said anything. "I'm not in love. If you just knew Oliver Otis, you'd realize — he isn't like that. I'm trying to tell you something important about your own father and you just make fun of me."

That wasn't really so. They weren't making fun of her. They hadn't said anything. She wasn't even home. And yet, she could already feel the tears stinging her closed lids.

Only Toby would try to hear what she was actually saying.

Suppose something happened before she got home and she wouldn't have the chance to tell her children the truth? They'd never know, all the rest of their lives, that their father had actually been a much nicer person —

Opening her eyes with a start, Loveday found Oliver standing before her, reaching, not for one hand, to shake it formally, as he'd done when meeting closed last night in Kendal, but for both. He stood holding them and looking down into her eyes.

The way he looked at her suddenly made Loveday feel full of possibility, with a treasure in her possession of which she was unaware, but which he recognized. This is how she remembered certain men looking at her before she was married, before she'd achieved anything, admiring her as she was, simply as an attractive young woman. Others were frankly acquisitive. But those particular men just looked at her in wonder, as they might observe a flower that was slowly opening, revealing an inner beauty they were content to gaze at without plucking. So did Oliver look at Loveday and what he appeared to see became reflected in his face. He seemed younger.

"You were right about the silence," she told him softly. "It didn't make me peaceful. It got me to thinking about things I'd never wanted to confront before — awful things."

If she were really such a bad woman, would a man like Oliver be looking at her this way?

"We all have regrets," he was saying. "Stewing over them is destructive. But when we face ourselves in the silence with companions who are also seeking guidance, we often find strength to begin anew. Beginning over is all that's asked of us."

"But it's too late."

"Never."

"There's no one left."

"There's you." His grip, so relaxed as to seem impersonal, tightened in reassurance.

How was he to know what a mess she'd made of life? She hoped he'd never find out.

"There's you," he repeated. "Your name endows you with a gift for reconciliation."

"Whom with?"

"Yourself."

What did he mean? Her name referred to a day in the Middle Ages when disputes were settled between serfs. How could it reconcile her to *herself*?

At least, she could be honest about the present.

"Oliver," she confessed, looking at him squarely, "I didn't just come because I wanted to help Rennie, though I'm glad I could do that. I'd been wanting an excuse to return. That's why I called you up — hoping you'd invite me."

"Whatever may have brought you to us, I'm glad you came."

"There's something here which — I don't know how to describe it."

He smiled down on her warmly. "Perhaps, after all, you've discovered your Quaker ancestors — in yourself."

"Yes. Only now I have to go home. I never intended to stay so long."

"You're leaving? This morning?"

"Oh no. I promised Rennie I'd stay till she gets back. Then I'll pack up my stuff in Boston and head home."

"To *Kansas?*" He looked stunned. "But," he argued, "even if you've discovered the spirit of your ancestors, you don't yet know what they did or where they lived. Your daughter-in-law won't be able to complete the family tree. How can you go back to Kansas without the information?"

"Sara Ann will be disappointed," Loveday admitted, "but, I have to go."

Oliver's hands, that had been grasping hers so affectionately, suddenly relinquished them.

10.

ALL THE WAY to Kendal, no one spoke except Ross, who chatted continuously. Oliver seemed strangely subdued. As for Loveday — she was beside herself. The peculiar mood that had enveloped her during the silence, the almost hypnotic spell, had vanished, but not before it betrayed her.

What got into me? she wondered, aghast. What made me say I'm going home when all I want is to be here? I could have written to the children. No need to *go*. Now I've burned my bridges. After telling Oliver in that solemn moment that I'm leaving, I can't very well stay.

If only he'd try to dissuade her! She'd capitulate at once.

He, however, said nothing till they reached the nursery school. Then he merely spoke to Ross.

"Loveday Mead and I'll be close by, at the Meetinghouse. Lunchtime, we'll pick thee up and drive to the cove to say hello to the swans."

Reluctantly yet manfully, Ross walked across the school yard. As Loveday watched the little guy go, her heart went out to him. She had resented his supervision during the silence, but as she thought about it, she felt touched. It showed he cared about her.

"I hope," she said to Oliver, "that I can win his confidence in the short time that's left — even his love."

Oliver didn't answer. When Ross was safe inside, he drove on.

In sunshine, the Friends Meetinghouse looked even smaller than last night — more starkly unadorned. But beautiful. On that bright October morning, the clear, antique glass in the windows glinted violet and gold. The sky was a cloudless blue. The leaves of the trees that shaded the dove-gray walls of the old building were crimson, saffron and brittle russet.

Oliver reached above a syringa bush for the key to the Meetinghouse, which was hanging from a nail in the wall. "We keep it here so anyone who wishes may open the door," he explained.

"Awfully trusting," Loveday commented. "In Boston, you'd be vandalized."

"There's nothing of value inside except those historic Minute Books. Who else would want them? We don't own communion plate or silver. Fire — that's the real risk. Youngsters have sometimes sneaked in to smoke. But we feel it's worth taking the chance so there'll be a quiet place to withdraw into, should some passerby feel the need to center down. In these troubling times — A place of worship ought to be open at all hours, to everybody. Don't you think so?"

Loveday shrugged. She didn't know what she thought about that. It sounded nice but dangerous. As she mounted the steps, she noticed a plaque beside the door which revealed that this Meetinghouse was erected in 1829. "Oh!" she cried. The date had significance for her in a different context.

Oliver was still standing at the foot of the stairs, gazing skyward. "Those gulls," he murmured. "It must be high tide."

The gulls didn't interest Loveday. She was running her finger over the numerals incised in the board. "Eighteen twenty-nine! Oliver, that's the year Nannerl Mozart died. She was blind, alone, penniless. And what memories she must have had! Regrets, too. I'm sure she had regrets."

Oliver came up beside Loveday and watched her finger trace the date.

"It was only a few months after Schubert's death," she told him dreamily.

For a second, Loveday was transported from Kendal to Vienna. She was sitting in a coffee house, listening to Lieder that articulated for all time the longing of the human heart. Then the orchestra struck up an irresistible waltz.

"That was the beginning of the waltz craze," she recalled, as Oliver unlocked the Meetinghouse door and stood aside for her to go in. "A young fiddler named Johann Strauss was composing such catchy tunes, they set the whole world dancing. After the stiff, impersonal minuet, reserved for courtiers, who kept a discreet distance from their partners, the waltz was liberating. Everyone danced it, even common people." Loveday giggled. "The man actually put his arm around the woman's waist. They gazed into each other's eyes and whispered secrets!"

Oliver laughed, too. "We older Quakers weren't allowed to dance when we were young. Well, my generation was the first to have that freedom. But I never learned. While all the gaiety you describe was going on in Vienna," he reflected, obviously fascinated by the contrast, "in this Rhode Island village, a handful of farm folk built a simple house of worship which still testifies to their faith."

How far apart we are, Loveday thought.

Their inner landscapes, the neighborhoods of their imagination were separated by the Atlantic Ocean and half the continent of Europe, as far apart in feeling as in space. Like the yearning refrain of a Schubert song, the words echoed in Loveday's mind: *How far apart!*

"Eighteenth-century Quakers were ahead of their time in many respects," Oliver was saying. "They befriended the Indians and recognized the equality of women. They renounced slavery a hundred years before the Emancipation Proclamation. But music, no! Music was excluded from their lives, even from their worship. A member who so much as happened to be present at a gathering where there was fiddling and dancing was termed guilty of 'disorderly walking.' As for owning a piano —"

"Disorderly —" Loveday repeated, shocked as well as amused. "You don't mean like — well —"

Oliver laughed again. "Inconceivable in this day and age, isn't it? Yet, in that period, Quakers dealt severely with petty infractions. The enjoyment of music and dancing was one."

"But why?"

"It was thought to distract from the main business of life, which was the cultivation of the spirit. Come in and I'll show you some examples of what those Friends called 'disorderly walking.'"

Halfway up the stairs that led to the gallery where the old Minute Books were stored, Loveday had an arresting thought. She stopped and looked back to share it with Oliver, who was coming up behind her.

"Music," she declared vehemently, "is what made life under the Hapsburgs bearable. For people who lived in poverty and constant fear of the police, what else was there but sensual pleasure? It was the only escape."

The narrow staircase made an inconvenient place for discussion. Oliver teetered precariously. Loveday hurried up the last few steps. The mustiness that greeted her in the gallery was so familiar as to be almost welcoming. When she was here before, she had decided privately that the faded brown cushions on the benches — stuffed with the original horsehair, Oliver told her proudly — needed a good airing.

As she looked down to the room below, where she'd sat with him last night, it struck her that, seen from here, there was something engaging about the very austerity. No altar, no pulpit, no regal armchair for a clergyperson (there wasn't any such person), just sunshine lying in stripes across the floor and glowing on the plain pine benches. Outside, autumn leaves blew against clear windows, creating a glory beyond the most sublime stained glass. There was a reverent aura about the simple, whitewashed room, as if the aspiration experienced there still permeated it.

And yet, there was also a lack of pretension, an acceptance of the people who came there as they naturally were. Children were expected to observe the silence, Oliver had told Loveday, not because they were restrained by their parents but because they themselves felt the solemnity. In his youth, he said, the benches at the front of the room — the "facing benches" — were reserved for Elders, but these distinctions had long since disappeared. Nowadays, children were often the ones who chose to sit up there. The narrow one in the center, he'd explained, was where the couple sat during a wedding.

In a corner of the gallery, Oliver was bending over a seachest. One by one, he lifted out the huge, leatherbound volumes and lined them up on a bench.

"There," he said, puffing a little. "Maybe we'll locate your ancestors this time." He sounded unenthusiastic.

Thinking of last night, Loveday turned to him and asked, "Does the Meeting still keep its Minutes in handsome books like these?"

"Afraid not. We could never afford the leather. We just use a modern record book with good rag paper so it will endure. Then," he added, with a twinkle, "if a descendant of yours should come here some day, he or she will find your name properly preserved in this year's Minutes."

This was exactly what Loveday'd been wondering about. Her name was recorded!

"These are the Minutes of the seventeen seventies," Oliver said, turning the tall, stiff pages carefully, stopping suddenly as he came to an item of interest.

"Loveday, here's a poor woman who was disowned for allowing her daughter to go to a non-Quaker wedding. *Barsheba Knowles, wife of Joseph Knowles,*" he read in his youthful voice with the crisp New England inflection, "*having a right of membership in our society and she giving liberty to her daughter to attend a marriage* — spelt m-a-r-a-g-e — *and notwithstanding Friends' labor, admonition, and advice, she not only neglected to condemn*" — laughing, Oliver made the word sound fierce — "*but rather justified her self and her child in attending the marriage, all which is contrary to and against the wholesome Discipline of our Society. Therefore we have denied Barsheba membership with us until she shall make satisfaction for her transgression, which is our hearty desire.*" Oliver looked up for a second. "Can't you just see them," he asked, grinning, "wanting her to beg forgiveness so they could be charitable and take her back? They didn't really intend to let her go, just to give her a bad time."

"They sound mean," Loveday exclaimed. "I always thought Quakers were gentle, like you."

"They try to be. Those old Friends felt they must enforce rigidly what they called the 'wholesome Discipline' of the Society. This nearly proved their undoing. Numbers dwindled. That was a pity, since the principles they stood for were actually noble. But, Loveday, what will our descendants think of us? We've gone to the other extreme, accepting every kind of behavior, even when we disapprove, even when we believe people are harming themselves. We're not beyond reproach."

As he spoke, Oliver turned some pages, then stopped. "Listen to this, recorded at the Yearly Meeting session held in Newport in seventeen seventy-four: *Divers Friends in this Meeting manifesting a Concern that the Liberty of the Africans might be fully restored* — think of it — seventeen seventy-four! Other Americans were fighting for their own liberty, while complacently owning slaves."

Loveday's eyes scanned the page as Oliver read the slanting script aloud. *"That such laws may be made that tend to the abolition of Slavery and to get such laws repealed as any way encourages it, we appoint these Friends to use their influence at the General Assembly of the Colony of Rhode Island or with members thereof: Thomas Hazard, Ezekiel Comstock, Stephen Hoxie, Isaac Austell* — Austell! Your forebear!"

Loveday turned to Oliver in disbelief. There was anguish in his face.

"Isaac Austell," he repeated. "There you are." Far from gloating over his success, he sounded bereft.

Now Loveday possessed the information that she'd come here for originally, that she'd since fervently hoped wouldn't turn up. It was on the page before her, plain as day. She was sunk.

"An ancestor to take pride in," Oliver was saying, "who labored to free the slaves nearly a century before most of his countrymen did anything. Not one" — he smiled wryly — "who walked disorderly."

Loveday tried to smile, too, but her face was frozen. She was in a state of shock.

"You're going home with something glorious to tell your grandchildren."

Loveday couldn't speak. Even if she hadn't already announced her departure, the discovery would have demanded that she go. There was no turning back now.

11.

AFTER THAT, the whole scene became blurred. All the things that made Firbank so appealing were the same, but Loveday couldn't savor them. In imagination, she was no longer there. She was already in Kansas, looking back with bittersweet nostalgia to her idyllic New England experience.

Peter came home early in the afternoon. He and Ross were invited to go sailing with the Hills.

Oliver rowed Loveday across the pond so she could see the ocean for the last time. The weather was glorious — sunny and clear, with a light offshore breeze. Yet, when Loveday stood on the dune beside Oliver, watching the waves roll in and cover the white sand with frothy fringes, none of the ecstasy she'd known on earlier occasions possessed her. All she felt was a dull ache.

In spite of her gloom, she enjoyed the evening with the Ludlows.

"When I was a young man," Oliver told her as they were driving to Kendal, "I considered Philip Ludlow, John's father, the embodiment of qualities I wished to possess. He was lovable, with bubbling humor. He held strong Quaker convictions, yet he was accepting of everyone, listening to their opinions, though he might differ radically. No one was afraid to talk honestly to Philip, even people who ordinarily felt rejected.

John's very like his father — quiet, compassionate, open."

"What does he do?"

"He's Ross's doctor. He's skillful and so tender that children give him their trust. But he's not very strong, himself. Picked up something in China during the Civil War. He was serving there with the medical team the Communist Government asked Friends to send over."

"You mean, Friends backed the Communists?"

"No. They didn't back anyone. It was because of their well-known impartiality that they were asked to take care of the sick and wounded on both sides. They didn't look into the political sympathies of the bodies they found, half buried in mud," Oliver concluded, turning into a driveway, "nor of the children with smallpox and pneumonia, who huddled together for warmth in the razed villages. The American Red Cross donated drugs to wipe out kala-azar, a disease that attacks children. John administered those drugs in a mud hut. Wheel-barrows full of children were brought in."

Loveday could see them in her mind's eye and she shuddered. John must be a wonderful man.

The Ludlows lived very simply in a little New England salt-box. Everything in the house struck Loveday as having been chosen with unusual taste. Clara served a delicious meal with a minimum of fuss, while John talked to Oliver and Loveday. She was as impressed by him as she had been by Clara the previous evening. He was a good-looking man, in spite of his pallor, with a humorous twinkle and a gracious manner.

But what Loveday was most conscious of that evening and what she would cherish in her memory was the happiness Oliver appeared to feel because she was with him. And the Ludlows treated her as if she belonged, simply because she was Oliver's friend.

Driving back to Firbank, he said little. When they stood on the upstairs landing, saying good night, he took both of Loveday's hands in his and, looking at her the way he had when she thought he was about to kiss her, he said, "Thy coming has enriched us all. We tend to get a little ingrown here." He didn't kiss her.

Like a bad dream, the finality of her departure troubled Loveday's sleep all night. In the morning, when she was packing her bag, she decided to leave right after Rennie returned. The sooner she went the less painful it would be. She'd have that talk with Rennie and take off.

The terrible finality wasn't all that made her severance from Firbank unbearable. This visit had been more affecting than previous ones. She felt uncritically accepted by Oliver. His manner seemed to imply that she was satisfactory, just as she was.

When Loveday entered the kitchen, Ross eyed her, apparently unperturbed. Then he returned to directing traffic on the kitchen table. Even he was beginning to accept her!

"Right on red," he commanded. "No turn on red."

"The fair weather's still with us," Oliver announced. "Indian summer, perfect for digging the last of the potatoes."

Tongue in cheek, he inquired whether Ross would mind staying home from nursery school to help. The joyful reply was deafening. More quietly, Loveday offered to go out with them.

"Hard to believe, isn't it," Oliver commented, when they stood in the field, surveying the rows of dead plant-tops, "that under those withered stalks there's a whole winter's sustenance for us?" He dug the prongs of the fork lightly into the soil. "So many things are like that. We only see a surface desolation, not the riches waiting beneath it for us to reach down and harvest."

They worked slowly, Oliver plunging the fork into the soil, then resting on it while Ross lifted each potato out of the ground with incredible care, laying it on the surface to dry.

Loveday brushed away the earth that clung to the skins, but her back wasn't used to that kind of activity and she soon had to stop. It wasn't long before Oliver had had enough, too.

Late in the afternoon, the rattle of Rennie's car, chugging up the lane, announced her return. Ross rushed out to greet his mother.

Peter, just home from work, rushed out, too, looking no less eager, if somewhat apprehensive.

The dogs bounded after him — Lion, the retriever, jumping on Rennie as she got out of the car and almost knocking her over in his delight; Duffy, the elderly fox terrier, bringing up the rear, limping, but wagging her stubby tail with consummate devotion.

"Poor old Duffy," Oliver exclaimed as he and Loveday watched from the doorway. "Before too long, we'll have to — "

"Oh no!" Loveday exclaimed. "The place won't be the same without Duffy."

She wanted everything to stay exactly the way it was.

The flowerbeds flanking the brick walk were bright with chrysanthemums and crimson roses. Beyond the walk, over by the old horse block, the three Hollands were locked in a passionate embrace. Their bodies seemed to say they could never get close enough to make up for the two-day separation.

Observing this touching reunion with what should have been the detachment of a visitor who had all but left, never to return, Loveday was surprised by the extent of her involvement. She watched anxiously as Rennie and Peter began speaking. What were they saying?

Viewed from the distance, the trio formed a compact unit. The individuals merged into an entity that was greater than the sum of its parts. Did Loveday really wish to see this unit disrupted?

She had barged in where angels like Oliver kept out. She had acted as if Rennie were single, instead of recognizing that she was an indispensable component of this ideal unit — ideal but frighteningly fragile.

No wonder Ross had regarded Loveday with suspicion! No wonder Rennie, who'd orginally been so friendly, had become reserved.

From this distance, Loveday couldn't make out what Rennie was saying to Peter, but she guessed it was a report of the Museum's offer.

Sickening fear gripped her.

Suppose the Hollands were to leave Firbank? Suppose they split up, even if only temporarily —

The brash assurance with which she'd intervened in the affairs of this family had been dictated by an obligation to support a younger sister, but now it became clear that the course Loveday was following threatened to destroy what she most wanted to preserve.

It's bad enough, being exiled. If I can't picture things here continuing the way they are —

Suddenly turning to Oliver, she blurted out, "I'm going to rewrite my life. Even before I write Nannerl Mozart's." Those were the last words she was to have with him alone.

He looked puzzled.

Before Loveday could explain — she wasn't sure herself just what she really meant — Peter and Rennie, holding Ross between them, came trooping up the front steps and surrounded Oliver and Loveday with their overflowing joy in being together.

Rennie reached out to them both.

12.

"Wow, it's good to be home! New York — I couldn't wait to get out of there. But it was wonderful in the Museum. Aquila sends thee her best, Oliver. Now that I'm going to be a colleague, she wants me to call her by her first name. Loveday, you got along beautifully. Thanks ever so much. You'll stay tonight, won't you?"

Loveday shook her head. "I'm leaving now."

"Not before we've had tea," Oliver declared. "The kettle's on. Come in the kitchen, everyone. We want to hear about thy trip, Serenity."

Hadn't she already implied that she was hired? What more was there to hear? Oliver seemed to be taking it more calmly than Loveday. But his whole future —

What would become of him?

While Ross climbed onto his telephone books and the grownups took their seats at the kitchen table, Oliver brewed tea in an antique pewter pot. Nicks impressed on it by many generations didn't detract from its elegance.

Setting the teapot down on the table beside the cake a neighbor had brought in, Oliver asked Rennie, "Did thee speak to Judy?"

"Yes. She was very touched by thy offer to come. But she doesn't want thee making that long trip. Thee needn't worry about her any more. She has a good job."

Loveday wasn't interested in Judy's job, only in Rennie's. "How was the Museum?"

"Marvelous! You ought to go there before you leave the East. It's easy to fly to New York from Boston."

Why not? Loveday was in no hurry to leave.

But Oliver didn't know that. "Loveday's impatient to return to her family," he explained to Rennie. "Yesterday, looking through the Kendal Meeting Minutes of the Revolutionary period, we found what she was hoping to discover when she came here — a reference to one of her ancestors. Now her daughter-in-law can add a biographical note to his name on the family tree. Isaac Austell was an ancestor to be proud of. Loveday's eager to get home and tell her children about him."

"Well," Loveday drawled, "there's no rush. As a matter of fact —"

"Never mind," Rennie broke in. "But the next time you come East, be sure to go to the Museum of Contemporary Art. I got so excited, seeing those pictures hanging there, after I'd helped Daphne pick them out for her Show! There were hundreds of drawings and paintings to choose from, you know. I'd hold one up and Daphne'd think about it, then nod or shake her head. That's how I knew which ones she wanted to exhibit. Now, the Museum owns some of her finest canvases."

"Including," Oliver put in, "the Second Serenity's portrait."

Until he said that, Rennie had looked so animated, so pretty, with that high coloring, the blue eyes and red curls, that Loveday could easily see why Daphne had wished to paint her portrait.

But when Oliver mentioned it, Rennie's expression became troubled.

"It's weird," she exclaimed, turning to Peter. "When I stand in front of the portrait, I —"

Peter grinned. "Thee hasn't got used to it yet!"

"No. I'm always afraid someone will recognize me and laugh. I don't know how it will be when I'm working there."

"Thee's accepted?" Oliver inquired in the same tone with which he had just asked, "Another cup of tea?"

"Yes. Well, I said I'd let them know definitely after I've talked it over with Peter. But I don't see how we can *not* accept. I'll be earning more than he's doing now. We'll have to live with Mother and Daddy, at least in the beginning. I'll commute to New York."

"*Me?*" Peter exclaimed. "Thee expects *me* to live with thy folks? I'm not about to give up my job and this home to go and live with them."

"Okay, Ross and I'll come here weekends. I hope Mother

won't mind taking care of him. Anyway, there's a day-care center in Neville where I can leave him while I'm at work."

"Rennie! Thee wouldn't do that to Ross?"

She looked down at her cup. Ross started to whimper.

"Would thee leave him with me?" Oliver asked diffidently. "Since thee'd be coming weekends —"

"Oh, Oliver!" The words escaped before Loveday could tell herself that this was none of her business. But how could an old man — Even she'd found it trying and she was a lot younger.

"That's sweet of thee, Oliver," Rennie said, raising her eyes. "But a child his age needs his mother. Anyway, Peter and I haven't had a chance to discuss this yet."

"Well, I'm not going to let Ross be pushed around just for a little extra money," Peter declared, taking the child on his lap.

Rennie's blue eyes blazed. "It's not just the money! This is the chance of a lifetime for me." Turning to Oliver, she changed the subject, making a noticeable effort to be calm. "How did it go the other night — the Called Meeting?"

"We had a good session. No unity as to the disposition of the bequest, but a variety of ideas. There's a general sentiment that we should tie the disbursement in with personal service. I agree."

Peter turned to him and asked, "What would thee like to see done?"

Characteristically, Oliver thought carefully before answering. At length he said, "Of course, what any one of us wants isn't decisive, only what appears best when the sense of the meeting is gathered. But I've been thinking for some time — Thee knows how many stranded walkers, cyclists, even motorists we've taken in every summer — total strangers. They've come for a pleasant stay at the beach, only to find at nightfall that there's no place around here to lay their heads. They've pitched tents in our woods, slept in the hayloft, even on the living room floor."

"There must have been hundreds."

Wistfully, Oliver murmured, "We may not always be here to take them in."

Rennie looked dismayed. In the very act of planning to leave Firbank, she seemed to have taken it for granted that she'd always be there. And in that moment, Loveday saw how much the place meant to Rennie.

"What's needed in this neighborhood," Oliver went on, "is simple, inexpensive accommodation, open to people of all ages. In England, Friends Meetings located in holiday centers often provide hostels for tourists. Friends staff them. To share the natural beauty one happens to be blest with seems to me to be as great a spiritual service as any one can render."

"Say," Peter cried, "that's a terrific idea! Melissa Gray's house is close to the beach. It could easily be converted into such a hostel. Maybe Neil Hill would build some little boats for those people to sail on the pond. There's a lot of land for camping. All of us in the Meeting could take turns being there to keep an eye on the place and provide an evening meal."

Peter's enthusiasm made Oliver look happier than he'd seemed all day. "I can just picture Lucas Lang sitting by the fire in that house after supper and telling the travelers about the history of this area."

"Afterward," Peter added, "I'd take them out and show them the stars. Ross can come with us. He'll have kids to play with there."

"That's just what he needs," Rennie exclaimed. "While I'm helping clean up, he can play — "

Oliver was laughing. "Sounds as though we'd benefit more from such an enterprise than the people we'd be doing it for."

I wish I were going to be here, Loveday thought. Then she remembered that she'd intended to return to Boston as soon as

Rennie came home. "I'd better be going," she said reluctantly. "I'll just run up and get my bag."

"Let me," Rennie urged. "I'm going up anyway. I can't stand these city clothes another minute."

They walked to the front hall together.

This was the opportunity Loveday'd been waiting for — to give Rennie the pep talk she'd planned ever since she heard about the job offer. It was now or never. Oliver and Peter were clearing away the tea things. They'd be joining them in a minute.

But the talk didn't come off the way Loveday'd rehearsed it — just the opposite. "I'm sorry," she said instead, surprised by her own words, "sorry if I seemed to be pushing you. The young women at college needed to be encouraged to find fulfillment. I'm afraid I kept forgetting that you're older."

"That's okay," Rennie said. "I knew you meant well. But I do have to have space to figure things out for myself. My parents were always trying to do that for me. Even now, they can't believe I'm grown up. But I am."

She threw her arms around Loveday. The reserve was gone.

As Rennie let go, Loveday said, "I just might fly to New York for a day or two. I want to see your portrait. Matter of fact, I'm not in such a rush."

Rennie started upstairs, but stopped and turned. "I'm glad I asked you to come home with me that day you were so frustrated by the librarian," she said, smiling. "And thank you for making Oliver happy. He's very lonely." Then she ran up the rest of the way.

I? Loveday thought. *I* make Oliver happy? *He* makes *me.* How could *I* — ?

Dazed by Rennie's last words, she slipped into the living room. She wanted to see The First Serenity's portrait once more and Daphne's other pictures, the Harvard chair which

Oliver occupied when they had those comfortable talks, the sampler.

She went over to the wall where it hung and reread the motto: *Walk cheerfully over the world.*

I must remember that, she thought. When I'm back home I'll remember everything here.

Rennie was coming down with Loveday's bag. They went out together.

Oliver, Peter and Ross were waiting in the driveway.

Fearful of breaking down, Loveday made short work of the goodbyes. Yes, Oliver did look lonely as he held the car door open for her. There was a tragic finality in the way he slammed it shut.

The motor was already running when, on an impulse, Loveday reached through the window, hoping for a last-minute sign of affection from Ross, now that he'd begun to warm up. Peter pushed him toward her and Loveday leaned out.

"Will you kiss me?" she asked, laughing.

"No."

She should have let it go at that. What possessed her to insist? "Don't you love me?"

He shook his head.

"Don't you?" Loveday pleaded, trying to sound as if she were joking, though she was in dead earnest.

"No." Then Ross said gravely, looking up at her, " 'cle Oliver loves you."

The little wretch! Trying to embarrass her —

Loveday drew back into the car. Her cheeks burned.

Shouting above the roar of the engine, Ross repeated, " 'cle Oliver loves you!"

"Ross!" Serenity cried. "Don't say things like that."

"But he *told* me. 'cle Oliver told me."

Without a backward look, Loveday stepped on the gas and sped down the lane.

PART THREE
Oliver

1.

*A*FTER ALL, Oliver wasn't required to terminate Duffy's life. It was rudely snuffed out at a moment when the little fox terrier and her infirmities were furthest from his thought.

As Loveday's car disappeared down the lane, he stood in the driveway with the Hollands, still seeing, in his mind's eye, her consternation when Ross made the startling disclosure.

Added to the pain he felt on parting from Loveday, this episode distressed Oliver so much that he was afraid he couldn't control his emotion. What must she think of him, confiding in a child, yet never declaring himself to her? Peter and Serenity — what must they think? If only Oliver had told them! Seeing the reproachful way they looked at Ross, seeing the child's response — fear and bewilderment — Oliver turned in anguish and headed for the house.

Ross started after him.

"Come, Ross," Serenity called. "Daddy and I are walking down to get the mail. Thee come with us."

Peter was whistling to the dogs.

Shut up in his study, Oliver collapsed into the chair by the window. He felt exhausted. Even with his eyes closed, he kept seeing Loveday's stricken face as she drove away. What she must think of him! But a declaration of love implied a proposal. And marriage wasn't what he'd had in mind that afternoon two months ago when, aching with loneliness, foolishly believing that his words weren't making any impression, he had confided in the sleepy child.

How could he have declared himself to Loveday? Why, he hadn't even told Heather. And this concerned her, too.

What if the unimaginable should occur and he were to propose? A marriage, he reminded himself, affects not only the man and woman who enter into it, but their families, as well. Without family unity, love, which ought to be sunny and free, will always be a little clouded and hemmed in.

Thinking of Heather added to Oliver's misery. In place of Loveday's stricken face, he saw his daughter's, as she sat at the massive Victorian desk in her London flat, reading an aerogram not as yet composed, in which he finally made a clean breast. The thought of her reaction to this unwritten letter gave him chills. Yet, how could he have withheld the truth from Heather?

Until now, he'd had a prick of conscience every time he wrote to her without mentioning Loveday. In his present state, he felt something far worse — abject remorse. What he had written was true, as far as it went. But it wasn't truth — the whole truth. And "speaking truth in love" was basic to his faith.

I've failed my own child, he thought guiltily.

No daughter could be more solicitous. Every week, she sent her father well-meant suggestions for improvement in his mode of living or thinking. To Oliver, most of these suggestions seemed irrelevant. Except for the short time Heather spent at Firbank each year, she actually knew little about what went on there from day to day. Yet, informed or not, she zealously offered advice.

Oliver's innate courtesy and his concern for everyone's self-esteem restrained him from letting Heather know how inept some of her tactfully worded admonitions appeared to him. He never argued. He simply did what he felt was right. Notwithstanding his age, he believed that he was managing his affairs properly — or had managed them, before Loveday came and upset his equanimity. Loveday's coming had made him less than forthright with Heather.

Patronizing — that's what it is, he told himself bitterly — withholding truth for fear of inflicting pain. That's unworthy. Heather could take it. I've let the trust run out of our relationship. Can it ever be restored?

Sitting in the armchair by the window, confronting regret upon regret, Oliver was struggling to keep from breaking down when Ross burst in without knocking — something he never did. He was sobbing.

Oliver took him on his lap and held the convulsing little body tightly. Peter and Serenity must have criticized him. That was wrong. How was the child to know that he'd been indiscreet?

"Don't cry," Oliver whispered soothingly. "It's all right. I know thee didn't mean — It's all right, Ross."

"But she's hurt!"

"Maybe not," Oliver managed to say — anything to calm the child. "Loveday Mead is a sensible lady."

Ross stopped crying temporarily. "Not her!" he burst out, as if Loveday wouldn't have mattered so much. "Duffy!"

"Oh. What happened?"

Ross started sobbing again. "Truck bop — bop — bopped Duffy."

Looking up, Oliver saw Serenity standing in the doorway. Her face was white.

"Ross told thee?"

"Yes. Is it bad?"

Serenity was slow to answer.

Oliver pressed her. "Is she suffering?"

"No. It was instantaneous. She couldn't have felt anything."

Instantaneous! So Duffy wasn't just hurt, as Ross thought, but dead. Oliver relaxed his hold on the child and shrank into himself.

Crossing the room, Serenity gently lifted her son off Oliver's lap and set him on his feet. Then she took Oliver's hand.

Held in her warm one, his hand felt icy.

"I know how thee loved her," she said softly. "We all did. But, Oliver, that truck just missed — " she caught her breath in a repressed sob — "just missed Ross."

This roused Oliver from his misery. "*Ross?*"

"He barely escaped. The truck came tearing down the Salt Pond Road so fast, he and Lion almost didn't get out of the way. They wouldn't have made it if Peter hadn't seen the truck coming. He grabbed Ross. Lion leaped after him. Duffy just couldn't move quickly enough."

"Trucks have no business on that road," Oliver cried angrily. "It's too narrow and winding. There's a sign forbidding them. But they pay no attention."

He withdrew his hand so he could grip the arms of his chair to stand up. His legs were like water.

"Sit still," Serenity urged, wiping her eyes. "Peter's taking care of everything."

"*Sit still?* When my dear companion is being laid to rest? I must go out and help Peter."

Again, Oliver tried to stand up and again he fell back. The room was spinning. Had he had a stroke? Perspiration broke out on his forehead.

"Sit still," Serenity repeated and this time it was a command. She sounded alarmed. "Hadn't I better call Dr. Liveek?"

"That won't be necessary," Oliver answered gruffly. But he wasn't so sure. "Do I look ill?"

Serenity didn't answer. All she said was, "I'm going to get thee a cup of tea. Come Ross, Daddy needs thee."

Oliver's shirt was drenched with perspiration and yet he was shivering. Had he really suffered a stroke? He tried moving his arms and legs, one after the other. They worked. Then he puckered his lips. Daphne's facial muscles had been paralyzed, twisting mouth. But his seemed to be all right. Daphne had had aphasia. He could speak. Everything was functioning. Could it have been a heart attack?

Serenity returned alone. "Ross is helping Peter dig the grave," she explained, handing Oliver the tea. "We told him he's taking thy place. That made him feel very proud. They're putting Duffy down at the edge of the orchard, under that big pine tree — thee knows. Peter said they'd have a little silence and maybe a prayer, just the two of them."

"But Ross — he's only a baby! Death's a shock, even for us."

Serenity perched on the edge of Oliver's desk. She looked at him earnestly. "Ross has to learn about death some time. I'd rather have it come early. My mother was so afraid, she didn't even want to hear about it. Daddy thought she wouldn't come to Daphne's memorial meeting, but she did and she told me afterward that it was the first time she saw death as anything but grisly. The fact that all those people were giving thanks for Daphne's life instead of crying made Mother aware of something she'd never known — that death is also — well — sort of sublime. I don't want Ross to be in his sixties before he discovers that."

Oliver nodded. "Thee's right."

Serenity looked at him pleadingly. "Oliver — " She hesitated. "Ross didn't mean to stir up trouble, saying what he did to Loveday. Thee knows that, doesn't thee? I can't imagine where he got the idea."

"I told him."

"Then it's true?"

"I'd been intending to tell thee and Peter all along, but

somehow, there never seemed to be a right time. I'm sorry now that I didn't just do it, regardless."

Serenity smiled lovingly. "We had a suspicion," she confessed. "As a matter of fact, we were hoping—"

"You *were?*"

"Of course! Peter and I think it would be an ideal marriage."

Oliver jumped. "*Marriage?* What has that to do with it? I'm not contemplating—"

"Loveday's great," Serenity exclaimed, disregarding this. "I did resent her putting pressure on me about taking the job. That's up to Peter and me to decide. But I think she understands now. From that first day, when I brought her home, it was obvious she was interested in thee."

"I doubt that."

"She is. Can't thee tell? She's always wanting to come back."

"Not any more. It was simply to find out about her ancestors. That's been achieved. There's nothing to come back for."

"Wait and see."

Baffled, Oliver peered at Serenity. What did she mean?

"Wait and see," she repeated, laughing. "Thee doesn't know much about women, Oliver. Loveday may not realize it herself yet, but she's gone on thee. She'll be back."

Unable to take this in, Oliver just stared at Serenity.

"With all her faults," she was saying, "Loveday's a really fine person. Still, doesn't thee think she was a bit silly to keep asking Ross if he loves her?"

"She was hoping to win his affection."

"How could he say yes, when he doesn't love her? Ross is truthful, but tender-hearted, too, and I think he wanted to console Loveday by telling her that, even if he didn't, someone loved her."

"It's all right," Oliver murmured, just as he'd done with Ross, though it wasn't in the least all right. "I hope thee and Peter didn't scold him."

"No. We were puzzled, though."

"It's all right," Oliver said again. "Only, Loveday looked so sad."

"Embarrassed, probably, with us there. It must actually make her radiantly happy to know that someone like thee — "

"She doesn't know."

"She *doesn't?*"

"I mean, she didn't, till Ross — Why should she? It doesn't change anything. What would she want with an old man like me?"

"Anyone would be honored to marry thee, Oliver," Serenity cried. "Thee's the most wonderful — "

"She's independent. She has all those musicians and a book to write."

"I don't know. Sometimes Loveday looks wistful. I often wonder if all that activity and her drive to run other women's lives isn't because she feels she's missed something herself. Now," Serenity commanded, walking toward the door, "thee take a nap."

"I must write to Heather."

"Later. Get some sleep first. When Peter comes in, he'll help thee up to thy room."

"No need for anything like that," Oliver cried after her indignantly. But, sinking back, he knew it was a false boast.

The click of the latch, as Serenity pulled the door to behind her, resounded in his ears like the shot of a gun, for it portended her departure from Firbank. Until he heard it, Oliver had been so preoccupied with Loveday's leaving and Duffy's death that he'd put everything else out of his mind. Suddenly he pictured what would happen when Serenity took that job. Peter might continue to sleep here on week nights for a time, but he would never choose to be separated very long from Serenity and Ross. Eventually, he'd be the one to capitulate.

He'd give up his university appointment to move to New York. Except for Lion, Oliver'd be quite alone.

Blackness closed in. Not since he was eighteen and the court-martial sentenced him to solitary confinement had he known such despair.

2.

AT SUPPERTIME, Oliver managed to drag himself to the kitchen. As soon as he was seated, Lion slid his long legs under the table and dropped his head on Oliver's shoes.

"He's grieving," Serenity decided.

Peter agreed. "He and Duffy did the same thing when Daphne died. Remember, Oliver, how thee had to take them with thee to meeting?"

"Dogs in meeting?" Ross exclaimed.

"Why not? They were very quiet, just lying at Uncle Oliver's feet."

"I believe they were gathered with us in worship," Oliver told the child.

When Serenity and Peter grasped his hands before beginning the meal, he recognized how deeply he was cherished and gave thanks. But he couldn't eat. Despite his earlier bluff, he was grateful when Peter, having finished, offered to go up with him.

Oliver ordinarily took the stairs easily. Tonight they were arduous. Peter hovered, one step below, apparently prepared to catch him if necessary.

When they reached his room, Oliver heaved a sigh of relief and he let himself down on the edge of his bed. He felt chilled.

Peter's nice, friendly face was unnaturally grave as he squatted to untie Oliver's shoelaces. He kept clearing his throat nervously.

"If what Ross told Loveday's a fact," he finally blurted out, pulling the right shoe off and dropping it, "what's thee waiting for, Oliver?" Flicking the bright yellow hair out of his eyes, he looked up questioningly. "Is it because of us — that thee doesn't want us to feel crowded out? We're leaving anyhow, thee knows."

Oliver stared at him. "You're *leaving?* Then it's settled?"

"No. But, sooner or later, we'll go. Rennie has her heart set on this thing."

"It's a wonderful opportunity," Oliver admitted feebly, as the left shoe hit the floor.

Peter stood up. "Rennie's a natural for that job," he declared, helping Oliver into his pajamas. "If she turns it down, someone else will get it and she may never find anything. The way the economy's going — "

Oliver crawled into bed and sank back on the pillow, too exhausted to cope with the economy.

"Believe me," Peter assured him, lingering by the bedside, "I don't want to go away and I don't want to quit my job. But I'm not going to split up the family, even for part of the week. That may work okay for some couples. We need each other. Besides, Rennie's parents aren't very good with little kids and Ross doesn't belong in a day-care center, where someone different might be looking after him all the time. He's kind of insecure, except with us and thee. Ever since that sitter — "

"I know."

"So, with us leaving," Peter went on, returning to the point he was trying to make, "it'd be neat if thee had Loveday."

"But, Peter, your leaving Firbank is no reason for me to marry. Ever since Daphne died, Heather's been urging me to come to England. She has a cozy retirement home all picked out, only an hour from London."

Peter dismissed the retirement home with a contemptuous shrug. "Why go some place like that when thee can be here? I'm not suggesting thee marry Loveday because thee's lonesome. It's because thee said thee loves her. What better reason?"

Oliver couldn't think of any.

"I like her," Peter declared. "Bit pushy sometimes," he conceded, grinning now and peering at Oliver to see how he was taking this frank appraisal. "That'll wear off when she's around thee. My Dad always says, 'Oliver Otis knows how to make plants and people grow to be their finest.' The way Loveday looks at thee sometimes — Rennie and I've both noticed it. We think, if thee'd propose, she'd be a pushover."

Oliver shivered. "*Propose? I? How?* She's taken off. What's more, all the vigor's gone out of me. I'd be no good to her."

How the roles were reversed! He'd been afraid the Hollands would laugh at his predicament. Instead, they were driving him to a conclusion he hadn't yet envisaged. Were they, perhaps, 'running before their guide,' as the old Friends used to say? Or was he slow to perceive his onrushing destiny?

Peter was edging toward the door. "Well," he murmured, sounding as if he'd shot his bolt, "see thee later. I have to give Ross his bath."

Even after Peter shut the door, Oliver looked at it fixedly, trying to understand.

Propose! he repeated to himself incredulously. Peter's so young, how can he know what an old man feels?

Oliver turned out the light and snuggled under the covers. On a clear night he could see the stars from his bed and the Fisher's Island light, but not in this weather. The fog signal was bellowing.

Gradually, he warmed up and relaxed. Maybe he was already asleep. At any rate, he began to dream. What if he actually did propose? What if, by some miracle, Loveday were to accept? For people their age, what would it be like?

She had lived alone so long. Would she want the intimacy of marriage that a young couple enjoyed? Maybe some sort of Platonic arrangement — Well, even so, they'd be together every day. What room would he give her? This was the one with the best view, the largest. He'd give it to her and move into the ell. This room would have to be repapered and refurbished, after all these years.

Would she come down to breakfast in that charming robe she was wearing the morning she surprised him in bed, when he was reading his Bible? With his eyes shut, he could still see the robe — pale green, the color of the meadow in early spring. No, of the ocean, toward evening when there was still a little daylight.

Loveday would write her book at Firbank. Perhaps when they sat by the fire in the evening, she'd read a chapter to him.

Just pretending it might happen gave Oliver unprecedented comfort. He knew he was dreaming, only half awake. But it was delicious.

In the morning, the fog signal was still going.

Must be thick out there, Oliver thought, turning toward the window and trying to see the pond. He could see nothing.

All those ships that were wrecked on the reef off the Point before those powerful warning signals were installed! He could only remember the names of one or two: the steamer *Metis* and, earlier, the patrol vessel sailing out of Newport under the command of Oliver Hazard Perry.

That Oliver was also of Quaker stock. But, in the agonizing dilemma faced by Friends — whether to support war or accept the punishment for upholding the testimony against participating in it — his father had left Friends and served as a naval officer in the Revolution. Oliver had taken the same course in the War of 1812.

In this century, most young Friends had, when obliged to do so, complied with the draft.

But the others, Oliver thought — those who can't accept military force — they should know that they're not alone. I ought to be listening as they struggle with their consciences. Instead, I'm just lying here, useless.

He reached for his Bible. His daily reading had brought him up to his favorite Psalm — 139.

> *O Lord, thou hast searched me, and*
> *known me.*
> *Thou knowest my downsitting and*
> *mine uprising, thou understandest my*
> *thought afar off.*

Oliver glanced at the door. It was shut, and yet, he could see Loveday standing out on the landing in her green robe, looking at him.

> *If I take the wings of the morning,*
> *and dwell in the uttermost parts of the*
> *sea;*
> *Even there shall thy hand lead me,*
> *and thy right hand shall hold me.*

That psalm spoke to Oliver's condition. He got up and found he was able to dress. He could walk downstairs.

Over the weekend, Serenity cared for him lovingly. Peter did his chores. This troubled Oliver. They both had too much to do already. And there were vegetables waiting to be harvested: broccoli, parsnips, brussels sprouts, kale. The asparagus bed had to be prepared for next year. The winter rye grass needed planting, and the flower bulbs were ready to be dug up and stored.

Serenity and Peter didn't conceal the fact that they were worried. Hadn't they better call Dr. Liveek?

Oliver refused. He had no pain, only this unusual malaise.

No doctor could cure that, he felt sure. If he was to recover, he must, with God's help, heal himself. He'd done it before.

"We don't like leaving thee alone," Serenity said after breakfast on Monday morning. "Peter had to go to his seminar and I can't cut my class. Sure thee doesn't want me to call Alice Hill and ask if she could come? She's usually free Mondays."

Oliver was sitting at the kitchen table, eating an egg. "I'll be all right," he declared bravely. "No, I don't want company. Too many letters to write."

One to Heather, telling her everything, even Peter's fanciful suggestion. It wouldn't alarm her. Now that Loveday had left Firbank forever, what was there to worry about? Maybe Oliver'd write to Loveday, too; inquire whether the traffic had been bad on her ride back to Boston. But how could he, when he didn't know her address?

Serenity and Ross were ready to leave.

"Come, Lion," she called, opening the back door. "Out!"

Lion remained under the table.

Serenity didn't insist. She gave Oliver one last, troubled glance and left. Ross followed her, looking over his shoulder with an almost paternal solicitude, which was both amusing and touching.

When Oliver finished eating, he disengaged his feet. "I'll be right back," he promised the dog, going to the hutch to get Fox's *Journal*. "There," he said, seating himself again and reaching down to give Lion a pat. "Thee can relax now. Running around takes too much effort today."

Sipping his tea, he opened the book and turned to the letter which Fox wrote to Lady Claypole when her mind was troubled. Parts of the letter had impressed Daphne so much that she'd drawn lines against them in the margins. After her death, these passages had sustained Oliver. Mightn't they restore him to his rightful mind now?

Be still and cool in thy own mind and spirit from thy own

thoughts, he read, savoring each phrase. *When ... the mind flies up in the air, and the creature is led into the night, and nature goes out of his course ... it comes to be all of a fire.*

Feeling depressed because life wasn't working out the way one wished might be a normal reaction. But it did lead the creature "into the night."

Therefore be still a while from thy own thoughts, searching, seeking, desires and imaginations, and be stayed in the principle of God in thee ... that will bring nature into his course ... thou wilt come to receive and feel the physician of value, which clothes people in their right mind ...

Oliver paused to take off his glasses and wipe his eyes, pondering the last sentence, yearning to receive and feel the physician of value, the "divine principle" within himself.

So then this is the word of the Lord God to you all, he read on, *what the light doth make manifest and discover — temptations, distractions, confusions, distemper — do not look at the temptations, confusions, corruptions, but at the light that discovers them ... and with the same light you will feel over them ... you will find grace and strength; and there is the first step of peace.*

Reading those words, Oliver was suddenly moved by an impulse which had nothing to do with either George Fox or Lady Claypole, but it felt like an authentic leading. It popped into his head so suddenly that it almost lifted him out of his chair: instead of writing to Loveday, why not telephone?

What an idea! Did it come under the heading of temptations or confusions, even — heaven forbid! — corruptions? Or might it be *distemper?*

That made Oliver smile. His sense of humor was coming back! He was "feeling over" the confusions, looking at the light instead, receiving the grace and strength required to bring nature into her (Oliver took the liberty of amending Fox's pronoun) course.

He'd never telephoned to Loveday before.

What would I say? he wondered, longing to hear her sweet voice again. Should I simply wish her a safe journey to Kansas — act as if nothing had happened? Oh, but it did! That look on her face as she was driving off —

Remembering that look, Oliver's resolve hardened. He'd telephone and apologize — not deny what Ross had said (how could he?) but ask forgiveness for causing Loveday embarrassment. One thing was certain: he mustn't let himself be carried away by what Peter had advised. It was unthinkable. Without Heather's approval —

He didn't know Loveday's number. Would Information disclose it? Some people's numbers were unlisted.

Information obliged.

Oliver almost lost his nerve as his trembling fingers dialed. Way off in Boston, the telephone began ringing. But Loveday didn't come. Oliver counted anxiously — six, seven, eight, nine. There was no answer.

She wouldn't have gone out so early in the morning. Had she already left for Kansas? But then, wouldn't the telephone have been disconnected?

At noon, Oliver tried again. No answer.

He warmed up the soup and unwrapped the sandwich Serenity had left for him. After lunch, he went to his study, followed by Lion, and settled himself in the armchair by the window, intending to call Boston every hour. But he promptly fell asleep.

It was late afternoon when Lion's barking woke him.

John Ludlow was standing by Oliver's chair, looking down on him kindly.

Oliver blinked. Then it dawned on him why John had come.

"Did they send for thee? They thought what I needed was a pediatrician? That I'm suffering from a disease of second childhood?"

John didn't seem to understand. The cheerfulness went out of his face and he peered at Oliver anxiously. "Thee sick? No one told me. We weren't in meeting on Sunday. Maybe thee'd rather I came some other time. I'm sorry. I just stopped by to ask — "

"What?"

John's eyes twinkled with mischief. "First tell me what's ailing thee." As Oliver didn't answer, John's bantering tone changed. "What's ailing thee, Oliver?" he demanded with the authority of a physician.

Oliver turned away and gazed out of the window.

3.

How could Oliver refuse to answer this man who was so open, so concerned, so tender in ministering to his patients? Even Ross gave him his complete trust. How could Oliver do less? Just because he didn't want to tell anyone that he yearned for Loveday —

He turned and faced John.

"It's nothing, really. I just had this sudden weakness. Could it have been my heart? I felt no pain."

John reached for Oliver's pulse. Then he drew his stethoscope out of his pocket. "Something upset thee?" he asked, unbuttoning Oliver's shirt.

"My little fox terrier was run over — Duffy. Remember her?"

"Of course. I was wondering where she was."

"And the Hollands are leaving." Oliver saw no need to mention Loveday. "How's my heart?" he asked, when John finished listening.

"Fine. Thee might have had a touch of this virus that's been going around. Boston's riddled with it."

So it wasn't just in his mind! Oliver was relieved. A virus had put nature out of her course, an invisible microorganism had led the creature into the night! Somehow, it was less damaging to his pride to be the victim of an invader than of his emotions.

"That good-looking woman who came to the Called Meeting with thee and to our house the other evening — she came from Boston, didn't she? I've forgotten her name. Something unique."

"Loveday. Means peacemaking."

"That's it! I remember, I was struck by the name the first time I heard it. So it means peacemaking — how nice! Was Loveday feeling all right?"

"First-rate. At least, she appeared so to me. Come to think of it, though, Serenity and Peter thought she did look a bit peculiar. Does thee suppose," Oliver asked, growing worried, "that Loveday might have been suffering from that virus?"

John folded his stethoscope and returned it to his pocket. "She could have been walking around with such a light case that she didn't even know she had it. Then, it might have been communicated to thee. Anyhow, whatever thy trouble may have been, thee's in good shape now." He turned the desk chair around and straddled it backward, facing Oliver. "Where's Ross?"

"At the Ashaways. They picked him up after nursery school. Peter will call for him on the way home. I wish I weren't failing Ross. He counts on me."

"Thee'll be up to taking care of him tomorrow. Just bundle up warmly when thee goes out."

"Really? *Tomorrow*? Ross is frightened of strangers, thee knows."

"No more than he should be at his age. A three-year-old

has a right to expect that some one person, whom he trusts, will look out for him — if not his mother, someone else, but not a string of people. Occasionally we see a kid who will take up cheerfully with anybody, but most of them still need some continuity at that age."

"So thee doesn't think Ross is — "

"There's nothing wrong with Ross. It's our society — mothers having to go to work or simply finding more satisfaction outside the home — pressures that put a small child's needs second. Ross will accept strangers like anyone else, when he's a little older."

"He still has the radiance of early childhood — thee knows what I mean? 'Trailing clouds of glory.' I hate to see that beautiful aura frightened out of him. It'll wear off soon enough, as it is."

"As long as he has thee when his parents are absent, he'll be all right. But don't worry today. He's probably having the time of his life, playing with the Ashaways."

Speaking of the Ashaways reminded Oliver of little Simeon, who died of meningitis years ago — how John sat at his bedside, night after night; how he smuggled Simeon's hamster into the hospital, hiding it in his coat pocket. Recalling the incident, Oliver laughed. "John, does thee remember Simeon's hamster?"

John chuckled. "I was almost fired! The head nurse was outraged. But it made the boy happy in his last days and that hamster didn't cause more infections than they always have in the hospital."

"Thee's what George Fox would have called a 'physician of value,'" Oliver told him, knowing full well that Fox was referring to the principle of God. But wasn't John simply an authorized agent?

"What's this about the Hollands leaving Firbank? I thought they loved it here. Has Peter been offered a job?"

"No, Serenity has. The Museum of Contemporary Art has asked her to be the first Curator of the Daphne Otis Collection. It's an irresistible opportunity. She first had the idea that she'd take Ross and live with her parents in the suburbs of New York. She was going to leave Ross with them or in a day-care center. Peter was to stay here, continuing in his job. They'd only have had weekends together. But Peter won't hear of it. He's decided to give up his faculty appointment."

"What a sacrifice!"

"I'm rather relieved. Dividing the family would have been bad for Ross. He adores Peter."

"And thee? What will thee do?"

Oliver's answer came slowly. "Heather wants me to move to England. She's found a retirement home she's keen on."

"Would thee like that?"

"No. I'd have more time with Heather and that would be a joy. But I couldn't forsake Lion, especially now, when he's grieving for Duffy. Besides, this is my home. What would I do with everything? Daphne's canvases, for instance — hundreds of them stacked in the woodshed. They speak to me. In that bedsitter, there wouldn't be space for more than two or three pictures. Very nice place, Heather tells me, but I'd miss Firbank. I'd never again row across the pond to behold the ocean, never go to meeting in Kendal again."

"I see no reason why thee shouldn't stay here as long as thee wishes," John said, folding his arms on the back of the chair he was straddling. "With someone coming in a few hours a day to help, thee could manage."

Oliver's spirits leaped. "Does thee really think so?"

"Yes. I happen to know that Judy Young's miserable down in New York."

"Serenity called her up when she was there and Judy said she was getting along fine."

"She'd like Austin to think so."

"I've been going to see him fairly regularly — just to give him some companionship. It's pitiful. He wants Judy so much, yet, when he had her, he didn't try to figure out how to make her happy. Does thee think Judy secretly wants to go back?"

"I don't know. What she says is that she's homesick for Kendal Friends."

"No one understands that better than I do. If I move to England — "

"Firbank might be just what Judy needs."

Oliver looked at John intently. "Does thee really think so?" he asked a second time. "I've been worrying about Judy, too. If she were to come here, she might feel that healing spirit of Grandmother's that seems to touch everyone who comes." Oliver was speaking of Judy, but thinking of Loveday.

"And thy spirit," John added.

"It would be a help to have Judy."

But Loveday — she was the one Oliver wanted.

"Oh!" John exclaimed, unfolding his arms and slapping his forehead. "Speaking of Judy — that reminds me — I clean forgot! Reason I came here today — Judy has sent in her resignation to the Committee that's reviewing the Queries. We've been asked to appoint someone in her place. As Convener of Kendal Meeting's Nominating Committee, I've been charged with asking whether thee'd be willing to finish out her term."

Oliver had served on hundreds of Quaker committees in his time and yet, each new appointment — the trust placed in him — made him feel humble.

"There's no committee I'd rather serve on," he confided. "Since we have no creed to keep us in line, we need the Queries to remind us of our obligations as decent human beings."

John looked delighted. "I was hoping thee'd accept."

"The Twelfth Query, John — thee knows: 'Do you live in

the virtue of that life and power that taketh away the occasion of all wars?' It's been troubling me. Now that young men
are obliged to register again, I ought to be helping those who
are torn between complying with the law and obeying the
command to love our enemies."

"There's nothing any of us can do to resolve their conflict,"
John murmured. "To influence them would be not only legally
but morally wrong. All we can do is listen, as they struggle to
make a decision which carries with it such grave consequences,
either way."

Oliver leaned forward and eyed John intently. "It does help
to have someone listen. I needn't tell thee."

"No indeed! Without my father's help, I couldn't have decided to become a conscientious objector. I don't mean that he
influenced me — not at the time, though we were brought up
not to fight or do violence, even with words. Of course, we
were actually no better than other kids, but we knew when
we scrapped and were hurtful that our parents disapproved.
My father didn't try to influence me as I was struggling with
the question of whether to enter the armed forces or apply
for alternative service. He simply urged me to consider my
position prayerfully. I was lucky in being allowed to work in
China."

"Thee paid dearly with thy health."

"I don't regret going," John declared. "This dysentery still
plagues me, but I have the comfort of having treated hundreds
of children who wouldn't otherwise have had any medical
care." John returned to his assignment. "I'm glad thee's accepting the appointment."

"That Committee meets in Cambridge," Oliver reminded
him, suddenly doubtful. "Does thee think I'll be up to traveling?"

"Three weeks from now? Of course! Just don't lug a heavy
bag. There's that lovely guest room in the Friends Center, up

at the top of the house, looking across the river to Boston. The Committee meets in that building. Thee won't have to worry about going out, should the weather be bad."

"Yes, I could stay there, if they have room. Daphne and I often did, years ago, when we attended meetings in Cambridge. As we got older, we traveled less and less."

"It's precisely thy age, thy lifelong concern for Truth that make thee valuable," John assured him. "As far as thy health goes — a few days in Cambridge might be the best thing in the world. Thee grew up there, didn't thee?"

"My father taught English literature at Harvard. But in vacation we generally came here to see Grandmother. I thought of Firbank as home."

"Do go, Oliver. Ross isn't the only one who's having to adjust to some pretty shattering separations. What with the Hollands leaving and Duffy — Thee's had a few blows, too."

The very thought that he might be active again was invigorating to Oliver. "I'll do what I can," he promised. "Thank thee for asking me."

John had discharged his duty now, but, busy man though he was, he didn't get up to go. Instead, he folded his arms on the back of the chair and rested his head on them dreamily.

For some time, neither he nor Oliver spoke.

The sun was setting. Oliver gazed at the bare branches on the edge of the woods, silhouetted against the sky. Even now, in November, when they were frigid and forlorn, even now they were gathering the strength that would send the sap running again. Could it possibly be like that for him? John seemed to think so.

How could he not confide in John?

Struggling with himself, continuing to look away, Oliver said softly, "The trouble *is* in my heart, John. But thee can't hear it with that contraption of thine. That's why I wouldn't let them call in Dr. Liveek. He's an excellent doctor, but I knew I must heal myself."

Oliver found it hard to go on. John waited, still resting his head on his arms.

"Thee sees," Oliver said, after a long silence, "the past few months, I've enjoyed Loveday's company. She's a seeker, like us, though not aware of it quite. But she's working to gain insight, to develop the art of living — living in the presence of God. It was a joy, being with her. Now all that's over. She left on Friday, under rather distressing circumstances. That's when I collapsed."

Out of the corner of his eye, Oliver watched for John's reaction.

John didn't stir.

Startled by having said so much, Oliver faced him. "Thee understands — this is just for thee. I haven't even told Heather, though I'm planning to write this very day."

John raised his head. He looked touched by the confidence. "Thank thee for telling me," he said, standing up and turning the chair in its proper direction. He moved closer to Oliver and stretched out his hand.

"Thy father," Oliver told him, shaking it affectionately, "was one of the best friends I ever had. Thee comes close, thyself."

John smiled down on him. "In that case," he said, "maybe thee won't mind my saying that if I was in thy place and saw a woman I took a shine to, believe me, *I* wouldn't *let* her get away. I'd run after her!"

"Run? I can scarcely walk."

"Yes, run!" John cried, laughing. "Thee can do it. 'Run and not be weary, walk and not faint.' "

"But Loveday's miles away. I've tried all day to reach her on the telephone. She must have left for Kansas."

"Then," John said, grinning, "thee'll have to 'mount up with

wings, as eagles.' Whichever means of transportation thee's
obliged to use, go!"

4.

TAKE HEED, *dear Friends, to the promptings of love and
truth in your hearts, which are the leadings of God,* Oliver
quoted to himself, remembering how, with Loveday at his
side, he had read these words at the Called Meeting.

For months, the promptings had resounded in his heart. Instead of listening and trusting, he'd tried to ignore them. Now,
thanks to Ross, they clamored irrepressibly. Oliver could no
longer delay acting on this quickening of love and truth.

The roles are reversed, he wrote to Heather, after John left.
*All those Clearness Committees I've served on, trying to make
sure the couples who wished to be married under the care of
our Meeting understood the nature of the promises they intended to make!*

*And Peter and Serenity — how Mother and I tried to help
them achieve clarity! When her parents were urging them to
marry although they were too young to know what they were
about, Mother somehow communicated her wise perception.
We counseled them. And now, THEY'RE counseling ME!
They, as well as John Ludlow —* Heather had gone to school
with John, had grown up with him in the Meeting and would
trust his judgment — *all three are encouraging me to ask the
widow I mentioned in an earlier letter whether she will take
me in marriage.*

Oliver couldn't quite bring himself to give her name. Not
that he feared Heather would be put off by the strangeness.
She wasn't superficial. But, after his long reticence, he found

it hard to expose so much at once and to Oliver there was something sacred in the name.

Thee mustn't think I've allowed myself to be persuaded, he assured Heather. *I resisted the idea out of fear that I might be behaving like a foolish old man. But my unremitting desire to cherish and serve her have at last convinced me that it's in right ordering. Peter thinks, if I were to propose, she'd be a "pushover." Thee knows how he talks.*

For my part, I have no reason to think that she reciprocates my feeling. Still, it's time I declared myself.

But not so precipitously as John recommends, Oliver reflected, resting his fingers from the exertion of jabbing his old typewriter. Before I can mount up with wings and fly to Emporia, I have a big hurdle to jump.

He braced himself for the leap.

It goes without saying, he went on, communicating his anxiety in a string of typographical errors, which he had to stop and correct, *that thee and I must have unity before I proceed. I know it will be hard for thee to imagine my wanting anyone after the glorious life I had with Mother. But I believe this is the course I should take. We shall need to write freely to each other until we are both clear that it is. Not until I have that assurance shall I make the offer. As a matter of fact,* Oliver had to admit, *I don't know her whereabouts. She's returned to Kansas without leaving an address.*

This depressed him. If Loveday had wanted to hear from him, wouldn't she have told him how to reach her?

She is the sort of woman — independent, dynamic, yet possessed of a lovable humility — whom Mother would have admired. Thee knows how, when Mother was doing a portrait, she could see beneath the features to the spirit of the person whose face she was painting. That's what made her portraits more than mere likenesses. They were universally appealing. Beneath my friend's competent exterior, Mother would have recognized her winning character. Her ancestors were South County Quakers, prominent in the eighteenth century, who married out. She adores Firbank.

Running on about Loveday gave Oliver so much pleasure that he had almost used up the space.

My dear, dear daughter, he concluded, removing his glasses to wipe his eyes, which had suddenly become misty, then putting the glasses on again, *nothing must ever be allowed to come between us. I hope thee'll write soon. Were thee to know the lady, thee'd love her, too.*

This last was more a hope than truth. Oliver was far from sure that Heather would appreciate Loveday, to say nothing of what she might feel about his remarrying.

I've been appointed to the Yearly Meeting Committee for Reviewing the Queries, he wrote at the bottom of the aerogram in longhand. *It meets in Cambridge three weeks from now. I look forward to going. I haven't been there in years.*

He didn't mention his recent indisposition. It was over.

Writing the letter was easy, compared to waiting for a reply. If, by some miracle, Heather should trust his judgment and approve of his plan without further discussion, what would he do then? Fly to Emporia, as John urged him to do? He hadn't flown in years. And yet, why not? Boarding a plane wasn't such a tremendous undertaking. To begin with, though, he'd have to get in touch with Loveday — ask whether he might come. And how could he do that when he didn't have her address?

And suppose, after he got out there and proposed, Loveday should turn him down — how would he ever manage the journey home?

The next day was overcast, but Oliver put on his boots and, as a concession to his recent illness, a scarf with his parka. He was going down to the edge of the orchard to see where Peter and Ross had laid Duffy to rest, under the big pine tree.

Being outdoors again restored Oliver, though he was disinclined to walk as fast as Lion expected. Making his way along the path between the apple trees, he could almost see Heather, a vivacious little girl, shaking the boughs, filling the bushel baskets. She'd been full of fun in those years, but when she entered adolescence she began to have strange ideas. Her father wished she'd been a boy so he'd have someone to take over the farm; her parents were so close, there was scant room in their hearts for her, though she knew very well how deeply they loved her. Until that time, the three of them had constituted a happy family. How could things have changed so suddenly, just because she'd reached a certain age?

Perhaps, Oliver thought, she needed more attention than we were giving her. Daphne was overwhelmed with commissions for portraits in those years and I had my hands very full. We decided Heather must be lonely, off here on a farm, an only child. So we sent her away to school, where she'd have the companionship of girls her age. We considered it a sacrifice on our part but perhaps it only confirmed her feeling of not being wanted. At any rate, things were never the same again.

Oliver had no trouble locating the grave. Peter — bless his heart — had sunk a short length of plank into the soil on which he had neatly carved, *Duffy*. It was a peaceful spot.

Not so long ago, Oliver reflected, leaning against the trunk of the old pine tree, Duffy was just a puppy, following Daphne around, communicating devotion with her eloquent eyes.

Faithfulness — that was the quality that distinguished them both. It wasn't the blind, servile attachment vulgarly ascribed to dogs and devoted wives, but faithfulness to *themselves*, to their own inborn vocation for selfless loving. It was as joyful and creative and independent as the highest work of art, bringing out the best in those with vision to perceive its beauty.

A stiff offshore breeze was bending the branches of the pine tree, swooping them from side to side. Although Oliver's feet felt like ice, he leaned against the sturdy trunk a moment longer, warmed by the legacy of love that these two had bequeathed to him. Lines from *Some Fruits of Solitude*, which Austin's mother read during the Meeting of Thanksgiving for Daphne's life came to his mind and brought renewed comfort.

They that love beyond the world cannot be separated by it ... Death is but crossing the world as friends do the seas. They live in one another still.

Yes, Oliver acknowledged as he made his way back along the path, love of that nature is the one enduring element.

It was time to leave for nursery school. Driving into Kendal with the wind buffeting the truck, he exulted over the new direction his life had taken. He was no longer just moony. Convinced by his younger friends that his secret impulse was in right ordering, he was beginning to act. Whatever the outcome, he had taken his destiny into his own hands. It was all thanks to Ross.

During the following weeks, he walked down to the mailbox every afternoon, hoping to hear from Heather and Loveday. Neither of the letters arrived before it was time to set out for Cambridge, only a fat manila envelope from the Clerk of the committee that Oliver had agreed to serve on. This contained suggestions for the revision of the existing Queries. Oliver put the papers in his bag, resolving to study them on the train.

By this time, he was quite a bit more realistic than when he wrote to Heather, confessing the state of his heart. In his eagerness, he had hoped then that Heather would have faith in his judgment and give him her blessing. But without knowing Loveday, how could Heather be certain that she'd make a good wife? He had asked too much of his daughter. No wonder she was slow to reply!

Furthermore, could people arrive at the kind of unity he felt he and Heather must have, by mail? Wasn't it imperative for them to sit down together, facing each other in love, and, with a sense of God's presence, discuss any differences they might have? Friends put their trust in this process — "gathering the sense of the meeting" — neither contending, nor bent on persuading one another, but simply seeking Truth together.

With letters meandering over the ocean and back, this would surely take a lot longer than if Heather and Oliver met face to face. It might even be impossible.

And yet, unless Heather was truly in accord, Oliver would feel that by going ahead and proposing anyhow, he was violating something very precious. She certainly wouldn't feel wildly enthusiastic about the idea — that was too much to expect. But, at least, she ought to be comfortable. Oliver saw no worthy alternative. He must discipline himself to wait until Heather could assent without violating her own integrity.

Only, at our age, he thought sadly, picturing Loveday, at our age, time is so very precious.

5.

MINDFUL of John Ludlow's advice, Oliver was traveling light — only the committee documents, his toilet articles and a change of clothes.

Ross watched him pack. Serenity came upstairs, carrying a loaf of freshly baked bread done up in a plastic wrapper.

"Thy contribution to the potluck supper this evening," she said.

"Oh, I forgot that I ought to bring something. This is beautiful."

"It's whole wheat, mixed with some meal from thy corn."

Oliver laid the loaf carefully on top of his fresh shirt, tucking the pajamas around the sides for protection.

"Friends will enjoy it," he assured Serenity.

Like Ross, she hovered over him. "Sure thee'll be all right?"

"Of course! I'm only going to Cambridge. John thinks I'm up to going all the way to Kansas. Do I look presentable?" Lifting his forearm, Oliver scrutinized the cuff of his jacket. "This suit's a bit threadbare." He'd worn it every winter First Day for over twenty years, never thinking, when he was about to go to Kendal, that it was shabby. But for going to the City — "I wonder," he said to Serenity, "whether, since I'm going to be passing through Harvard Square tomorrow morning on my way home, I shouldn't drop in at the Coop and see whether they have anything appropriate."

"Do! And splurge, Oliver. Thee hasn't spent anything on thyself as long as I've known thee."

"At my age, investing in clothes hardly seems justified. But since I'll have the time, I'll just look."

"Why doesn't thee stay till tomorrow afternoon? Have lunch with thy old friends — the Rothchilds and the Bartrams."

"That would give me pleasure. I'll telephone to them when I get there — see if they're free."

"The best train leaves Boston at five o'clock. We'll meet it and have a late supper."

Oliver frowned. How could he wait till tomorrow evening to find out whether Heather had written? "I'd hoped," he confided to Serenity, "that I'd hear from Heather before leaving."

"Let me call the post office. If they haven't yet put our mail on the truck, they can hold it and when Alice comes to take thee to the station, she can stop while thee goes in and gets it. If Heather's letter has arrived — "

She must have seen the joy in Oliver's eyes, for she left immediately to telephone. He thought she looked troubled.

Ross followed him down the stairs, looking so ruefully at the bag when it was set down by the door in the front hall that Oliver took his hand and squeezed it.

"I'll be back tomorrow," he promised, leading the way into the kitchen.

Serenity was standing at the counter. Yes, she looked sad, too.

Turning, she murmured, casting her eyes down, "Oliver, if thee and Loveday — Could we always come back here on weekends and in vacation? We'll miss thee."

Oliver went over to her. Laying his hands on her shoulders, he looked lovingly into her eyes. "This is your home," he told her. "Whatever I do has no bearing on your being here. If Loveday should come — and I still can't believe that will happen — I'm sure she will want you as much as I shall. Thee would be of help to her with some of those ideas — the way she was trying to persuade thee to take the job. Her inclination is to think all women must follow along the same lines. That comes from having had responsibility for great numbers at a time. She needs to learn that each case must be prayerfully considered."

"I think she understands already. We had a talk before she left. What I'm wondering is: would it be fair to expect her to live under the same roof with us? We four are so close — she might find it hard."

"I hadn't thought of that," Oliver admitted, stepping back. "But isn't it what Firbank stands for — 'No Nukes'? Doesn't that apply to nuclear families as well as missiles?"

That made Serenity laugh.

"After all, thee and Peter have been able to build a good marriage with me around," Oliver insisted earnestly. "Daphne and I lived with Grandmother. Why shouldn't Loveday fit in with the Hollands?"

It sounded reasonable, but how would Loveday feel? That was the main consideration. And Ross — being obliged to share

Oliver's attention would be quite an adjustment for him.

He was sitting at the kitchen table, watching Oliver eat an early lunch.

"Oliver," Serenity burst out suddenly, sounding as if she couldn't hold it back another second. "Peter's definitely decided to give up his job so the three of us can stay together. He hopes to find an apartment in New York."

"He told me."

Serenity was almost in tears. "I don't want to ruin his future. That's what it comes to. When I came back from New York, I was so excited by the offer that I really didn't stop to think what it was going to do to him. But he'll never get a job in New York." She twisted her fingers in agony. "I want to work at the Museum so badly. I don't know what to do."

"No need to decide yet, is there?"

"I have to give them my answer by Monday."

A car drove into the driveway. Alice Hill had come to take Oliver to the station. He put on his overcoat, noticing for the first time that it was shabby, too. The buttonholes were fraying. But the old Irish tweed hat that Oliver loved still looked pretty decent.

Serenity and Ross saw him off with hugs and kisses, plus the puckering of Ross's mouth which, Oliver knew, foreboded a gush of tears.

"I'll be back before you know it."

Obligingly, Alice stopped at the post office. She waited in the car while Oliver hurried up the steps.

The postmistress was so pleased to see Oliver that, as she handed him the Firbank mail, she tried to engage him in conversation. But he was distracted.

There was Heather's letter! Oliver would have ripped the thin, blue paper open on the spot, with neighbors milling around him in the lobby, had he not been afraid of missing the train. Tingling with excitement, he put the aerogram in his breast pocket.

Alice insisted on getting out and waiting with him on the platform. He'd known her since she was a little girl with pig-tails — one of the Lancashires — and he'd always been especially fond of her and Neil. They were forever doing nice things for him.

"How's Neil?" he asked. "Business quieting down, now that the boats have been hauled out?"

"Yes. He's busy, though, sending out the bills for winter storage. They trouble him, Oliver. With inflation increasing so rapidly, he has to charge more than he used to do but the people whose boats he's stored for years don't have more money. Some of them don't even have jobs. Neil doesn't take care of fancy yachts — he won't touch those — just small boats people have fun in, sailing around Little Narragansett Bay."

Oliver nodded sympathetically. "It's a sport for the soul. So much of our activity is dependent on motors and batteries, while sailing is determined by Nature. Our movements are in obedience to her moods."

This seemed to please Alice. Her hazel eyes shone. "Exactly! Take our *Katrina*, for instance — washed ashore in a hurricane, her hull stove in. The owners didn't want to bother with her. Neil towed her to the Yard and repaired her, giving her back the dignity of the old schooners, and our whole family has grown up learning to live on the water."

The train came in.

Oliver threw his arms around Alice and kissed her — something he was ordinarily too old-fashioned to do to women outside the family. But he felt ridiculously happy, going to Cambridge again after all these years, and he had that letter in his pocket, which filled him with hope, though with apprehension too.

As soon as he was settled in the train, he pulled it out, fumbling with his glasses. His hand was unexpectedly trembling.

What disturbing news! the letter began, without preliminaries. *I'm quite upset. I certainly don't approve of your —* Oliver's hand shook so that he could barely make out Heather's scrawl. He went back to be sure he hadn't misread "don't" for "do." *I certainly don't* — his hopes collapsed — *approve of your living at Firbank alone. If Rennie and Peter decide to move to New York —*

Oliver glanced at the top right-hand corner of the aerogram and everything came clear: this wasn't Heather's response to his last letter but to the one before, in which he'd written about Serenity's job offer. The mails were simply slower than he, in his eagerness, had allowed for. Greatly relieved, he read on.

The minute your letter came, I rang up Margaret Fell House and by great good fortune, someone died last week. Well, it wasn't such good fortune for the person who died, I suppose, though probably not unexpected, since everyone there is well along in years, but lucky for you that I put your name down five years ago as there's a long waiting list.

It's a lovely, sunny room with —

Oliver stuck the letter in his pocket again, leaned back against the seat and, pulling his hat down over his eyes, went to sleep.

6.

BY THE TIME the train reached Boston, Oliver had recovered from Heather's letter. Whatever happened, he was not going to live in England among strangers who were momentarily expected to die. He intended to remain at Firbank with Lion, Daphne's paintings, his garden and the ocean.

The sleep was refreshing. But he hadn't read those documents.

Emerging from South Station, he stood a moment on the littered sidewalk, letting the sun shine on his upturned face. It tempered the chill of reproach he felt for not appreciating Heather's efforts. She'd gone to a lot of trouble, even to putting his name down five years ago, without consulting him. He ought to be more grateful.

Serenity had urged him to take a taxi to Cambridge, but the Query Oliver had heard read in meeting all his life — *Do you observe simplicity and moderation in your manner of living?* — unfitted him for incurring the expense of a taxi when the subway stop was right in front of the station and he was quite able to walk the short distance at the other end. He descended into the bowels of the earth just as the train was coming in.

When the car surfaced beside the Charles Street Jail, Oliver's heart ached. Those grim, stone walls! Weren't there better ways of reclaiming people?

A minute later, the Jail with its heavily barred windows disappeared. The car was rumbling over the Longfellow Bridge. Oliver wondered whether children still called those squat turrets salt-and-pepper shakers. College crews were rowing on the Charles and sailboats heeled gaily in the sparkling sunshine.

Then the car dove into a tunnel again. Years ago, when Oliver lived in Cambridge and he had occasion to go to Boston, he always took the subway — the "T" they called it now. He still knew the order of the stations by heart: Kendall (with two Ls, unlike his town in Rhode Island), Central, Harvard.

He was already there. Dragged forward by a phalanx of rushing bodies, he landed on the platform.

The stairs to the street were steep. His heart thumped. Halfway up, he had to stand still. When, at last, he reached the top, he found Harvard Square greatly changed. The Coop was there, just as in former times, but the clock out in front, beneath which, in his day, many a tryst took place, was gone. Not that Oliver had ever met anyone there. Daphne was his first love and he'd courted her abroad.

After traveling underground, he sniffed the crisp air greedily. It wasn't so fragrant as at Firbank, but wonderfully exhilarating. It made him feel almost young. He was glad he'd decided to walk, instead of rolling up to the Friends Center in a taxi.

Tomorrow morning he'd come down here again. He'd go into the Coop and look at the suits. But how would he know which to choose, whether the quality was good, whether the color became him? Daphne'd always gone shopping with him. Being an Englishwoman, she had readily recognized a good wool and her artist's eye was unerring about the shade. To make such a decision on his own — If only he'd been appointed to that Committee while Loveday was still doing her research in Cambridge! She might not have minded going with him. Or would that have been too personal a request to make of her?

Crossing the street at the risk of his life, he made his way through the crowd in Harvard Square. When he was a boy, this had been the focal point of a tranquil college town. Now it teemed with people and cars, bumper to bumper, horns blaring. Dignified Brattle Street had been taken over by theaters, restaurants and clothing shops.

Oliver stopped to look in the window of a book store. The titles displayed there gave the impression that Cambridge readers were largely preoccupied with eroticism rather than with romance, of which, in his eyes, sexual performance was but the fruit.

Wouldn't people prefer to savor love in all its aspects? he wondered. Why just the one?

Jostled by the crowd of students hurrying by, he had so much trouble keeping his footing that he gave up and turned away.

These days especially, he said to himself, still thinking of the books in the window, these days, when the most passionate relationships are proving impermanent, most couples want more than instruction in technique. They want to discover the qualities they must cultivate to live happily ever after. Those publishers don't know beans about human nature. No wonder their business is bad.

He crossed the street at the spot where Longfellow's Village Blacksmith had had his forge. The spreading chestnut tree was long since gone, as well as the Cock Horse, that charming tearoom where, in his childhood, Oliver used to be taken for a treat. One landmark remained, though: the undulating brick pavement, which had never been repaired. It was perilous but delightfully familiar.

Beyond the Radcliffe Yard and the Divinity School, Brattle Street was little changed. Many of the older mansions still stood, like Craigie House, where those Rhode Island Friends petitioned General Washington for leave to pass through the lines with relief and where, later, the poet Longfellow lived.

Now, at last, Oliver was in Longfellow Park and there, in a quiet corner, nestled close to the earth, was the Friends Meetinghouse, joined by a porte-cochère to the Friends Center. Of warm rose brick with white trim and a slate roof, it welcomed Oliver as it had done for over forty years.

He thought of Loveday again — what joy it would have given him to show it to her and to see her reaction to its simple beauty. His father had been a member of the Building Committee and Oliver knew what loving care had been taken to make this place of worship express the longing for harmony of those who were to use it.

He felt suddenly lonely. With the turnover characteristic of Friends Meetings in university towns, surely no one would remember him. But as he mounted the steps of the Center, the door opened. Ellen, the secretary, must have spotted him through the window.

"Oliver Otis! It's good to see you! You haven't been here in so long."

He set his bag on the bench by the door. Breathless from the walk, he could only beam down on this old friend and shake her hand.

She was not young, but she had the figure of a little girl and a face that Oliver thought of as both innocent and acquainted with grief, though quick to light up in a smile, as it did now. Her dark eyes glowed as she looked up at Oliver.

"Ellen!" he managed to exclaim finally. "I feel like Rip Van Winkle."

She laughed. "You haven't been here since the Sanctuary, have you?"

"Except for an urgent concern like that, I stayed pretty close to home during the Vietnam War. After Daphne had her stroke, I never left. Since she went — well, I don't know where the time has gone. And how has thee been?"

Ellen wasn't a Friend, but she was so devoted to the Meeting and held such a warm place in the hearts of its members that addressing her in the plain language came naturally. Oliver could remember when she and her diminutive mother arrived here, refugees from Nazi Germany, having escaped by way of Shanghai.

"I'm fine," Ellen was saying. "But my mother had the flu. She's better. Still, at ninety, it's worrying. The flu's been bad this year."

"I had a touch myself."

As he spoke, Oliver noticed the copper bowl that was standing on the table in the front hall. Some Friend, who probably lived in the country, perhaps out Walden Pond way, had made a breathtaking arrangement of wildflowers and grasses. Golden yarrow, brown burdock, teasel, yellow-gray tansy — even dried they had a strong, woodsy smell. Dusty-white sweet everlasting and sprigs of sea lavender gave the whole thing a cloudy, airy feeling.

It was beautiful, but it so reminded Oliver of Daphne that it hurt.

"My wife used to go to the woods in the fall and pick things like these," he confided to Ellen. "She'd dry them in the barn and later she'd bring them in and arrange them in a blue vase on the coffee table."

"I remember Daphne Otis's flowers. She always brought me a bouquet when you came."

Ellen's tone and expression conveyed such pleasure in re-calling Daphne that she endeared herself even more to Oliver and he felt moved to say things that he usually kept to himself.

"She painted them, too — not in the style of those botanical plates she'd been taught to make at the Academy — flat, faith-ful specimens. Daphne painted flowers the way she painted people — less to reproduce their shape and color than to com-municate their essence, 'their flowerhood,' she used to say."

"Excuse me a minute," Ellen broke in, dashing to her office to answer the telephone.

Waiting by the newel post at the foot of the stairs, Oliver visualized the wildflowers and humble grasses Daphne used to glorify in winter — goldenrod, fluffy, white four-o'clocks, redtop, witch grass, timothy. They sat for her as people would sit for their portraits — in the living room. They sat very still with upturned faces, projecting their personalities, linked to Daphne in silent communion, while she dipped her brush in water, ran it over blobs of color and lightly touched the paper.

"Daphne loved to paint cattails," Oliver told Ellen when she returned, continuing where he'd left off. "Thee knows? Those tall marsh plants with fuzzy brown spikes and leaves like reeds? Most people think them gawky. But Daphne brought out their elegance. And sea lavender! She never picked it, of course."

Carried away, Oliver had allowed himself to go on too long. Ellen appeared interested, but he ought to let her go back to work.

"Well," he said, "I mustn't keep thee."

"Let me take you to your room. The Resident Friends are away for the weekend. They were sorry to miss you."

Before Oliver had a chance to protest, Ellen picked up his bag. She went to the front door and locked it.

"We have to do this nowadays," she told him sadly. "Too many typewriters have been stolen out of my office and the cash box — So when I leave, even for a few minutes, I lock the door. We never used to, but now — "

7.

OLIVER was still thinking of Daphne as he followed Ellen up the stately staircase. Long before the Second World War, long after the Korean, they had come here together to help with resettling refugees or to witness to the Quaker Peace Testimony.

Cherished friends of theirs lived at the Center in those days — George and Florence Selleck. George fostered the religious life of the Meeting for decades, looked after the buildings and reached out to the college students in the area.

"I miss George and Florence," Oliver told Ellen, as they passed the apartment on the second floor, where the Sellecks used to live. "Something of their aura still seems to be here. They invariably gave Daphne and me a warm welcome, just as thee did today." Aware that he had another flight to climb, he lingered on the landing. "We'd be tired from traveling, we'd open the front door and there the Sellecks would be, coming to greet us. They seemed always poised on the stairs when we arrived, as if they'd been waiting there for us since our last visit."

"Yes! Florence used to say the Center should be home to everyone. She had a gift for friendship." About to proceed, Ellen also lingered, apparently as happy as Oliver to have someone with whom to share reminiscences. "You know, it was George who gave me a job, when I first came to this country."

"I remember very well. I can see thee as if it were today — thy frightened face. Thee thought Friends were scary, when we're actually so harmless! How could anyone be afraid of George?"

Oliver smiled, remembering the gentle humor, the endearing simplicity of their old friend.

And Ellen laughed at her former self. "You can't imagine how frightened I was. My English was terrible and I was so ignorant. The first day I came to work, George gave me some cards to file. I didn't know the difference between Harvard and Bryn Mawr — they were both colleges! With his firm and quiet kindness, he guided me through those difficult years and introduced me to Quakerism."

"That radiant spirit! It shone in his face," Oliver murmured, thinking how difficult it is to give thanks for a life without also begrudging its passing.

There were tears in Ellen's eyes. "George Selleck was my teacher and my friend," she said softly. Then she led the way up to the next floor.

Glancing back as he started to follow her, Oliver wondered who was now living behind the door of that apartment.

These were back stairs and he found the high risers daunting. But he reached the top not too far behind Ellen. They passed through the nursery. He could picture toddlers playing here on First Days while their parents were worshipping over in the Meetinghouse.

Ellen opened the door of the sunny guest room, placed the bag on the luggage stand and left.

As John had said, the south window, fitted into an alcove, looked out over the Charles River to Boston. Oliver remembered how the lights of the City twinkled at night. There were twin beds on either side of the north window, which faced the Meetinghouse lawn.

Daphne had invariably chosen the bed to the left. Oliver had nominally occupied the other one. In actuality, only his clothes did. He himself had always squeezed in with Daphne and they'd slept, blissfully entwined all night, just as they did at home.

The sight of that bed triggered the most overwhelming longing.

To avoid looking at it, Oliver walked over to the wall beside the door, where a notice, beautifully hand-lettered and framed, related the history of this guest room. He was familiar with it, but he always read the account with fresh pleasure.

FROM THE WILL OF NICHOLAS UPSALL OF BOSTON

Dated Eighth Month 9, 1660

I do order and give for the use of such servants of the Lord as are commonly called Quakers, my new feather bed, bolster and pillows, with a good pair of sheets and a pair of blankets, with the new rugg, and bedstead fitted with rope, Matt and Curtains, in that little room in my house, The Red Lyon Inn, called the parlor, or in the chamber over that parlor...

I give to the said Society of Quakers my chest, with all my books and papers therein lying, with a small table in the room ...My will is, if my executrix or my daughter Cook shall see meet to set a house on any part of my land for the use of the Quakers, that then it shall be built 24 feet in length and

18 feet wide, with a chimney. And said bed, bedstead and table shall be for their company.

*　*　*　*　*

Four years earlier, the *Swallow* had sailed into Boston with two Quaker women on board whose luggage was found to consist chiefly of books, which were declared to contain "most corrupt, heretical and blasphemous doctrines." The books were burned by the hangman. Mary Fisher and Ann Austin were imprisoned. Hearing that they were being starved, Nicholas Upsall bribed the jailer to give them food. After five weeks, the master of the *Swallow* was obliged to take them away.

Meanwhile, more Quakers sailed in. They had a brutal reception from the authorities, but their message of the Divine Light in the soul touched the heart of Nicholas Upsall.

Oliver could never read the account without being deeply moved. To think that this earliest colonist, who had been admitted to the privilege of a freeman at the first General Court held in America, should have forfeited his freedom to shelter the "servants of the Lord commonly called Quakers"! He read on:

The General Court then passed a law imposing a fine on any sea captain who brought in a Quaker or any colonist who entertained one. This was proclaimed before the Red Lyon Inn. Standing at his door, Nicholas Upsall remarked that it was "a sad forerunner of some heavy judgment to fall on the country." For this, he was fined and banished. Returning to Boston three years later, he was sentenced, though already in his sixties, to "perpetual Imprisonment." He died Seventh Month 20, 1666 and was buried at Copp's Hill, near the Old North Church.

In 1694, the Yearly Meeting of Friends for New England recorded this Minute: Whereas Nicholas Upsall of Boston did formerly bequeath unto us, the people of God in scorn called Quakers, a chamber and furniture in Boston; but not having received the benefit of it, we do now give power and order our friends Edward Shippen and Edward Wanton to agree and sell the aforesaid privileges and rights in the same.

Persecution continued. Nevertheless, in 1695, Friends built a Meetinghouse near the present City Hall, "the money from Nicholas Upsall's chamber to go towards it." This was superseded in 1710 by a Meetinghouse in Quaker Lane, which was sold in 1808. Funds were passed on from one Meetinghouse to the next until, in 1937, the fifth in the Boston area was erected in Longfellow Park, Cambridge.

In recognition of Nicholas Upsall's concern for the use of the little room and furniture in his Inn, which stood on Richmond Street in Boston, above what is now the entrance to the Callahan Tunnel, Friends Meeting at Cambridge has set aside this room for the refreshment and repose of its guests.

How thoughtful of Friends to post this notice, Oliver said to himself, as he unpacked his bag.

Carefully lifting Serenity's bread from its nest of pajamas, he recalled the day last January when he ran the corn through the sheller and took it over to Perrytown, where it was ground into the meal, which was added to this loaf.

He didn't even know then that such a person as Loveday Mead existed. Next January, when it came time to go over to Perrytown with the corn he and Austin cut this year, where would they be, he and Loveday? She in Emporia? He at Firbank? At the Margaret Fell House? (Perish the thought!) Would they both be at Firbank? This last, he simply couldn't imagine.

As he took the documents out of his bag and sat down in the armchair to study them, it required an effort of will to detach his thoughts from this speculation.

There were pages of Minutes covering the Committee's proceedings. There was the Yearly Meeting's charge to the Committee: from time to time, it was to review the Queries which were presently being read in Meetings. *The intent of the Queries*, it pointed out, *is to direct the attention of Friends to the source of their spiritual strength and to encourage them to consider whether their personal lives witness to their faith.*

While the Queries refer to eternal Truth, which does not change, the language in which they present Truth and the concerns they address belong to a given age and must therefore be periodically reviewed.

Glancing up from the page, Oliver found himself looking directly at Daphne's old bed.

Yet, instead of disturbing him, as it had when he first entered the room, seeing Daphne's bed gave him singular comfort. Daphne was there with him, taking his hand, as she used to do when they lay together. But now she was leading him on, leading him into the future — as much of it as there might be for him. She was sending him on his way, unafflicted by regret.

This was her legacy of love.

Shutting his eyes, feeling her dear presence, Oliver had an access of understanding that shook him: before he could marry again, he must enshrine Daphne in a much deeper recess of his heart, where her absence would no longer be such a sorrow. In this recess, he could abide with her in the same love that had blessed him for over fifty years, but without the yearning for her that still beset him. Only by letting go this way would he be worthy of another wife. Until then, he had no right to ask Loveday for her hand.

Up to now, he had believed that only one thing stood in the way of his proposing: securing Heather's approval. Suddenly he saw that the greatest obstacle lay in himself: he wasn't ready. There was so little time. And yet, he wasn't ready.

Without altering his feelings, without diminishing the love he treasured, he must reeducate his heart.

Was he capable of doing this much for Loveday?

8.

IT WAS SO LONG since Oliver had been out of Kendal that he felt a little confused when he came downstairs and was intro duced to about ten members of his Committee, who looked very young, though most were probably middle-aged. He knew only two of them, but they all welcomed him warmly.

The contributions everyone had brought for supper were spread on the long oak table in the kitchen. Oliver added Serenity's loaf. Then he served himself and joined the others in the Children's Library. It was a jolly meal, with joking and teasing and a show of high spirits which would be checked later, when Friends became engrossed in the work they had come to do.

Oliver was quickly drawn into the conversation. He had a feeling that he was going to enjoy being with these people.

When the meal was over, they all moved to the Far Parlor.

The somber, antique pictures in that room bespoke the style and outlook of another age. On the north wall hung a portrait of plump Elizabeth Fry, the early nineteenth-century English Quaker, who initiated the movement for prison reform. Between the east windows, an engraving showed her reading the Bible to the women in Newgate Prison, while their ragged children lay on the stone floor.

Before beginning their work, the members of the Committee settled into a dedicating silence. Oliver felt conscience-stricken. His mind was wandering.

Heather's letter — when would it come, freeing him — he fervently hoped! — to declare himself? And if it did, how was he going to locate Loveday? These personal desires engaged his thoughts rather than the serious task he'd been called to do and he reproached himself.

Unable to center down, he studied the faces of the Friends around the table. They were, he thought, simple, good people, concerned with means, rather than ends.

The Clerk raised his head. The Committee was about to get down to business.

There was a great shuffling of papers.

"We're considering the Ninth Query," the Clerk told Oliver. "This is how it reads at the present time: 'Do you regard your possessions as given to you in trust, and do you part with them freely to meet the needs of others? With reverence for life and for the splendor of God's continuing creation, do you try to protect the natural environment and its creatures against pollution, abuse and harmful exploitation? Do you actively promote just distribution of the world's resources through frugality in your own life and through your support for social and economic practices which will sustain and enrich life for all?' "

Oliver listened attentively.

"Awfully long," someone murmured and Oliver was inclined to agree.

Someone else suggested deleting the phrase "with reverence for life and for the splendors of God's continuing creation."

This provoked a discussion. There were those who agreed and those who liked the phrase.

Oliver was trying to decide where he stood on this point when a bearded young man stuck his head in the door.

"Anybody here named Otis?"

Oliver looked up swiftly.

"Telephone."

"For me?" He jumped to his feet.

No one in Cambridge knew he was here. He'd meant to call his friends when he arrived, but it slipped his mind.

Wouldn't be Serenity. I left only a few hours ago. If it is, something's happened.

Or was she simply anxious about him, wanting to make sure he'd arrived safely?

Ellen's office was closed. Oliver looked around the front hall, wondering where to go.

"The pay phone," the bearded man told him, pointing to the cloakroom by the stairs.

The receiver had been left dangling from the wall.

Yes, it was Serenity and she did want to know about his trip. Had the train been on time? He didn't feel too tired? She sounded casual, but the deliberate way she enunciated her words made Oliver suspect that she had more on her mind than mere solicitude.

"Has something happened?"

"Well, yes. I just had a call from —" She sounded uneasy. "From Loveday."

"*Loveday?*"

"Unhun. She's been very sick. That's why we didn't hear from her. She went to New York intending to stay two days and came down with flu. A really bad case. Sounds to me like pneumonia."

"No! I was afraid — Pneumonia! Is she out of danger, Serenity? Will she recover?"

"She's okay. Got back to Boston this afternoon." Serenity hemmed. "Oliver — Why doesn't thee phone to Loveday?"

"I shall. I'll call right away." What was he saying? "Does thee think she wants to hear from me?"

"I don't know. I tried to explain that Ross is just a baby and he didn't understand what he was saying; that he was only trying to make her feel good. But she changed the subject. Still, if she hadn't hoped to speak to thee, she wouldn't have phoned, would she? I mean, a polite note would have been enough."

Oliver's anxiety overcame his diffidence. "Does thee know her number?"

He had to get out his address book, find his pencil, put on his glasses before he could write down the number Serenity gave him. Then she hung up.

Oliver replaced the receiver and fished in his pocket. Luckily, he had a dime. He dropped it in the slot and dialed.

A moment later, Loveday was saying a healthy-sounding, "Hello."

Standing in the narrow cloakroom, wedged between racks of bulky coats, a pile of folding chairs and a mound of backpacks, Oliver tried to collect himself. His taut emotions couldn't adjust to the speed with which joy had overtaken his frustration.

"This," he finally managed to say, "is Oliver. How are you feeling, Loveday?" Without giving her a chance to answer, he persisted, bewildered, "Are you all right?"

His anxiety caused the instrument to vibrate.

"Yes. Yes, I'm fine. Well, a bit wobbly, but much better. Did Rennie tell you? I had the flu."

She sounded so beautiful, so entirely like herself, that all Oliver's longing came over him in a rush, unfitting him to speak. But she sounded guarded, too, as if not quite sure how she should respond to him. No wonder!

He must reassure her.

"John Ludlow thought you might have been coming down with something when you were at Firbank."

"How did he know? Did I look awful?"

"Not to me, Loveday. No, John just feared you'd caught the bug that was going around."

"But how could he tell?"

"I had a touch."

"Oh! You mean I gave it to *you?* Oh, Oliver, I'm sorry. I didn't know. Was it terrible?"

"Nothing to speak of."

"I had no idea I was exposing anyone. I was feeling all right at Firbank. Well, not quite like myself, but I never dreamed I was coming down with something. It wasn't till I reached New York and was staying with these people — Kitty and Maurice — that I suddenly got sick. It was embarrassing. I'd come for a couple of nights and stayed weeks. The Woman Who Came to Dinner, they called me, trying to laugh it off, so I'd feel better. But it was no joke. Kitty was a student of mine in the sixties. I'd never met Maurice. They weren't getting along well together, but they were very good to me. They called in a doctor, who gave me an antibiotic and told me to stay put for a week after the fever came down. I cheated a little because the children are so anxious for me to get home."

"I remember how urgently you felt you must go."

"Yes. I meant to write to Rennie while I was in New York, but didn't have the oomph. So, soon as I got back here, I phoned and she told me you — "

"Loveday, may I come to see you?"

A heartless telephone operator intercepted the reply. Oliver's three minutes were up. He must deposit another ten cents.

Anguished, he wailed, "I don't have a dime. Will a quarter do?"

"You're calling from a pay phone?" Loveday broke in. "Why didn't you say so? Give me the number and I'll call you back."

As he waited for the ring, Oliver's heart pounded.

"I'm glad you got in touch with me," Loveday said, when they were reunited. "I didn't want to leave the East without saying goodbye and — "

"When are you going?"

"Day after tomorrow. If I can get packed."

"Are you really strong enough? Why don't you come back to Firbank with me and recuperate before setting out?"

Heather's letter might arrive tomorrow. If Loveday were at Firbank —

"Thanks. That's sweet. But the children are expecting me. They've been worried."

Should he stay and help her pack, see her off? But Ross — Oliver had promised him he'd be back tomorrow. Besides, she hadn't answered his question.

"I didn't want to leave," she repeated, "without thanking you for helping me find out about Isaac Austell. You're right. He really is an ancestor to be proud of."

Her disregard of his desire to see her made him unnaturally aggressive. "Loveday," he asked again, more tentatively this time, "may I come to see you?"

"*Tonight?* It's nearly ten. I only got in a short while ago. The place is a mess. My neighbor took in a whole shopping bag full of mail. I haven't looked through it yet. Why don't you wait till tomorrow?"

How could he? Evidently, she found it easy. But he —

"Come for lunch."

"That will be first-rate, only I don't want you to bother cooking when you have so much to do and you're still not strong. We'll go out. I'll pick you up. What time shall I come?"

She seemed to be thinking it over.

"I have a lot to tell you," Oliver added, hoping he wasn't pressing too hard. "And I'm leaving on the five o'clock train. The Hollands are meeting me."

Perhaps she'd urge him to stay over till Sunday. Would Ross understand?

"In that case," she said, "we'd better meet early."

"*How early?*"

"What about ten? I'd come to Cambridge and get you but I don't have that rented car any more. I gave it up before going to New York."

"That's all right," Oliver cried, elated. "I'll take a taxi."

Surprised by joy, he thought rapturously, squeezing the receiver.

A taxi! All the way to Boston! That Query about frugality — What had got into him?

"Do you know where Chestnut Street is, on Beacon Hill?"

There was a sudden burst of conversation and activity in the front hall. The Committee must have adjourned. For the pleasure of conversing with Loveday, Oliver had neglected his duty. He should have waited till now to call her. But how could he have done that?

Men were coming into the cloakroom for their coats. With all the commotion, Oliver had trouble hearing what Loveday was saying.

"Will you repeat that, please?"

"Do you know where Chestnut Street is? Runs between Beacon and Mount Vernon."

"Yes. Yes, I know."

Someone placed a hand on Oliver's arm. "Good night," he whispered. "Glad to have you with us."

Someone else was working his way into a parka. Then he assembled his belongings noisily and left. "See you next time," he called over his shoulder.

Loveday was still talking. Oliver didn't like to ask her to repeat the directions again. But he had no choice.

"I live at Eight Chestnut Street, near the corner of Walnut. Second house on the right as you face the Common."

"Oh! That must be next door to Friends House. I know quite well where that is."

"I'll see you then." She didn't suggest his staying an extra day. At least, with all the goings-on in the cloakroom, Oliver hadn't heard it.

"Good night, my dear," he murmured, forgetting himself. "Rest well."

"Good night, Oliver."

Aghast, he hung up the receiver. He'd called her, "my dear." Would she take it amiss? She hadn't sounded offended as she answered, formally but not coldly, "Good night, Oliver."

His knees were buckling. He had to get out of the stuffy cloakroom.

With difficulty, he made his way to the bench in the front hall and sat down. Everyone had left.

Before Oliver could climb those long flights of stairs, he needed to recover.

Tomorrow — tomorrow morning, he was going to see her! He hugged his happiness to himself, wishing he were home so he could rush to Serenity and Peter with his news. There wasn't a soul here to talk to.

Surprised by joy, he quoted to himself, *impatient as the wind, I turned to share the transport* — *Oh! with whom?*

No, he thought then, not even the dear Hollands could understand what I feel. Only Loveday — she is the one to share my joy. Unless she does —

9.

HALF THE NIGHT, in that strange bed, Oliver thought about the flowers he intended to bring Loveday. Choosing them would, in itself, be an act of love. They had to be just right. Roses? The hothouse varieties wouldn't be nearly so lovely as the ones that grew in summer on the south wall at Firbank, but they'd do.

What would it be like when he and Loveday met? How would they act; what would they say? Oliver would have to explain that, while Ross's assertion was absolutely true, he wasn't yet free to propose.

His loyalty to Heather forbade his mentioning how long he had had to wait for her letter. But he could confide the sudden revelation that had come to him in this room — that he had no right to ask Loveday for her hand until he had enshrined Daphne in a much deeper recess of his heart.

These thoughts went through his head when he should have been sleeping. Nevertheless, in the morning, he woke up refreshed and eager.

> And all the windows of my heart
> I open to the day,

he quoted to himself happily, as he opened the curtains and looked out over the Meetinghouse lawn.

While he dressed, the light slanting through the north window made him even more aware of his fraying cuffs. To visit Loveday, he ought to be looking his best. On the way to Beacon Hill, he'd stop at the Harvard Coop and glance at the suits, though there wouldn't be time to try one on.

It was a magnificent day, cold but sunny. Oliver felt buoyed up as he left the Center and walked down Brattle Street.

What color roses? Pink? Yellow? Red? He considered each in turn, visualizing it, wondering which Loveday would prefer.

At Church Street, he rounded the corner and stepped into the narrow flower shop. As soon as he looked through the glass doors of the lighted case at the profusion of flowers, blooming bravely in November, he forgot all about roses. There was a tall vase with sprigs of acacia — mimosa, Daphne used to call it. Clusters of small, feathery, golden balls implored Oliver to install them in the room which Loveday graced.

The florist took out a sprig and held it at arm's length. "Yes! That's the very thing! What shall we put with it? Babies' breath?"

"Beautiful together, aren't they?" the florist commented, when he'd added some sprays of tiny, white flowers. "How about a little statice? The soft purple will go good with the gold. Surrounded by laurel — "

Oliver took such pleasure in the colorful combination that he felt sad when the bouquet was rolled up in a cornucopia and stapled shut at the top. The florist handed it to him with a knowing smile, as if to say that the men from the University came here, too, when they were in love. He knew the signs, his smile said. He had recognized them in his elderly customer.

Oddly enough, the smile didn't discomfit Oliver. Quite the contrary — he would have liked to tell the whole world of his love

Elated, he left the shop, holding the bouquet with tender care, hardly able to wait till he could present it to Loveday. But if he set out for Boston now, he'd arrive too early. So he walked around the corner to the Coop and took the elevator to the Men's Clothing Department. There, while he balanced the flowers in one hand, he slid the clothes hangers along the racks with the other, glancing at his watch every few minutes, rapidly surveying the suits.

Suddenly, his hand was arrested. *Beware of all Enterprises that require new clothes,* had popped into his head.

Thoreau was challenging him. Was he thinking of buying a suit because he needed it or was he mainly trying to impress Loveday?

Troubled, he left the department and walked down the stairs, through the haberdashery, out onto Massachusetts Avenue. There he climbed into a taxi that reeked of stale cigarettes. He leaned back against the upholstery, barely containing his impatience to reach Loveday, as he was driven down Memorial Drive, across the Longfellow Bridge and through the narrow streets of Beacon Hill. Past Louisburg Square, up

Mount Vernon Street, almost to the summit, the taxi climbed, stopping finally at the corner of Walnut and Chestnut Streets.

Once out of the taxi, Oliver was in another world. The handsome, early nineteenth-century brick mansions were of modest height, elegant in their Georgian simplicity, with the golden dome of the State House visible above the rooftops.

This was familiar ground. At Number 6, Friends maintained a residence for students and young working people of every faith. Years ago, when he was serving on the Board of Managers, Oliver had come here regularly. To think that, all these months, Loveday was living right next door! Had Oliver known, he would have been able to picture her there and that would have given him pleasure.

A curving flight of stairs led to the door of Number 8, which was overhung by a columned portico.

Be still and cool, Oliver admonished himself, as he pressed the button marked *Mead.*

But he wasn't, not the least bit. He was, in Fox's words, *all of a fire.* He leaned against the outside door so it would open the moment the buzzer sounded.

Loveday's apartment was on the ground floor. Even before she opened her door, Oliver was there, waiting.

Suddenly, to his intense surprise, they were in each other's arms. How had this happened? The bouquet, which, till now, had been carefully held upright, dangled down Loveday's back.

Oliver would have been happy to remain that way forever, but she quickly let go.

It was too dark in the entrance hall to see her face clearly before she turned to lead the way into the apartment.

Who was responsible for that embrace? It seemed to have occurred spontaneously, almost without the intention of either one — at least, that's how it felt to Oliver.

In the living room, he handed her the flowers, watching

eagerly as she tore the stapled fold and unwound the paper.

"Oh," she exclaimed. "Oliver! How beautiful! I'll take them home with me — they'll keep."

Her pleasure couldn't have been more gratifying.

But she looked pale. Oliver longed to carry her off to the bracing air of Firbank.

"Sit down," she urged. "I'll just put these in water."

As she headed for the kitchen, the ease with which she moved made her seem young. Her haircut — shorter than Oliver remembered — reenforced this impression.

While she was gone, he looked around the room at the Victorian furniture, which had lost its original distinction. It was just shabby. Moreover, it was uncomfortable. He thought he could tell the difference between the rented stuff and Loveday's own — the boxes of books, ready to be shipped to Kansas, the paisley throw that lay across the back of the couch.

She returned, carrying a vase with the flowers attractively arranged, placed it on a drop-leaf table and sat down across the room.

Oliver's heart was beating fast. Much as he'd thought about Loveday, indulging in imaginary conversations, now that he was with her, he couldn't think of the appropriate things to say and he only had a few hours in which to explain himself. He studied her face. His utter pleasure in seeing her again was clouded by the need to assess her feelings.

They sat there, looking at each other.

He was searching, frightened of what he might find. She seemed more self-possessed than she'd ever been at Firbank.

The creases in her face deepened suddenly and she did the most incredible thing: she burst out laughing!

Weighed down as Oliver was with the gravity of the situation, nothing could have surprised him more.

"Don't be so glum," she begged. "Let's forget the whole business. It did upset me, I admit. Then I put it out of my mind, pretending it never happened. Why can't you do the same thing? We only have a short time to spend together. Let's enjoy it."

He saw the rightness of her plea. And yet, he had to make amends.

"I couldn't bear to think of your being hurt," he protested. "Ross didn't mean any harm. In a moment of loneliness, I confided in him, never dreaming that he'd remember. In fact, I thought he was half asleep."

She pointedly ignored this. "How are things at home?" she asked.

He told her about the Hollands — their plan to move to New York and how this troubled Serenity; about the arrangements Heather had made for his future in England.

"Are you going?"

The way she asked — the unmistakable anxiety in her tone — set all his fears at rest. She cared!

"No!" he assured her. "How could I leave Firbank? And Kendal Meeting? I'll manage with someone coming in to help. Judy Young, perhaps." Then he added, though this hadn't occurred to him at all before, "Besides, there may come a time when the Hollands will need me — will need to return to Firbank. Tell me about yourself, Loveday. I'm distressed to think you were so ill."

"I was. But I'm fine now. And, Oliver, I have the most wonderful news! After I spoke to you last night, I opened the mail. There was a letter from Mary Day, one of my students who's an editor now, right here in Boston. She spoke to the head of her department and he's very interested in my book — I mean, the one I'm going to write."

"That *is* wonderful!"

"Yes. They want me to come in and talk about it before I go home. I called Mary last night and we made a date for

Monday noon. Then I called Emily and told her I'm postponing my return a few days."

If only Oliver weren't obliged to leave this afternoon! They might have spent Sunday together. But he'd promised Ross; Peter ought not to be asked to do the extra chores again — he'd done so much already; the only clean shirt Oliver'd brought with him was on his back. How could he stay? Besides, Loveday wasn't urging him.

This one precious day was fast passing. It was already time to take her to lunch.

"There used to be a little French restaurant over beyond the State House. Do you know if it's still there?"

"I believe there are several."

They walked out into the sunshine together, down the hill to Beacon Street and along the Common. Oliver had the impulse to take Loveday's arm, but he was afraid that might be too forward.

He could never come here without recalling the four Quakers who were hanged on the Common for their faith. It made a man who professed to believe in the same principles ask himself how he would stand up to the test, should that be demanded of him in his time.

"Have you seen Mary Dyer?" he asked, as they reached the State House.

"Her name is *Day*. I just told you — I'm seeing her on Monday."

"The Mary I'm referring to was named Dyer. Her statue's on the State House lawn. When the hedge needs clipping, it's hidden. Look, there — see it? That's Mary Dyer, who was hanged here in sixteen sixty for coming back after she was banished."

Oliver led the way up the State House walk and stopped. They had a good view of the statue — a woman, wearing the simplest dress and a small cap, sitting on a bench with her hands in her lap — a Quaker at worship. Solitary, exposed to the ultimate cruelty, she seemed to be gazing beyond the anguish of her life here to the love beyond.

"Oh!" Loveday exclaimed. "Isn't there a photograph of this statue on the cover of that book you put by my bed at Firbank — the one about Quakers in Boston?"

"Yes. Can you read the words chiseled in the base?"

"My life not — "

"That's the seventeenth-century spelling for 'nought.' "

"My life nought availeth me in comparison to the liberty of the Truth," Loveday read.

She looked thoughtful, obviously moved by the awesome words. Her previous experience had possibly not required that she consider the price she would be willing to pay for "the liberty of the Truth."

They found a restaurant and were given a table by the window, but the outlook was principally on traffic.

When they were seated, Loveday opened the conversation. "How's Ross?"

"Doubly precious."

She frowned, as if she were trying to understand how this were possible.

Oliver braced himself to tell her what had happened.

"We almost lost him."

"*Ross?*"

"Yes. A truck came racing down the Salt Pond Road. They're not supposed to be there. Peter snatched Ross to the side just in time."

"When was this?"

"The day you left Firbank. Just after you drove off, in fact. Peter and Serenity went down to get the mail, taking Ross and the dogs."

It was too hard to continue. Oliver looked at Loveday, imploring her to infer the rest, so he wouldn't have to say it.

She saw his distress, but couldn't guess the reason. "Oliver! What happened? Was Ross hurt?"

"No, he's fine. And so is Lion. With his long legs, he was able to get out of the way. But Duffy —"

"Oh, Oliver! You mean — ?"

"Serenity says it was instantaneous. I hope so. She was a dear little thing, Loveday."

"I know."

Her sympathy emboldened Oliver. He reached across the table and laid his hand on hers for an instant. "Loveday, please hear me out. I don't want to hurt you, but there are some things I have to say. Will you let me?"

She looked at her plate. "I didn't mean to shut you up," she murmured apologetically. "It's just been so painful. You see" — her self-possession vanished — "I care about you, too. But —" She didn't go on.

The emotion that rose in Oliver then must have been apparent to her. He was forced to wait and compose himself before continuing to speak, rearranging the silverware at his place, moving the knife and fork, then moving them back to their original position.

Finally, he risked looking at her squarely. "Until a few weeks ago, I never thought of marriage as a possibility. At my age — I simply felt this high regard for you and acknowledged to myself that it was, indeed, love. I didn't expect it to change anything. Lately, I've been encouraged to think that I might dare to ask you to consider marriage, but there are certain matters to be settled first. Once those are cleared —"

He was almost silenced by her expression. It was one he had seen before. She was at war with herself, being pulled in two directions. She looked so unhappy that he almost stopped speaking.

"I'm not proposing," he assured her. "You needn't be afraid.

I'm not proposing — yet. But you went off without leaving your address and I do look to a day when I shall ask whether I may come to see you and talk about marriage."

"Come to *Kansas?*"

"Why not?"

Now it was out! His heart was racing. He left the knife and fork where they were and leaned back, looking down into his lap. When he was at last able to face Loveday, she was taking a little notebook out of her purse and writing in it. Then she tore out a page and handed it to him.

"That's my address," she said. "I don't want you to think I'm running away from you. As a matter of fact, I guess I was so slow getting over that flu because I felt crushed. Being at Firbank has been one of the greatest experiences of my life — being with you. And I was sick, thinking it was over — gone out of my life. But as long as you aren't proposing, I don't see why we can't continue to be friends."

"And if way should open for me, may I come?"

She seemed to find this very hard to answer. "It's a big trip," she said finally, "and I wouldn't want you to come all that way for nothing."

He didn't feel he could say more. Glancing at his watch, he found that it was almost three o'clock. He had to get back to Cambridge, collect his belongings and hurry to South Station. At least, he had declared what was in his heart. Had it offended her? Or was she simply unable to reveal her feelings?

They said very little after that. What was there to say?

Oliver paid the bill and they left the restaurant. He was planning to walk back to Chestnut Street with Loveday, but she explained that she had an errand to do and would leave him here. It would be a more likely place for him to pick up a taxi.

They stood on the pavement, feeling, Oliver thought, closer

than they'd ever been, now that they were parting, perhaps forever.

And he hadn't been completely candid. "I should have been more explicit," he said hurriedly. "What stands in my way — partly — is the realization that came to me yesterday — how unfair it would be to ask anyone to marry me as long as I'm still grieving for Daphne. I must learn to love her without being so regretful."

"But, Oliver, I don't see how you can do that until you have someone to take her place — I don't mean in your love but in your present life."

"Do you think so? Do you really think so?"

"I'm certain."

"Bless thee, Loveday," he said, reaching for her hands. "Thee has put great joy in an old man's life."

Still holding his hands, she lifted her face and kissed him.

10.

IT WAS A MERCY that the taxi drew up to the curb just then, for Oliver was in danger of breaking down. All the way to Longfellow Park, he struggled with his emotions, telling himself that he must control them or he'd get rattled and miss his train. But that goodbye kiss had undone him.

When he reached the Center and got out of the taxi, he felt so weak that he did a rash thing: he asked the driver to wait while he went in and got his bag. He was in no condition to take the subway. He'd let himself be driven all the way to South Station!

Inside, there were a lot of people.

As Oliver started up the stairs, he noticed that the three-by-five card, which was taped to the newel post, bore his name. *Oliver Otis, please call your home.*

Now what? Something very serious must have occurred if he had to be reached before he got home. Would the taxi driver be patient while Oliver fished for the money and dialed?

In the stuffy cloakroom, he stood counting the rings anxiously. At last, Serenity answered.

"Oliver — " Her voice had that same uneasy inflection he'd noticed yesterday, when she told him about Loveday's call. He braced himself. "Oliver, Heather phoned this morning. I tried to reach thee at once, but thee must have gone out early."

"Heather *phoned?* What's the matter? Is she sick? Is one of the children?"

"No, everybody's all right. She called to say she's coming. Monday."

"Heather's coming? How wonderful!"

"Yes, her plane gets in to Boston at two o'clock."

"Heather's coming?" Oliver repeated, but now he saw the reason and it unnerved him. This was just what, months ago, he'd feared would happen if he wrote about Loveday.

"She's worried," Serenity was saying. "She says, getting married's a big step. She wants to talk to thee about it."

"Yes, it's a big step. I'm by no means sure I'm going to take it. Loveday doesn't seem interested. So Heather's coming may be all for nothing."

"Well, don't tell her not to. It will do thee good to have a visit."

That was true. Oliver had thought all along that they must seek Truth together. But if she trusted his judgment, would Heather be coming just now?

"We thought," Serenity was saying, "thee might like to stay over and meet her plane. Peter says he'll drive up Monday afternoon and bring the two of you home, so there won't be a problem with Heather's bags, only he can't leave till five. With the traffic and all, it may be pretty late. You'd better get supper there."

"But I promised Ross I'd come today."

"That's okay. I'll explain it to him. He'll understand. Don't worry about things here, Oliver. Peter will take care of the chores. Thee'd enjoy going to meeting in Cambridge tomorrow, wouldn't thee?"

"Yes. I haven't been here since the Sanctuary. Yes, I'd like that. Only, I don't have a fresh shirt."

That made Serenity giggle. Obviously, it wasn't as grave a matter to her as it was to Oliver.

"Will Loveday still be there when Heather arrives?"

"I'm not sure. She has an appointment Monday morning. I don't know whether she's leaving directly after that or not. Her children are impatient for her return."

"If she's still there," Serenity suggested, "why not have supper together, the three of you? Heather complained that she doesn't know anything about Loveday. Thee never mentioned her till a couple of weeks ago. She can't figure out what's up. So if she got to meet Loveday — "

Oliver was overwhelmed with remorse. "I did hold out on Heather. But, Serenity, what was the use of worrying her?"

"Thee sounds pretty worried thyself. Is something wrong?"

"Yes, very wrong." Oliver didn't know how to identify what he was feeling. "A man my age," he began, hunting for a rational explanation, "a man my age has no business falling in love. It just upsets the people he cares about."

Serenity laughed out loud.

"Oliver darling, I'm not upset. I think it's the most beautiful thing in the world. So does Peter."

Only after he'd hung the receiver on the wall did Oliver remember the taxi. He went out to pay the driver and tell him that, after all, he wasn't going to South Station today.

The driver's disappointment was volubly expressed in language quite unfamiliar to Oliver, who luckily had too many other things on his mind to be perturbed.

He returned to the cloakroom and dialed Loveday's number. She wasn't home yet.

Several young people were in the Center kitchen. Oliver went in and asked the bearded young man who had called him to the telephone last evening whether it would be possible to keep the guest room two more nights. The young man said, "It's okay. If you need anything, I'm Jim."

"Stay and have supper with us," one of the girls urged. "It's just about ready. You're Oliver Otis, aren't you?"

"How did you know?"

"I heard you were coming. I've wanted to meet you ever since I was in a workshop on peacemaking. We're trying to figure out positive things to do and somebody told about your working to restore the vegetation in Vietnam. That's neat. I'm Nancy." She rattled off a string of names.

There were eight of them. They included Oliver as if he were their age, sharing their meal, laughing and telling about themselves.

Oliver forgot his worries, cheered by the companionship and exuberance of these young people. When the meal was over, he invited them all to come to Firbank. Then he tried Loveday's number again. She wasn't home.

By the time Oliver had climbed to the top of the house and closed the door of the guest room behind him, he was too exhausted to do anything but throw himself onto the bed.

If he only knew where he stood with Loveday, he'd be in a better position to reassure Heather. But he didn't. Loveday was obviously struggling. Part of her seemed to be withdrawing. Part of her was warmly disposed toward him. Otherwise, why would she have kissed him?

How was he to convince Heather that he wasn't simply a

foolish old man? She evidently felt she must rush over and protect him. It was a temptation to persuade himself that this was a matter to be decided entirely between himself and Loveday.

It was a great temptation, yet were Oliver to disregard Heather, he wouldn't be true to himself. He must try to join with her in seeking Truth, respecting her judgment, even if she questioned his.

Besides, assuming that Loveday were to accept him and she wished to be married under the care of Friends, if the family had reservations, the Committee appointed to look into the clearness for marriage of the couple might discourage the Meeting from accepting this responsibility. To Oliver, too, it was of the greatest importance that Heather and Loveday's children be in accord, else how could it be a happy marriage? Firbank had always been a place of harmony.

Patience — that was what this situation required. Heather was not unreasonable. Eventually, she'd understand. Only, there was so little time. At his age —

Fragments of James Nayler's words echoed in Oliver's head, those incomparably beautiful words of the early Friend who suffered so much: *There is a spirit which I feel that delights to do no evil ... but delights to endure all things, in hope to enjoy its own in the end ... it takes its kingdom with entreaty and not with contention ...*

He must have fallen asleep, for suddenly it was ten o'clock.

Loveday! He had to get down to the telephone before she retired; tell her that he was still here; that he'd be remaining till Monday. Maybe she'd see him again.

She was home!

"Heather's coming," he announced, explaining why he was prolonging his stay.

"Your daughter? From London? I thought she only came in the summertime."

"Well — Generally — "

"Is it something special? Your birthday?"

If Oliver were to admit why Heather was coming, wouldn't it be terribly embarrassing for Loveday when they met? She'd feel she was being looked over.

"Heather has something to discuss that she doesn't want to put in a letter," Oliver said lamely. "She's arriving Monday at two and Peter's coming to pick us up that evening. Loveday, would you have supper with us? I'd like you to know Heather."

"That would be nice. But let's not go out. Bring her here. It'll be more relaxed."

"Not when you're getting ready to leave."

"I'll make it very simple."

Oliver felt pushy as he asked Loveday whether she had plans for tomorrow, but, more than ever, he needed to be with her.

Unfortunately, she was going to be busy in the afternoon. A neighbor had offered to come in and help her pack. But she was free in the morning. Was Oliver thinking of going to Friends Meeting? Would he like her to join him?

Would he!

"Where is it?"

"Right here. I'll come over and call for you."

"No. I can find it. I know my way around Cambridge. I'll be there."

His spirits soared as he replaced the receiver. She was coming to meeting with him!

11.

THIS FIRST DAY, Oliver told himself when he opened his eyes the next morning, was a gift. He would spend part of it with the woman he loved.

And in the healing quietude of the meeting, he'd have a chance to bank the fire that raged in him; to abandon the feverish pursuit of his desire and turn instead to his Inward Light. He and Loveday, sharing the silence, would perhaps return from the hour in God's presence with a deeper understanding, not alone of themselves but of each other.

He saw her coming up Brattle Street even before she recognized him and he all but ran to meet her. She looked beautiful. And happy — nearly as happy, he dared think, as he was.

They turned into Longfellow Park together, walking toward the Meetinghouse, hardly speaking, except with their eyes. As they neared the building, Oliver felt a sense of expectancy so profound that it almost held the promise of fulfillment.

Unlike remote Kendal Meeting, where strangers seldom come, Cambridge Meeting, with its hundreds of visitors, needed a doorkeeper, a Friend appointed to welcome newcomers. As Oliver and Loveday mounted the steps of the Meetinghouse, a spry, elderly woman gave them a dazzling smile and reached out to shake hands.

The meeting room was already quite full. At the door, Oliver stood still, looking around for two empty seats. Then he led Loveday to a bench under one of the windows. When they were settled, he turned to her with gratitude, for he felt complete now. This was what he'd observed about Loveday the first time he mentioned her to Heather — that she made him feel whole, as he hadn't felt since Daphne died.

Centering down in a strange Meetinghouse always took a while. There was too much to notice — the affecting sight of so many children sitting beside their parents for the first half hour, swinging their legs occasionally, yet obviously caught up in the still reverence; the grave, often deeply troubled faces of the college students.

Oliver hadn't been here in years, not since the late sixties, when he came up from Firbank to take part in the Sanctuary. At that time, a soldier who was absent from the Army without leave was sitting near the fireplace, awaiting arrest.

The young man — Oliver kept trying to remember his name — had been ordered to go to Vietnam. Convinced that he could not kill, he had disappeared. Frightened and sick, he'd decided after a couple of months to give himself up. Though not previously known to Friends, he had appealed to the Meeting for sanctuary until he should be apprehended.

Eric — that was the soldier's name! Recalling it, Oliver remembered, too, the dramatic sequence of events that had later been reported to him. It was in this room, during a meeting for worship on a First Day in August that Eric came out of hiding. Toward the end of the hour, the Clerk introduced him. Eric stood up and declared his position. Then the Clerk announced that the handshaking which customarily signaled the close of meeting was being postponed. Friends intended to continue worshipping in support of Eric as long as he was with them.

They remained in their seats. Eric went over to the Center, where he held a news conference in which he stated his conscientious objection to war.

Everyone expected the Meetinghouse to be immediately surrounded by the police, but nothing happened. Toward evening, some Friends prepared supper for Eric, his mother, his girl, his personal friends. Others maintained the worship, participating in turns.

At midnight, Eric was bedded down in the basement of the Meetinghouse where, by day, volunteers clean and mend castoff clothing for the needy. On a cot set up between the sewing machine and the button boxes, Eric waited.

All night, the witness continued. Some Friends went home to sleep; others came to take their places.

In the morning, Eric's picture appeared on TV and in the newspapers, even in the Kendal *Sun*. Tall, likable, he was described by the reporter, evidently with surprise, as "just an ordinary guy."

Oliver, reading the article at Firbank, was indignant. "No such thing!" he cried, showing it to Daphne. "He must be *extra-ordinary* or he wouldn't have the courage. I wish I were in Cambridge, helping to support him. But even if I left right now, by the time I got there, it would be too late. The police would have come."

The police didn't. A second day, a second night, a third —

Oliver kept in touch by telephone. On the fourth day, he simply had to go. When he arrived, he found this Meetinghouse full, for it had suddenly become a focus for people who had never set foot in it before — nuns in their new, short habits, rabbis, priests, Protestant clergymen, hippie-types, anguished parents. Suddenly, they had a place where they could go and pray silently for peace.

No sooner had Oliver been seated in the Meetinghouse that day — it was, he recalled now, the summer of '68 — than he was carried back fifty years to the First World War. *He* was that young man who refused to bear arms, though he never ran away. He went to prison, as Eric was destined to do.

It was a shattering identification. All that day, Oliver hadn't really been upholding Eric. He'd been reliving events in his own life, the cost to him of being a conscientious objector in the First World War. Yes, it was shattering.

By evening, the police still hadn't come. August was a busy time on the farm. Oliver couldn't stay longer.

Back at Firbank, working in his field, lying in bed at night, he thought of nothing but young Eric, awaiting court-martial.

On the seventeenth day, Oliver couldn't bear it any longer. "I'm going back to Cambridge," he told Daphne.

"Stay as long as thee's needed," she urged. "I'll ask one of Austin's boys to come over and take care of things while thee's gone." She placed her fingertips on Oliver's shoulders and looked lovingly into his eyes. "Thee's a good man," she said, confirming the rightness of his decision.

Cambridge was in the throes of a heat wave. Some Friends had gone on vacation. Those who remained were dog-tired. They greeted Oliver gratefully.

He stayed all night. It seemed as though daybreak would never come. He could still remember the cricket that was stuck in the hot air register — how its chirping threatened to put him to sleep. He'd thought of Czechoslovakia. Only the week before, the Soviets had invaded that country, ruthlessly crushing all resistance.

If we were in Czechoslovakia, Oliver'd thought that night, we wouldn't be allowed to support a man who refuses to obey the military. We wouldn't even be allowed to gather for worship.

He'd given thanks for his country, which could tolerate dissent.

The cricket chirped all night.

In the morning, other Friends arrived. Oliver went down to the Square for breakfast. It was so good to be out in the air, he wanted to take a long walk. But something drew him back.

At eleven that morning, two men in plain clothes entered

the Meetinghouse. From their bearing, Oliver guessed they were "the feds." Nevertheless, they sat down quietly on a back bench. Later, Oliver learned that, before coming in, they'd been told about the meeting for worship — how it had continued for eighteen days and nights. Would they wait five minutes while it drew to a close?

So the officers sat there, listening to Friends speak of their willingness to suffer rather than to kill; of the loving nature of God and the brotherhood of all people. The silence that followed throbbed with tragedy. Eric's hour had come.

The officers stood up and marched to the front of the Meetinghouse, where he was sitting beside his girl. They presented the warrant for his arrest. They didn't lay hands on him. Eric got to his feet. His girl reached up and touched his arm. He looked back at her as he walked out with the officers.

For a few more minutes, silence enfolded Friends. Then they shook hands. The long meeting was over.

Today, a good decade later, the occasion was as vivid to Oliver as if it had just happened, for it had opened the wound in him that never quite healed. In 1918, had it not been for the Armistice, he would have remained in solitary confinement.

He'd never been able to talk about what he had endured, not even to Daphne, though that wasn't necessary. She knew.

But Loveday — after reading his book, she'd asked about his imprisonment and he had declined to answer.

He, who professed to stand for Truth, had held out on the woman he loved, just as he'd held out on his daughter. The remorse he'd felt in the cloakroom, when Serenity relayed Heather's fears, was nothing to the shame that assailed him now, sitting beside Loveday in the Meetinghouse. He wasn't worthy of her confidence.

Peeking at her, he wondered whether he could make amends this late. She looked very serious, preoccupied, no doubt, with her own spiritual search. How badly they needed to be redeemed in the light of each other's unqualified acceptance!

Oliver could hardly wait for meeting to close. He'd take Loveday to a nice, quiet place for lunch and there he'd entrust to her the pain he'd kept bottled up all his adult life. A very few words would suffice. But, for him, it would be a momentous event.

There was a sudden stir in the room, a scraping of feet. The children were leaving, midway through the hour, going to their classes in the First Day School. The empty places they left on the benches looked forlorn.

Some Quaker parents said frankly that they could only begin to center down after their wriggling children had gone. But Oliver never quite forgot the small ache he always used to feel, when Heather was a little girl and the moment came for her to slide down from her place between him and Daphne. After she followed the other children out of the room, meeting lost some of its radiance for him.

Remembering Heather back in those days — her merry giggle and springy, red pigtails — he felt a wave of love sweep over him. She was coming! She loved him so much, she wanted to be sure that Loveday would make him happy.

A smoldering log, crashing in the fireplace, drew Oliver's attention outward.

At the back of the room, a young woman had risen to speak. She was apparently so frightened that her voice was barely audible. Much of what she said escaped Oliver, yet he heard enough to conclude that she was crying out in despair. The hazard of nuclear waste, the arms race —

She had hardly taken her seat again when a man got up and cited statistics of the weapons being manufactured today. What were Friends doing to stop the threat of total annihilation?

There was a hopelessness in all this that went to Oliver's heart. These young people felt completely impotent, for they had no part in the decision-making which, they believed, was leading to destruction.

For we know that the whole creation groaneth and travaileth together until now. And not only they, but ourselves... Since Biblical times, this was a fact of life. But, Oliver told himself, in Romans, those words are followed by the assertion: *For we are saved by hope.*

Coming here to air their fears undoubtedly relieved these young people. Still, the meeting for worship was more than a therapy session. It was a testimony to Friends' reliance on that divinity in all humankind which could never be annihilated. Regardless of the evil in the world, the indwelling God filled men and women with hope and joy.

Oliver had never been more conscious of this than at that moment. Joy moved him to the point where he felt called to share it with the despondent young people around him. What were Friends doing to stop the threat of total annihilation? Simply trusting in the supremacy of that reality which nothing could kill.

To his intense surprise, because he rarely felt moved to speak in meeting, he found himself on his feet.

"When Jesus was taking leave of his disciples, aware that he was going to his death," Oliver began, not sure what he would say next, "he left to them the greatest legacy he had to bequeath. It must have been precisely the opposite of what the desolated disciples expected. Yet the words spoken in that tragic moment were to enhance the lives of men and women throughout subsequent centuries.

"*Abide in me, and I in you*... *These things have I spoken unto you that my joy might remain in you, and that your joy might be full.*"

Oliver sank to the bench and drifted away on a sea of silence, of infinite light, where all thought was suspended. He didn't return until there was a sudden ripple in the room and the old lady sitting beside him extended her hand. Oliver took it automatically. Meeting was over, but his spirit lagged, lingering on the sunlit sea.

When, at last, he turned to Loveday, it seemed to him that she was coming back from afar off, too. Then her earnest expression changed to an endearing smile. She was telling him something very softly — so softly that it was drowned out by the deep voice of a middle-aged man, who had walked to the front of the room.

"Welcome to Friends Meeting at Cambridge," the man said. "If you are here for the first time, or returning after an absence, we would like to know who you are. Will you stand and tell us your name and where you come from?"

The two young people who had voiced despair both said that this was their first Friends Meeting. Obviously, they'd come because they were troubled and this was known as a place where one was free to express what was on one's mind. Half a dozen others introduced themselves. Then Oliver rose and said, "I'm Oliver Otis from Kendal Meeting, in Rhode Island, returning after a long absence, and this is my friend, Loveday Mead, from Emporia, Kansas."

"Glad to have you with us," the man at the front of the room responded.

Friends stood up, chatting, heading for the door.

Oliver was eager to get away, to take Loveday to that quiet place he'd dreamed of. But as they left the Meetinghouse, they were stopped under the porte-cochère by Friends who had known him years ago. They wanted to tell him that his ministry had been favored. He feared Loveday might be feeling ignored, for she had stepped away and was surveying her surroundings.

"Look," she cried, when they were finally alone. She pointed up at the roof of the porte-cochère. "See what it says there? It's the same thing that's on your sampler at Firbank: *Walk cheerfully over the world, answering that of God in every one."*

Oliver lifted his eyes to the eaves, where the children of the First Day School had carved Fox's words.

"I never even knew there was anything like that in me," Loveday confided, turning to him, "till I came to Firbank and you answered it."

12.

Oliver had never considered himself worldly, so it shocked him to discover how much pleasure he took in a new suit — the first he'd ever bought by himself.

During the night, he wondered whether it wouldn't be more prudent to postpone purchasing it till Heather came. She'd like helping him make up his mind. But, in the morning, he decided to go ahead on his own. He could no longer deny that he wanted to look his best for Loveday. Besides, if Heather thought he was neglecting his appearance, wouldn't she fear her father was growing senile?

Her plane wasn't due till two o'clock. With the whole morning free, Oliver had gone back to the Coop.

After he made the selection, he was glad he'd relied on his judgment. The suit was of pure wool, gray, as befitted an elderly Quaker, but a vibrant shade, with a herringbone weave that gave it quiet elegance. Oliver felt lucky to have found it, half hidden amongst the flashy plaids and checks, snubbed by younger men, waiting to be possessed by *him.* Daphne would have loved it.

Running his fingers over the soft nap, he was so carried away that he did as Serenity'd urged: he disregarded the price.

The tailor was able to turn up the trousers while Oliver, chilly in his briefs, stood in the fitting room, changing shirts. Each evening, at the Friends Center, he had rinsed out the briefs along with his socks. But there was no place to drip-dry the shirt. So, he'd bought a new one.

Buttoning it, he was repulsed by his reflection in the mirror. Who'd marry an old codger like thee? it asked him. A scarecrow! Those knobby knees —

The tailor returned. Oliver tried on the suit. What a transformation!

"I'll wear it," he said, elated. "Will you send the old one home, please?"

He walked out with a springy step. Loveday'd approve. Even Heather might.

This encounter between the women he loved — what would happen when Loveday opened her door? One thing was sure: in Heather's presence, Oliver wouldn't fall into her arms again!

Halfway down the stairs, he realized that, should Heather's plane be on time, it would be too early to go directly to Loveday's apartment. Where could they spend an hour? The tearooms that used to abound were gone.

Beacon Hill Friends House, Oliver thought suddenly — the student residence next door to Loveday's apartment — the very place! He was known there. He found a pay phone and called the Director, explaining his dilemma. She was delighted to help. Unfortunately, she had to go out, but one of the students would gladly give Oliver and his daughter tea.

Having found a satisfactory solution to that problem, Oliver cut through the haberdashery, heading for the street. In a narrow aisle, his arm brushed against a stand of neckties and he stopped, merely curious. He owned dozens of ties and rarely wore one; he didn't need another. Spinning the stand, he came upon a dark red silk with silver dots. Wouldn't that go beautifully with the gray wool? It was irresistible.

After spending so much, Oliver felt forced to take the subway. He had to make three changes, from the Red Line to the Green, to the Blue, to the airport bus — laughing at himself each time for making this small economy to offset the enormous outlay.

In the men's room at the airport, he put on the new necktie. The effect pleased him. Would Loveday notice?

A crowd already waited at the gate through which Heather was scheduled to emerge. Standing there, Oliver wondered how she would act when she met Loveday. Would she be gracious? Or uncommunicative? If anxious or displeased, she could be aloof to a degree that was downright discourteous. Then again, she might be the well-bred British matron, socially correct, secretly hostile. Either way, if that was how Heather behaved, the dinner would be a fiasco.

And Oliver was desperately eager to have it turn out a success. For, since yesterday, Loveday had become still more dear to him. As they sat in the corner of a restaurant after meeting, he had confided to her the pain he'd kept locked away for over sixty years.

"If it hadn't been for my training in using solitude to cultivate the awareness of God's presence," he'd declared, agitated as he remembered the stockade, "I should have lost my mind."

Loveday had listened with a sympathy that made him feel as though she were reaching out to draw him to her in comfort. That felt healing.

Perhaps he should have told her why Heather was coming. At least, she would have been prepared. How could she help suspecting that she was being looked over? Wouldn't that make her self-conscious, defensive, even silly, the way she was when she kept asking Ross if he loved her?

By the time the plane from London was announced, Oliver's apprehension had reached fever-pitch. Buffeted by the crowd, he was suddenly overtaken by extreme weariness. If Heather didn't come soon — His knees were shaky.

It took the passengers forever to go through customs. Finally, a few people appeared and walked toward the gate.

Scanning each face, continually disappointed, Oliver began to wonder whether Heather had changed her mind at the last minute. Why hadn't he stayed at the Center all morning, in case she wanted to notify him?

Then he saw her, wedged in a mass of slowly moving people. She was wearing a plum-colored coat and hat. Forgetting his fatigue, Oliver rushed forward to embrace her before she was even halfway through the gate.

"My dear," he murmured, reviving, "my dear." He held her tightly.

She kissed him, but quickly backed off. "Let's move on," she urged. "We're blocking traffic." She looked tired, too.

Oliver took her suitcase, balancing it with his bag. It was heavy. He didn't know how far he could carry it.

"Well, Father," Heather exclaimed with relief, when they had worked their way clear of the crowd, "how are you?" Before Oliver could answer she went on, "I'm glad you're here. I was afraid I'd have to get to Kendal alone. Rennie wasn't sure you'd wait."

"Of course I'd wait for thee! Thank thee for coming."

"I tried writing, but I just couldn't think of what to say. Three aerograms — I tore them up, one after the other. With postage what it is — So I decided to fly over. It's not a convenient time. Stephen's in Scotland on business. But —"

"How's Stephen? How are the children?"

"All in good form."

They reached the street. Puffing, Oliver put down the suitcase.

"Beacon Hill," he managed to tell the driver, when they got into a taxi. "Six Chestnut Street."

"Where are you taking me? Aren't we going to Firbank?"

"Tonight. Peter's coming for us. Now we're having tea at the Quaker student house. Let me get a good look at thee before we enter the tunnel. Was it a bumpy flight?"

"Planes always make me seedy."

"I hope thy appetite will return by dinnertime. Loveday has invited us."

"Loveday," Heather repeated, drawling the syllables. "What an odd name. You never mentioned it. I didn't have the foggiest notion what she's called till I rang up and Rennie told me." She sounded piqued.

Oliver meant to explain how hard he had found it to speak about Loveday — he, who was usually so open — but they were nearing the end of the tunnel and he remembered the Red Lyon Inn, which once stood overhead.

"Quick," he cried, grabbing Heather's arm. "Look up." He pointed to the dim vault of the tunnel.

"What is it? I can't see anything."

"No, it's on the street above us. That's where Nicholas Upsall lived. His bequest, made over three centuries ago, provided for my comfort, the past three nights."

Now Heather looked thoroughly annoyed.

Don't fob me off with ancient history, Father, she seemed to be saying, withdrawing visibly. Here I've come all the way across the ocean, airsick in the bargain, simply to find out about this woman. And you — Why are you so evasive?

She didn't say this, but the look she gave Oliver conveyed it and brought him to his senses.

"I'm sorry if I've worried thee," he said, patting her hand. "I had no thought of marrying until I wrote. At my age — "

"Yes," she broke in, suddenly showing all her pent-up feeling. "If you were ten years younger, I could understand. But unless she's a schemer, what reason would any woman have for marrying an — "

"None, I'm afraid. Loveday doesn't seem inclined. Though, sometimes, I'm bold enough to think — Till I ask her, I can't be sure and till I know whether thee's comfortable, I don't feel free to ask her." Oliver glanced at Heather, hoping for some hint of approval, but she simply looked upset. He sighed. "Thy journey may turn out to have been in vain," he warned.

To his relief, the touchy conversation ended, for the taxi had stopped. They got out.

If Heather only knew how ardently an old man can desire a woman, Oliver thought, fishing for his wallet. What a shock it would be!

She was exclaiming over the architecture of Friends House. "Reminds me of Hampstead," she murmured, as they mounted the steps and rang the bell.

They were welcomed by a smiling girl in blue jeans and a heavy sweater. She introduced herself as Carol. They left their things in the entrance hall and Carol led the way down the majestic staircase to the dining room.

Through French doors, Oliver and Heather looked out at a brick courtyard, under a dull, November sky.

"Snow by morning," Oliver predicted.

Places had been set for two at the end of a table long enough to seat twenty. Carol brought in the teapot and a platter of cookies. Then she disappeared.

Sitting beside Heather, watching her pour, Oliver noticed that her hair was almost white. He found it hard to grasp that his child was middle-aged. Wasn't it only yesterday that she was swinging from the branches of the apple trees, her red pigtails flying?

He took her hand in his, happy to have it again, silently praying that they might find unity; that, with God's help,

they'd come to an understanding which wouldn't violate
Heather's feelings or force him to repress his own.

"Oh, Father, thank you for the tea," she said, after her
second cup. "I feel ever so much better. This is a lovely place."
She turned and studied him. "Isn't that a new suit? I don't
remember seeing it before."

"Does thee like it?"

"Very much." She reached over to feel the cloth, taking a
little fold of the sleeve between her thumb and forefinger.

"It's my first since thy wedding."

"About time! That's almost thirty years ago."

"Well, the old suit had grown a bit shabby," Oliver admitted,
laughing. "I'm glad thee approves. I was a little afraid to trust
my judgment. Mother and I always used to shop together."

"You're becoming independent," Heather observed, with
what sounded like a touch of sarcasm. "I never did understand
why you refused to take more initiative. You and Mother
couldn't seem to do anything alone. Stephen and I love each
other, too, but I'd never dream of going to his tailor with him
and I certainly wouldn't want him choosing my frocks." She
made a face. "You two were always so close."

Her adolescent notion — that her parents had no room in
their hearts for her because they were wrapped up in each
other — hadn't yet been lived down! In her fifties, Heather
was still clinging to the fantasy she had created at fifteen.

Oliver looked at her, begging her with his eyes to face the
truth at last. He never had felt free to discuss this with her.
Now he took a daring resolve.

"Heather," he began, putting down his cookie and squeezing
her hand, "thee knows very well that we loved thee as much
as we loved each other. We weren't adept at dispelling the
strange notion thee concocted in thy adolescence, but the love
was there."

"I know," she conceded grudgingly. "You really were good parents. It's just the way I felt at the time. You and Mother were never able to convince me. Later, when Rennie came to Firbank, I couldn't see why you two did so well with her, while, with your own daughter —"

"We were a lot older then — old enough to have been Serenity's grandparents. Suffering may have made us wiser. And maybe it's necessary to skip a generation. Serenity's parents couldn't help her, either."

"Oh, Serenity's parents! They're the end. But you and Mother should have —"

"I wish I could help Serenity now," Oliver murmured. "She's very troubled. Peter's prepared to sacrifice his job, which he loves. She knows that isn't right. And Ross still needs his mother. But she wants that job."

"It looks like a situation in which everyone is going to be hurt."

"Possibly," Oliver admitted. "I've worried a good deal about them. But, thee knows, Peter and Serenity have a sturdy marriage. Somehow, they'll come through."

"Tell me," Heather said, changing the subject, "is this woman —"

"Loveday?"

"Yes, Loveday — is she anything like Mother?"

"Not at all! Except for that short depression after her stroke, Mother had equanimity and a clear sense of purpose, while Loveday is sometimes torn by conflicting impulses. She's been doing research for a book which she means to start writing, but, so far, I don't believe she's done much."

"Sounds like a difficult person."

"Oh no! She just hasn't quite found her niche yet."

"*At her age?* Didn't you say she's in her seventies?"

"*Early* seventies."

"What do you see in her?"

How could Oliver answer that? He twiddled his teacup, determined to be forthright, yet incapable of characterizing Loveday objectively.

"It's — well — I simply fell in love, practically at first sight. I haven't been the same since."

"So I gather. I just can't understand. You used to be so reasonable."

Oliver ignored the reproach. "I'm convinced," he assured Heather, "that Loveday would blossom at Firbank."

Heather looked down at the table. "You always were self-less," she murmured. "That's why I came — to make sure you weren't overlooking your own welfare. It shouldn't be all one way."

"It's not. We're seekers together. And Loveday's companion-ship makes me supremely happy. But the past few days," Oliver confided, dropping his voice, "I've realized that it wouldn't be fair to marry while I'm still grieving for Mother. So I may not be ready, though Loveday thinks I can't cease grieving till I have someone else to cherish."

"You seem to have discussed this with her pretty thoroughly. Well, I'm disappointed. I really counted on your coming to England. With the Hollands leaving, it seemed the natural thing."

Tears blurred Oliver's vision. Heather hadn't come because she mistrusted his judgment. She'd come because she wanted him near her. He let go her hand and reached in his pocket for his handkerchief.

Noticing his emotion, she looked touched. "It will seem very strange," she murmured, "having a stepmother. Still, I'm not going to prevent you. How could I? All I want is to make sure that this wom—, that Loveday won't take advantage of you."

"Thank thee, dear. When thee meets her, I believe thee'll feel easy. The real question is: will she have me?"

Heather dropped her British speech and reverted to the slang of her New England youth. Her eyes narrowed with mischief, as she quipped, "Wanna bet?"

13.

TENSION gripped Oliver as he and Heather walked next door. When he pressed the button above Loveday's mailbox, his hand shook so that he wondered whether the buzzer had sounded. Waiting, he glanced at Heather. She looked scared. Sensing, perhaps, how nervous he was, she reached out and patted his coat sleeve.

Loveday welcomed them with the poise Oliver had observed the first time he was here. In her own home — shabby and transitory though it might be — she was very different from the insecure visitor at Firbank.

"I'm glad I didn't miss your visit," she said to Heather, hanging up her coat. "I've heard so much about you." She led the way into the living room, scarcely looking at Oliver, leaving him to take care of himself.

"So good of you to invite us when you're just about to go a journey," Heather murmured politely.

"Good of you to come. You must be tired. Jet lag — "

They were both embarrassed, Oliver decided. But whereas Loveday appeared self-possessed, Heather's exaggerated British accent gave her away.

Standing just inside the living room door, Oliver waited for them to be seated. Then he dropped into one of the lumpy armchairs, feeling left out, an observer rather than the cause of the whole odd confrontation. Not till Loveday offered him a glass of tomato juice did she give him one of her charming smiles. But she took no notice of the suit.

Heather was going on about the resemblance of Beacon Hill to certain parts of London. The superficiality of her conversation bothered Oliver. There was too little time to be engaging in small talk. Peter would be calling for them soon. It was important that Heather get to know Loveday. How else could she appreciate her?

Loveday didn't volunteer anything meaningful, either. She was apologizing quite needlessly for the state of the apartment.

"These boxes! They're all ready to be shipped home. The man was supposed to pick them up this afternoon, but he never came."

She was simply making conversation. Didn't she wish to be friends with Heather? Gradually, something dawned on Oliver: Loveday had guessed why Heather came and she was hurt.

"Father says you're flying west tomorrow," Heather was rattling on, as she threaded her way between the boxes.

"I *was*. But everything's changed. I'm flying east, soon as I can get my passport."

"East?" Oliver cried. "You don't mean to Europe?"

What could have caused this sudden change of plan? Only yesterday —

"Yes. I'm — Oh! Excuse me. Something seems to be burning." Loveday flew to the kitchen.

She soon returned, carrying an orange casserole between charred potholders. The movement of her hands as she carefully placed the casserole on the card table by the living room window, the tilt of her head expressed an assurance that revealed a new, highly attractive side of her character.

But when the three of them were seated around the table on tippy folding chairs, she seemed uncertain whether to suggest that they have grace.

Oliver took the initiative, reaching for her hand and Heather's, bowing his head.

After the nervous chatter, the silence was of itself a blessing.

Oliver thought of Firbank — how good it would be to get home. Tonight he'd sleep in his own bed. Tomorrow he'd put on his work shirt and chinos. He'd walk down to the pond with Lion and look across the dunes to the ocean. It might be snowing, but he'd go, anyway.

Right now, behind his closed lids, he unaccountably saw last summer's carpet of purple loosestrife, growing by the wayside between Firbank and Perryville, with early morning dew sparkling on the whorled leaves. The vision recalled Thoreau's remark about all true greatness wearing the homeliest dress and speaking the homeliest language. *Its theme is gossamer and dew lines,* Oliver recalled Thoreau writing, *and loosestrife, for it has never stirred from its repose and is most ignorant of foreign parts. Heaven is the inmost place.*

Oliver ought never to have stirred from his repose. And what was Loveday doing, traveling to foreign parts, when he so passionately wanted her to stay at Firbank?

As he opened his eyes and raised his head, he found that she was looking at him intently, but it was impossible to read her thought. *How could you do this to me?* — was that what she was asking him?

"What's this about your going to Europe?" he inquired, in a tone that was more testy than he meant it to be.

Her face lit up. "The most wonderful thing happened today! I couldn't wait to tell you. Heather, help yourself to salad. You remember," Loveday continued, speaking only to Oliver, "I had this lunch date with Mary Day? I thought it was just going to be the two of us, but her boss came along. She'd told him about my research and he wanted to meet me. After lunch, they took me to the office and talked business. The upshot of it is, Oliver, they're sending me to Salzburg — paying my expenses. Isn't that *something?*"

It was indeed something.

Oliver tried to tell Loveday that he was pleased, but he didn't think he sounded very convincing. Austria was much farther from Firbank than Kansas, much too far. Had she forgotten that she must go home?

"It's what they call an option," Loveday explained. "Not a contract — I'll get that when the book is finished. I hadn't dreamed of actually going to Salzburg, but they think it will stimulate me. In return, I have to give them the first chance to publish the book. There's no point in my going to Emporia first. I'd just have to fly east again. Besides, they're anxious to bring the book out as soon as possible."

Heather looked very impressed. "How long will you be staying?"

"I don't know. I did want to be home for Thanksgiving. The children certainly won't like it if I'm not back by Christmas. I haven't had a chance to phone and tell them yet. Won't they be surprised!"

"Do you have an address?" Oliver asked, taking his little notebook out of the unfamiliar pocket.

"There hasn't been a minute to think about things like that. I guess I'll have to hunt up a room when I get there. Last time, I got my mail at the post office. *Postlagernd* — General Delivery — it's probably the best address."

"What was that German word again?"

She spelled it for him.

Oliver wrote it down with care. When he looked up, he saw that she was pleading with him silently. What was she trying to tell him?

Aloud she said, "You're the one I have to thank for this,

Oliver. You encouraged me. Hadn't been for that, I might have given up. The children thought I was wasting my time here on a crackpot idea. But you inspired me."

Heather glanced at her father.

"I didn't do a thing," he protested, secretly flattered.

"Yes, you did," Loveday insisted, getting up to clear the table. "You knew only too well what's involved in writing a book and you made me feel I could do it, too."

Giving Oliver a smile that went right to his heart, she carried the dinner plates out to the kitchen.

"You evidently don't know how much she's already accomplished, Father," Heather whispered, while Loveday was gone. "Publishers are shrewd. They wouldn't invest all that money to send her to Europe if she didn't have something—" She stopped in mid-sentence.

Loveday was returning with the dessert plates.

Oliver jumped up to help her.

"Let me," Heather begged, as if she really wanted to.

"Sit still, both of you. There's nothing to do. Really."

They were eating some very special ice cream when the Hollands arrived.

Heather left the table and went to the door to meet them. Peter and Serenity greeted her affectionately.

But Ross ran to Oliver. He was angry. " 'cle Oliver!" he cried reproachfully. "Thee promised." He kicked the card table, which teetered, then righted itself miraculously. "Thee promised to come back tomorrow and thee didn't."

Risking the collapse of the folding chair, Oliver reached out, drew the boy onto his lap and held him close.

Loveday joined the little group that was standing across the room. "Come and have some ice cream."

"No, thanks," Serenity answered. "We have to go right back. It's starting to snow and Ross is dead tired. He and I weren't going to come but he couldn't wait any longer to see Oliver. He's been upset all weekend, terribly upset. He's so dependent on him. It worries me."

"What better model could a kid have?" Peter asked. "He'll get over this need, Rennie. He's still so little and Oliver's the one who looks out for him when we're not there."

"Father always was a baby spoiler," Heather observed. "My children adored him, following him around, when I brought them over years ago. They still care, but now they're so engrossed in their holiday plans that they don't want to come."

"Thee promised," Ross reproached Oliver again, manfully keeping back the tears.

"I know," Oliver whispered, bending down to the little ear. "I missed thee, too. Aunt Heather surprised us, thee sees. That's why I was delayed. I went to the airport and met her plane. But I'm not going away again, not for a long time. Will thee run over and say hello to her?"

It was Oliver's only chance to have a word alone with Loveday, who had come back. There was so much he wanted to say. How compress it into one final moment?

"I'm sorry," he said softly, "if I've ever caused you pain or annoyance. I never would give you a minute's distress, if I possibly could avoid it."

"But why can't we just go on being friends? It's been such a beautiful experience for me. Why does it have to become complicated by outsiders?"

Ross returned and tried to climb on Oliver again.

"Sit here," Loveday urged him, getting up and indicating her chair. "I'm going to get you an ice cream cone. You can take it with you and eat it in the car."

Across the room, Heather was congratulating Serenity.

"I'm so pleased that you're going to take care of Mother's Collection at the Museum. It's altogether fitting. But what a pity, Peter, that you have to give up your faculty appointment. I should think you'd find that a hardship."

"Well, I do. But this is too good a chance for Rennie to miss." He turned to her. "I'm just going next door to pick up the bags. When I get back, let's shove off. Oliver thinks the snow may keep up all night."

Oliver observed the look that passed between them — the pain of being parted, though it was only for a few minutes. He saw it every morning, when they were parting for the day.

I shouldn't worry about them, he told himself. Their love is being tested. They're not going to have an easy time. But it's a generous, maturing love.

"If Ross makes such a fuss when Oliver's gone for just three days," Serenity said to Heather, after Peter left, "how will he survive when we move?"

"Give him time," Heather, the educationist, advised. "Don't make the break till he's ready. If you do, it could be traumatic."

"I know," Serenity wailed. "That's just the trouble — there isn't time. I'm starting work next week. Luckily, we don't have to go house-hunting. Judy Young's had it with New York. We're taking over the lease on her apartment."

Serenity still sounded disturbed. Oliver wished he could console her as readily as he did Ross. He called her and she came.

"Has Loveday told thee her news? Something wonderful happened today."

Serenity's face brightened. "Does thee mean thee —"

Oliver shook his head sadly. "No, I'm afraid that's out of the question. No, she's going to Europe. Her publishers are sending her. What's Judy going to do? Is she coming back to Kendal?

"I don't know."

Loveday appeared with the cone and a handful of paper towels.

"Oliver's just told me your terrific news," Serenity exclaimed. "You must be happy."

"I am."

Peter was standing in the doorway. "Let's go, folks. It's snowing real hard."

"We're coming," Serenity called, taking Ross by the wrist. "But, Peter, first listen to this: Loveday's got an offer for her book. She's going to Austria!"

"Great!"

At the door, Serenity kissed Loveday. "Have a good trip. Send us a postcard. And come to see us at Firbank when you get back."

"We won't be there," Peter put in.

"Oliver will. And we'll come weekends. We'll have to for Ross. And for me. I'll be homesick."

Ross reached up and gave Loveday a hug.

She was visibly touched. She was also plentifully smeared with ice cream.

Oliver wished he could embrace Loveday, too. There was no opportunity for a private farewell.

"Thank you," Heather said, "for a delightful dinner."

"I'm glad you came," Loveday told her. "I was eager to meet you." Then she did a most surprising thing. She took both of Heather's hands and looked into her eyes reassuringly, really looked at her for the first time. "Enjoy your stay," she said. "And don't worry. You have nothing to worry about. Believe me."

The click of Loveday's door closing behind them sent Oliver's mind flying up into the air.

And the creature is led into the night, echoed as he and Heather stepped into the dark street. *It comes to be all of a fire.*

The brick sidewalk was already slippery. Oliver took Heather's arm, lifting his face to let the snowflakes cool his cheeks.

"Well, Father," Heather said, as they walked toward the car, "you were right about one thing: I needn't have come. I'm sorry for you, but you have to realize that she's not interested in marriage. What a pity! She's charming. And so able."

PART FOUR

Loveday

1.

*M*ORE THAN ANYTHING else, the bells of Salzburg transported Loveday into the eighteenth century. Throughout the Old Town, they rang hourly, never in unison —too soon, too late, on pitch, off key—hurling a beautiful dissonance into the sky.

They were so fascinating that, during her first week there, Loveday would stand still in the street when the bells began ringing and try to determine by each one's timbre which church it resounded from—the Cathedral, St. Peter's, the Franciscans', or the Collegiate Church, which stood diagonally across from the house where she was staying.

To capture the atmosphere she hoped to communicate in her book, she had rented a room in the Sigmund Haffnergasse. It was on this street—Kirchgasse it was formerly called—at Number 12, that Nannerl Mozart, who was by then the Baroness Berchtold zu Sonnenburg, lived, after her husband died.

Loveday's little room looked out onto the cobblestones of the Green Market and the casements of the Mozart children's birthplace. Across the way, she could just glimpse the convex facade of the Collegiate Church, where, in 1826, Wolfgang Amadeus Mozart, Junior, conducted his father's *Requiem,* as a memorial to his stepfather. What a privilege, to be living in the center of these historic places!

When the chatty landlady showed her the room, Loveday

knew at once that she wouldn't be happy anywhere else. She was trying to be practical, wondering whether the mattress under that fat eiderdown was lumpy, when suddenly, without warning, the bell of the Collegiate Church struck the hour right outside the window, reverberating in the room, shaking the furniture and rattling the glass on the washstand. It was unnerving. Yet, because of the associations, Loveday wanted to live there. Now, after a week, she was just getting used to the hourly commotion. She was even falling under its romantic spell.

So it wasn't surprising that the bells of Salzburg rang repeatedly in Loveday's book. She was still hunting for a catchy title — some echo of the wild tintinnabulation.

Sitting in her little room at the end of that first week, she read the opening chapter over to herself.

On the thirtieth of July, 1751, the bells of Salzburg — muted, because it was midnight — announced the entrance into this world at Number 9, Getreidegasse of Maria Walburga Ignatia Mozart, known all her life as Nannerl.

Having lost their first three children in infancy, Leopold and Anna Maria Mozart hovered over this baby. The two who were born next died before they were a year old.

Then, when Nannerl was four and a half, on St. John Chrysostom's Day at eight in the evening, the bells celebrated the birth of Joannes Chrysostomos Wolfgang Gottlieb. At first, he was simply called Wolfgang. It wasn't till he went to Italy that he added the Amadeus, Latinizing Gottlieb.

Because five babies had died so quickly, it was imperative that this one be baptized immediately. Papa bundled him up the very next morning and, running all the way, carried him through the January weather to the Cathedral.

Loveday had seen the huge baptismal font. It was supported by four Romanesque lions. Ought she to include a description here? She decided not to.

Eager for her eleven o'clock coffee, she glanced at the traveling clock. Only ten-ten.

Her feet hadn't been warm since she arrived. Sitting still in a house whose walls retained the dampness of centuries and trying to write with stiff fingers was turning out to be less fun than she'd imagined, back in Boston.

She thought of Oliver and his book. He'd spoken as if writing took no effort at all. It had been pure pleasure. How had he done it? But he wasn't alone in a strange country. He'd had Serenity with him, typing and talking things over.

Loveday knew no one in Salzburg, other than her boring landlady and the people at the Mozart Library, who were obliging when she went there and asked to see some original manuscripts. They showed her pages of the diary Nannerl kept when the family went on tour in 1762. But the librarians were obviously too busy to engage in conversation with an unknown author — an American and a woman, at that — an old woman. She longed for someone knowledgeable with whom to discuss her work. Now that she was beginning to write, the story had taken on a different coloration.

She turned her attention back to the chapter, crossing out a word here, putting in a comma there. On the whole, it pleased her.

Leopold Mozart was a violinist in the orchestra of the Archbishop. As soon as he could make his little daughter sit still, he began teaching her to play the clavichord. She proved an apt pupil. But her baby brother, standing on tiptoe at the instrument, played without instruction what she had to work hard to learn.

The children were eleven and six when Papa realized that their extraordinary talent might prove to be lucrative. Consequently, he took his little prodigies on the road to perform before royalty, at the court of Schönbrunn for the Empress Maria Theresa, at Versailles for King Louis XV, and even across the formidable English Channel to play at Buckingham House before King George III and Queen Charlotte.

Maria Theresa's private secretary drove up in state before the Mozarts' Vienna lodgings, bringing imperial presents, hand-me-downs from a prince and princess: a violet satin suit edged with gold braid for Wolfgang and a white taffeta gown for Nannerl. Papa deplored the fact that there wasn't enough material in the gown to make it over afterward into anything but a petticoat.

At the Palace, Wolfgang slipped on the polished floor. It was Princess Marie Antoinette — herself only seven years old — who picked him up. Wolfgang promised to marry her. Instead, she was to become the bride of Louis XVI of France and to end her life on the guillotine.

In London, Leopold also felt less than content with the royal gift, although he made the best of that.

"The honorarium was only twenty-four guineas," he wrote home, "but the graciousness with which His Majesty the King and Her Majesty the Queen received us cannot be described." In a subsequent letter, he cited another consolation for the meager recompense: "It's satisfaction enough that, although she's only twelve years old, my little girl is one of the most proficient players in Europe."

Nevertheless, it was Wolfgang who got the attention. He kissed the ladies and composed sonatas for the Queen. He looked adorable in a powdered wig.

The fuss that was made over her little brother irked Nannerl. In another letter, however, Papa reported: "Nannerl isn't jealous of the boy any more because everyone raves about her playing and admires her talent."

Loveday glanced at the clock again. Ten-forty. In a few minutes, she'd stop work and go to the Residenzplatz to hear the carillon.

Every morning at eleven, it played a tinkling tune, accompanied by the monotone church bells. Loveday had formed the habit of going to hear it, sitting in the café across the

Square, sipping the delicious Austrian coffee, indulging in the pastry. In the States, she'd never dream of consuming all that rich cream. Here, it was irresistible. When she got back to Emporia, she'd diet.

She was already dreaming of the coffee. But she returned to her chapter, trying to listen with a critical inner ear to what she'd written.

For three and a half years, the Mozarts were on the road, traveling in uncomfortable coaches, which tended to break down. The clavichord they had to carry with them took up most of the space. It was often bitter cold. Papa and the children got sore throats, infected teeth, scarlet fever. And they lived in constant anxiety, lest the remuneration for the concerts be insufficient to cover their expenses; lest the Archbishop of Salzburg, who was also the ruling prince, would dismiss Papa for staying away too long. A musician was only a servant, whose place at table was above the cook's, but below the valet's. And this master was a tyrant.

Yet it all seemed warranted. Wherever the children performed they were showered with praise.

The tour was educational, too. In London, Nannerl wrote in her diary:

I saw a donkey. He had white and coffee-brown stripes. They were so even, one would have thought they were painted on.

She became desperately ill at the Hague. Papa and Mama didn't expect her to live. They sat by her bedside, describing the delights of heaven, while Wolfgang amused himself in the next room, composing a symphony.

Nannerl recovered, but then Wolfgang contracted an illness which, "in four weeks has made him so wretched that he is not only unrecognizable," Leopold wrote to his Salzburg landlord, "but has nothing left except his tender skin and little bones." Nevertheless, before long, the children were once more playing in public. Wolfgang's Symphony in B-flat was performed in Amsterdam. On the long journey back to Salzburg, he fell ill again. A week later, he and Nannerl gave another concert.

Finally the weary family reached home.

Loveday leaned back in the chair. Just writing about the rigors of that journey wore her out. But she had felt it necessary to sketch this account of Nannerl's early success in order to show how unfair it was that, after she was older, such a gifted artist was given no chance to perform, because of her sex.

At last, the time had come to go out. Loveday locked the manuscript in her suitcase, put on her raincoat and overshoes, and walked through the Old Market to the Café Glockenspiel.

Apart from the bells, Salzburg was less attractive than it had been when Loveday was here before, in the spring of the year. Lilacs were in bloom then. Fountains played in the squares and, along the narrow, medieval streets, window boxes were crammed with red geraniums and deep blue ageratum.

Now it was winter, with an icy wind coming down from the Alps. The fountains were boarded up; some of the museums and theaters were closed. In the rain, the churches looked streaky and stark.

But the coffee and pastry were as fabulous as ever.

Loveday always chose a table in the same corner of the café and was served by the same bald waiter, who usually exchanged a few words with her. She was so lonely that she looked forward to this chat with absurd eagerness.

"*Kaffee mit Schlagobers, bitte,*" she said, when the waiter came to take her order. She invariably asked for the same things. How could anything else possibly be better? "*Und*" — feeling guilty — "*Kremschnitten.*"

The waiter nodded knowingly. But he was rushed today and hurried off before she had a chance to inform him in her college German, which was better suited to reading than conversation, that it was raining again — a fact which could not have escaped his attention.

The coffee and pastry hadn't arrived before the carillon started playing in the octagonal tower across the Residenzplatz.

Loveday listened, enchanted. According to the guidebook, the eighteenth-century clappers were wrongly installed. That's why the chimes sounded out of tune. Still, they were beautiful in their antiquity and the atmosphere they created, reverberating among the Baroque buildings.

Was it presumptuous, Loveday wondered, to cherish the hope that, above the ground bass of Salzburg's bells, her story of Nannerl's life would, in its modest way, also sing out to the world?

2.

THEY WERE SINISTER, too, those bells, Loveday had to concede, as the carillon died away.

In the eighteenth century, they rent the air with provincial pettiness, with disregard for the unempowered, with religious bigotry. They chimed unfeelingly while Loveday's Protestant ancestors were sent into exile. But she doubted that any of these bells existed when the Jews were driven out.

Even if the Jews were persecuted without benefit of musical accompaniment, Loveday said to herself, they left their own resonance behind. The medieval ghetto is still called Judengasse, though it's nearly six centuries since they were there.

St. Peter's tolled when the witch was being executed behind the cemetery, a befuddled country girl, not much older than Nannerl, who was nine at the time.

Had this gruesome episode instilled such fear in Nannerl

that she became fanatically obedient, even to renouncing the man she loved when she was in her thirties, because Papa wouldn't have him? Wolfgang, who was living in Vienna by then, offered to help her. Earlier, when she was helping him, sending money she'd earned, her father warned that, should he die and leave her penniless, the Archbishop would press her into domestic service.

Incensed, Loveday asked herself, What chance did a woman have, in such a society, to take control of her life?

For Wolfgang, too, Salzburg's bells clamored of domination, both by his father ("Next to God comes Papa," he said as a child, but when he grew up, he did what he pleased, even marrying against Papa's wishes) — and by the Archbishop, who treated him shamefully. Wolfgang's irrepressible genius couldn't flourish within hearing of those bells. And yet, Loveday reflected as she waited for the coffee, Wolfgang was cradled in their sound as snugly as in the arms of sweet, self-effacing Mama. Salzburg's bells were the matrix from which both the glory and the anguish of his music sprang.

This morning, the other lone customers in the café were all men. They came in, went to the newspaper rack, selected one and sat down at a table by themselves. No one preferred to join Loveday. Austrians were friendly, easygoing people, but they had good manners, too. Who would strike up a conversation with a foreign woman in a café?

It was just that Loveday was so lonely.

While she waited to be served, she unobtrusively bowed her head, trying to draw in her scattered self, recalling the grace at Firbank — the unexpected current that electrified her, as Oliver took her hand. Alone, she just felt numb.

The waiter arrived with a heavy tray, balanced on his upturned palm.

"*Bitte sehr,*" he said, as he set the coffee and pastry on the table. Then he rushed away.

Loveday sipped slowly. On account of the calories, she only allowed herself one coffee a day. She didn't want to gain five pounds again, the way she did the last time she came to Austria. As for the *Kremschnitten* — sheets of puff pastry with creamy filling — what Loveday would have called a napoleon — well, she wouldn't eat any lunch.

As soon as she'd finished, she got up and walked to the post office. She went there several times a day, hoping to find a letter from home. None had come so far, but she'd only been in Europe a week. There wasn't really time for mail to have crossed the ocean. Still, she couldn't wait.

She might have to. The children were never good about writing. When Loveday was in Boston, they phoned occasionally. At this distance, except in an emergency, phoning was out of the question. Writing to their homesick mother, just to keep in touch, to comfort her — would that occur to them? But, of course, they didn't know she was homesick.

All those months that she stayed in Boston after she'd completed her research, simply hoping to be invited to Firbank again — she hadn't missed the children then. Now, all she thought of was getting a letter from home.

No. All she really thought of was Oliver — how wonderful it had been, knowing him; how his touching confession of love had almost undone her.

She longed for his reassuring presence. She could picture him — his youthful bearing, the unusual aliveness of his expression. When he looked at her, his whole face crinkled into a rapturous smile. They might be discussing some heavy subject and suddenly this joyous look would overspread his face. Loveday hadn't taken it personally before. Oliver was cordial to everyone. Only now did she realize that the way he looked at *her* was more significant than she'd thought at the time. She remembered the night she was coming down the stairs at Firbank and he stood at the bottom, waiting for her with outstretched arms. Before she reached him, he dropped his arms to his sides, but his impulse had been clear.

It made her proud to be held in affection by a man like that, to be admired in his chivalrous way. No one had ever made her feel so worthy. This wasn't an acknowledgment of achievement or status, but an appreciation of some inner worth, which he perceived.

Nevertheless, Heather's suddenly flying across the ocean simply to pass on Loveday, when Oliver hadn't even proposed — that was an insult to them both. What business was it of Heather's? Oliver wasn't senile, in need of a governess. He could decide things for himself. Well, Loveday had made it perfectly clear to Heather that she wasn't interested in marriage.

Ought she to write to Oliver? Or would it be more fitting to indicate by her silence that the fortuitous friendship had terminated as suddenly and unexpectedly as it began?

She didn't want it to end — ever. Why couldn't they continue to be friends? Shouldn't she, at least, send him a postcard, one of those beautiful views of the town taken from across the River, with the grim fortress towering above everything and the sky an unnatural blue?

She might even write a letter, telling about her work. When her book came out, she'd send him an autographed copy. He'd be impressed!

But *marriage!* What for? Wasn't she getting along fine on her own? With a publisher *paying in advance* for her first book — Late in life, she was starting a second career, one that was even more prestigious than the first. How could she possibly think of settling down to domesticity in a little backwater, even one as charming as Firbank?

Being with Oliver had been wonderful. Loveday just never dreamed he'd fall in love with her. Well, she guessed she loved him, too, in an uninvolved way. He was attractive — very. That morning at Firbank, when she'd started down to get the coffee and caught him sitting up in that big, old bed, reading his Bible, her feelings had been far from spiritual. He had roused something in her that she'd had to fight, ever since.

Had she been right to burn her bridges, telling Heather off? "You have nothing to worry about," she'd assured her. "Believe me."

Did Loveday mean it? Or had she just said that out of spite — because she was so angry at Heather for coming to look her over?

She meant it.

She thought of those long wedding certificates, hanging on the wall at Firbank. *To be unto thee,* they both said. *Promising to be unto thee —*

Defining oneself in terms of a relationship, rather than wholly as an individual — it was a concept Loveday had considered out of date. But maybe —

She did wish she could see Oliver. It wasn't true that she was getting along fine. She was on the brink — she, who'd always been in command.

At the post office, there was no mail for her. She must go back to the room and settle down to work, forget.

It was always a tossup whether to go around the north side of the Cathedral or the south. The distance was about the same, either way.

She decided on the south side, passing the Franciscan Church, not stopping to notice the famous doors, thinking only of herself in faraway Cambridge, having lunch with Oliver, after the Friends Meeting.

Speaking with obvious difficulty, he had told her there, in the restaurant, why he went to prison in the First World War. He had explained that, while he would have been willing to lay down his life for his country, if need be, he could not take someone else's, or threaten other people. Making the decision to refuse military service, accepting the consequences had entailed so much suffering that it was hard to speak of it. But he wanted Loveday to know.

She remembered the wine-colored tablecloth in that restaurant. She'd fixed her gaze on it, unable to bear the pain in Oliver's eyes, as he confided what — he went on to say — he had kept bottled up all his life.

He had chosen to confide this to *her!* It was as if he were offering his whole self, without reservation. No one, not even Bill, had ever done that. It had moved Loveday so deeply that she was unable to finish the meal. If they hadn't been in a public place, she would have taken Oliver in her arms.

Thinking about it now, though, she wondered what to make of a man who refused to defend his country. Even if the Bible commanded one not to kill, weren't there occasions when it was justified? If she were attacked, would he protect her?

"Violence only begets violence," he had said. "The more we arm, the more vulnerable we become, for those who are threatened by our power will react by arming even more. Eventually — Our only hope lies in friendly cooperation."

Loveday knew her Quaker ancestors had paid a high price for the same testimony. But that was years ago. There was no nuclear threat then. Today —

Was it a flaw in Oliver's character?

Or was this belief the key to his stature? Was this what made him reach out to a total stranger? Was it what made him capable of "answering that of God" in her?

3.

BACK IN THE ROOM, Loveday began writing about the Mozarts' second visit to Vienna.

The young Emperor enjoyed having Nannerl at court. She was just seventeen, pretty and vivacious. Joseph teased her. He said things that made her blush. Nannerl liked the attention, but Leopold thought the young Emperor stingy.

These Vienna concerts were the last public performances sister and brother gave together. Nannerl never played in public again.

The historian in Loveday reflected that the year the Mozarts returned to Salzburg — 1769 — a boy was born in Corsica whose soldiers would one day capture Nannerl's only son. And the following year, Beethoven was born. His whole work, as well as Schubert's, would be produced during Nannerl's lifetime.

For she was to live another sixty years after that last public appearance — years in which Marie Antoinette, whom she'd known as a small princess, was guillotined; George III, the Mozarts' old friend, lost not alone his colonies in America, but his mind. And Napoleon, Nannerl's bitter enemy, died at St. Helena.

Had Oliver's conviction prevailed, none of the violent events would have occurred in those years, only the creation of immortal music.

It almost seemed as though he were collaborating with Loveday. He, who knew little about music, was actually contributing from a distance to this book.

For he had awakened a sensitivity in her that she'd repressed when she was pushing ahead in the world. His awareness of latent beauty — like a composer's — influenced her writing, even more than those bells.

Until she met him, she had never dared tell anyone about her fantasy in St. Gilgen, for fear of being thought flaky. Oliver's cordiality made her blurt it out at once. He'd taken it very seriously.

"When the bus stopped in St. Gilgen and I stood before

the house where Nannerl and her mother had lived, studying their faces on the bas-relief, both so wistful — You'll think it queer — "

Why had she imagined *she* was chosen, out of the whole bus full of tourists? She had felt rather flattered. She didn't tell Oliver that.

She'd gone on to explain about Nannerl — how sex discrimination had ruined her career. But Mama Mozart — Loveday had overlooked *her*. Yet, Oliver would have identified with Mama. They were both loving, giving people. Why hadn't Loveday told him? Was it because Mama hadn't had a career, other than making up to the children in tenderness for Papa's ruthless ambition — was that why Loveday wasn't interested? How disgusting! Now that she was living in the Mozarts' feelings, no longer trying to prove something, she wished she could tell Oliver about Mama.

When she began the project, she was determined to be objective, dispassionate. Through his influence, she'd become very, very involved. How could she have known, that day at St. Gilgen, that it would lead to this?

She wrote on, letting the record speak.

A young man came in from the country to court Nannerl. She thought him too rustic. Wolfgang, writing from Milan, chided her in brotherly terms for breaking the man's heart. "I'm glad you enjoyed the sleighride...but I have one regret: that you let Herr von Mölk sigh and suffer so and that you didn't go sleighriding with him so he could dump you in the snow. What a lot of handkerchiefs he must have used that day, crying over you!"

Loveday laughed — not at Wolfgang's humor; at herself. Who would have thought, a year ago, that, with her ideas, she'd become fascinated by a farmer?

But he's not a rustic, she thought. Son of a Harvard professor, author of a book —

When Wolfgang was twenty-one, Papa asked for a leave of absence in order to take his son on another concert tour. The Archbishop refused. Since the parents considered Wolfgang incapable of handling money, Mama went with him.

Furious, Loveday threw her ballpoint on the table. Why didn't Leopold let Wolfgang grow up?

She could imagine the departure, as Leopold described it in a letter: Nannerl weeping, Leopold so overcome with emotion that he forgot to give his son a father's blessing. He ran to the window. As the carriage was already out of sight, the blessing had to be transmitted through the air.

Leopold wrote regularly to his wife and son, directing them. "Wherever you stay," he reminded Wolfgang, "you will always get the servant to put the boot-trees in your boots, won't you?" He added that the boy had forgotten his gray trousers.

Picturing Anna Maria and Wolfgang traveling through the Hessian countryside, Loveday reflected that they would have seen few able-bodied men. For twenty-two thousand had been recruited by the Elector and hired out as mercenaries to George III of England, who sent them to America with orders to subdue his rebellious colonists. In one day alone, a thousand of these Hessians were captured at Trenton.

Here was Loveday, acting like an historian again! She must stick to the narrative. But it was getting boring. Nannerl kept house for her father. Her chief activities seemed to be: going to Mass, having her hair done and walking the dog.

"The day you left," she wrote to her mother and brother, "I spent mostly in bed because I was vomiting and had a dreadful headache. On the 24th, at half-past seven I went to early Mass at Holy Trinity... On the 25th I went to the half-past ten Mass... On the 26th lit.. Victoria Adlgasser dressed my hair... I went to the half-past ten Mass and in the afternoon from four to five I took Pimperl for a walk..."

On the 27th I went to the half-past eleven Mass in Mirabell and in the afternoon I went to market with Katherl Gilowsky. Afterwards we played cards until four o'clock with Abbé Bullinger. Then Katherl combed my hair and I took Pimperl for a walk."

The Mozart Museum was full of portraits of Nannerl, wearing the towering hairdo made popular by her contemporary, the Marquise de Pompadour.

Loveday was beginning to wonder what a good hairdresser might do for her. Ought she to get a permanent? She hadn't considered that in years. Would it make her look better? But here, in a foreign country — who knows what they might do?

Why did she want one, anyway? she asked herself, as she finished copying Nannerl's silly letter.

"Today, October 4th, Victoria did my hair. I went to the half-past ten Mass and now I shall take Pimperl for a walk and then go to the play with Papa. Keep well. I kiss Mama's hands and beg you not to forget me."

Mama's hands suffered as winter approached. "I can hardly hold my pen, I'm freezing so," she wrote from Mannheim. "Wolfgang is lunching with Herr Wendling today so I am at home alone, as I usually am, and have to put up with the most horrible cold. For even if they light a small fire, they never put any more coal on it... A little fire like this costs twelve Kreutzer," she explained in answer to her husband's constant inquiry as to how much they were spending. "Only death costs nothing—and even that's not true."

Tears were running down Loveday's cheeks. She wished she'd told Oliver about Mama.

Mama was homesick for everyone, including the fox terrier. "This very moment, Nannerl will please stop whatever she is doing and give Pimperl a kiss on her little paws and make it smack so loudly that I can hear it in Mannheim. I wish I could be with you just for one day...

Loveday was homesick, too. She thought of the wild reception Lion and Duffy used to give her at Firbank. Dear little Duffy!

"I have no other news," Mama concluded, "beyond what you already know, that the English have suffered a crushing defeat at the hands of the Americans."

Wolfgang, she reported, was very popular in Mannheim, but he was not finding work that paid.

Leopold blamed him for not giving enough attention to business. "I do hope," he wrote to Mama, "that Wolfgang's head isn't always full of music."

Loveday laughed out loud. How lucky for the world that it was! Nannerl's head, on the other hand, was full of foolishness.

Looking forward to her mother's return, she wrote, "Mama was kind enough to tell me that the coiffures and caps they wear in Mannheim are much prettier and that the women dress much more stylishly than in Salzburg... I should like to ask her to watch closely how that coiffure is made and to bring a toupee cushion with her and whatever else is necessary for it and, if possible, a cap in the very latest fashion and anything else she may like to bring."

Mama asked that two Masses be read in Salzburg for her protection on the journey. "I put my whole trust in them, for I shall certainly not be forsaken," she wrote to her husband. But she never got back to Salzburg.

Wolfgang needed money again. Nannerl sent him her earnings from the piano lessons she gave. Leopold sent him a scathing letter.

"Your old father of fifty-eight should run around from house to house for a miserable fee, so that he may support you."

Fifty-eight! Loveday thought. Oliver's *seventy*-eight and he's not old. But, in those days, people's life expectancy —

"Were it not for your sister," Leopold expostulated, "I should probably not have the strength to write this letter." Leopold rallied enough to remind Wolfgang that, as a child, he had always said, "Next to God comes Papa." Now he had "too much pride and self-love" to take parental advice.

Not surprisingly, Leopold reported two days later that he suffered from nervous palpitations. "Your sister is my only support now," he lamented.

Loveday's room was almost dark. She got up and switched on the light. But there was only one bulb and that was so dim, she could barely see. Still, she pressed on.

Then the inexcusable happened: Wolfgang fell in love.

Mama tried to shield her son from the wrath that would be visited on him when this news reached Salzburg. What could she say? "When Wolfgang makes new acquaintances, he immediately wants to give them his life and worldly goods," she wrote to Leopold. "In short, he prefers other people to me, for I remonstrate with him about this and that, and about things which I do not like; and he objects to this."

As Mama had easily foreseen, Papa was beside himself.

"Now it depends solely on your good sense and your way of life whether you die as an ordinary musician, utterly forgotten by the world," he wrote to Wolfgang, "or as a famous Kapellmeister, of whom posterity will read; whether, captured by some woman, you die bedded on straw in an attic full of starving children, or whether... you leave this world with your family well provided for... You know, and you have a thousand proofs of it, that God in his goodness has given me sound judgment... What has prevented you, then, from asking my advice and from always acting as I desired?"

Loveday sank back, exhausted. What happened next in the story was so sad, she couldn't bring herself to write about it. Leopold had ordered his wife to take the boy to Paris. "From Paris, the name and fame of a man of great talent resounds through the whole world," he reasoned. But in Paris, where

Wolfgang composed incessantly, success came no more readily than in Mannheim. Only tragedy awaited the Mozarts there, for on July 3, 1778, self-effacing, devoted Mama died.

This was supposed to be Nannerl's book, but Mama had eclipsed her in Loveday's affection. How had that happened? As a matter of fact, Loveday was sorry for every one of those Mozarts, even arrogant, self-deluding Papa.

Identifying with them, she was sorry for herself, too. Sorry and a little afraid.

4.

ONE MIDNIGHT in the following week, Loveday woke up, sobbing. She must have dreamed — She couldn't remember. Her mind was blank, but her heart ached. For what?

Was it for poor Mama, who had given Nannerl and Wolfgang the only gentle, unselfish love they were ever to know?

The heavy eiderdown was oppressive. Loveday tossed it off. Now she was freezing, but she had nothing to cover herself with. The top sheet was fastened to the eiderdown. She jumped out of bed and got her coat. Lying down again, she pulled it up around her shoulders. Her feet stuck out. She couldn't go back to sleep.

Yesterday was Thanksgiving.

It still is, Loveday suddenly realized. In Emporia, it's only five o'clock. It's Thanksgiving and I'm not there.

That must be what made her cry. Right now, her family was eating turkey and cranberry sauce at Emily's house — Will and Sara Ann, with their two boys, and Toby. Were Emily's children home? Or was this the year they spent the holidays with their father? Loveday wanted to picture them at home, not in Los Angeles with that scoundrel and his new wife.

She should have phoned. It would have cost a lot, speaking to each of them. She couldn't have done that in three minutes. But it would have been worth any amount of money. Why didn't she think of that before she went to bed? Should she dress and go out now? But where would she find a pay phone? They were in the post office. It was closed.

In Salzburg, who even knew this was Thanksgiving?

Why wasn't Loveday in Emporia, where she belonged, helping Emily with the dinner? What was she doing here? Just because of that crazy fantasy —

Oliver didn't consider it crazy. He called it a "leading" — divine guidance, which drove one to embark on an enterprise without knowing how it would end. Maybe Loveday was obliged to come here in order to find out something — not about Nannerl — about herself. If so, she wasn't getting very far.

Hadn't she told Oliver the last time she was at Firbank that she must go home? As they sat in the silence that morning, it had seemed imperative. She must go at once and tell her children the facts — how she had misrepresented the character of their father all these years, allowing her harbored grudges to distort the truth. Yet, when she was unexpectedly offered a brilliant opportunity, she put all that out of her mind, telling herself it could wait.

But could it?

She'd allowed herself to be pressured into flying to Europe, instead of going home first, spending Thanksgiving with her family, setting the record straight. What difference would it have made if she'd come to Austria a few weeks later, even after Christmas? She always spent Christmas at home.

Something might happen to her here. She might have an accident. There'd be nobody to notify her children. She didn't know a soul. The only people who ever spoke to her were Frau Scheibl, her elderly landlady, and the bald waiter. She might even die in a strange country, like Mama Mozart. Her children would never know what she'd intended to tell them.

Loveday's teeth began chattering. She threw off the coat and reached over to retrieve the heavy eiderdown.

Something might happen. Oliver wouldn't know what had become of her.

He'd said something to Serenity the night before she went to her job interview that had had the power of a charm, "Be still and cool." Loveday was annoyed with him then. She'd wanted Serenity to be assertive and on fire.

Now she needed the charm. Be still and cool, she repeated, over and over. But without Oliver, it didn't work.

When morning came, the sun was shining. It was market day down in the Square. Standing at her window, Loveday watched the farmers erect their stalls and trestle tables. Huge red-and-white umbrellas sprang up; baskets of fruits and vegetables, pots of plants and flowers cluttered the cobblestones.

The Collegiate bell struck eight, battering Loveday's eardrums, almost lifting her off her feet.

In Nannerl's diary — Loveday had seen some of the original pages at the Mozart Library — there was an entry for September, 1779 which told about the Night Music that she and her father and brother had heard played in this very Square: a March of Wolfgang's and his Haffner Serenade. Just knowing that she was looking down on the spot where Mozart had listened to his own music, over two hundred years ago, gave Loveday goose pimples.

From all directions, women were coming to market with their cloth shopping bags. One held a little boy by the hand. He was bundled up in an Alpine cloak. Loveday couldn't see his face, but he made her think of Ross.

How was Ross taking the separation from Oliver? Loveday's

heart went out to the little guy. She knew how he felt. She wished she hadn't pressured Rennie about taking that job. Where had Ross eaten Thanksgiving dinner? Probably in Neville, with Rennie's parents, or in Ohio, with Peter's.

In that case, Oliver was alone, unless Heather stayed to keep him company over the holiday. Why was Loveday so angry with Heather? Sitting on that folding chair in her elegantly tailored suit, fidgeting, she had looked pathetic. She evidently loved her father so much that, when she imagined he was being threatened, she hastily flew across the ocean to try to protect him. What was wrong with that? She was inept and absurd, putting on that British accent, but she was a good daughter.

Why dwell on that now? Loveday had work to do. She sat down at the wobbly table and looked over the manuscript. It was growing hefty.

When the news of Mama's death reached Salzburg, *she'd written yesterday*, Nannerl had her hands full, comforting Papa. Wolfgang needed money again and she sent it. Six months later, he returned to Salzburg, broken-hearted.

Nevertheless, he composed the most beautiful music that year: the Post Horn Serenade, the Sinfonia Concertante for violin and viola, the Concerto in E flat for two pianos.

Loveday remembered the morning at Firbank, when she was trying to center down in the silence and the Rondo of this concerto kept running through her head.

She began humming the Finale now — the violins introducing the theme, then the pianos coming in, one after the other, an octave apart — a lighthearted conversation between two players.

Wolfgang dedicated that concerto to Nannerl. But he didn't invite her to play it with him at the first public performance in Vienna. He chose another young woman, whom he didn't care for. She was simply a good musician.

This was a bit of information Loveday had just picked up. It shattered her contention that Nannerl's gifts were underrated solely on account of her sex. As a matter of fact, Maria Theresia Paradies, the blind pianist, for whom Wolfgang wrote the Concerto in B flat, was having great success, too.

The whole point of the book was to show the unfair treatment Nannerl received because she was a woman and Loveday's theory had collapsed. The more she learned about Nannerl, the more she realized that this wasn't a very dynamic artist. Perhaps she didn't merit more success. Her tragedy wasn't really attributable to sex discrimination so much as to the fact that she wasn't strong enough to stand up to her father and — more importantly — that she was next of kin to a genius. Years later, Wolfgang's son was to experience the same disappointment. He was a competent musician, but the critics always compared him to his father and declared him inferior.

This was such a distressing discovery for Loveday that she would have abandoned the whole thing. What kept her going now was the desire to have a book in print. And so she continued.

Wolfgang was appointed Court Organist in Salzburg, but after a row with the Archbishop, he was literally kicked out. He went to live in Vienna.

Back in Salzburg, love was eating at Nannerl's heart — the tender attention of a man who did not, in Leopold's estimation, have sufficient means to support her. He was Franz D'Yppold, the tutor to the Archbishop's pages. Nannerl began to ail. In the summer, Leopold wrote to Wolfgang that she was seriously ill.

Deeply concerned, Wolfgang suggested a remedy: "Now I'm going to write to you frankly. Believe me, dear sister, in all seriousness, the best cure for you would be a husband, and because it is affecting your health, I wish with all my heart that you could marry soon. But it will never work out for you in Salzburg. Couldn't D'Yppold find something here? Ask him. I'll do the impossible to help. Then you could surely marry, for you could earn plenty here. My father would have to consent and come along. Then we could live together happily again."

Leopold wouldn't hear of it. Nannerl acquiesced dutifully. But it took her a long time to recover.

As Loveday pulled out a fresh sheet of paper, she asked herself how Nannerl could have turned down the man who loved her and whom she loved, judging by her disappointment. Just because her father was a tyrant — Love should have made her courageous, like Wolfgang.

Just before Christmas, *Loveday went on,* Wolfgang wrote to his father about Constanze.

"I love her and she loves me...you surely are happy when I am? My dearest father...please take pity on your son."

Leopold was livid.

Later, Wolfgang wrote to Nannerl, enclosing a clumsy letter from Constanze, begging his sister to reply. Her father wouldn't let her.

Loveday was so angry, she wanted to strangle Leopold. How could he treat his children this way? She was interiorizing the Mozart saga far too much, allowing it to engage her emotions.

In August of 1782, Wolfgang and Constanze were married in Vienna. Wolfgang pleaded with Nannerl, but she couldn't forgive him for disregarding their father's wishes.

"Congratulations," Wolfgang wrote to Leopold the following June. "You are a grandfather! Yesterday, my wife was delivered of a fine, sturdy boy, as round as a ball." And, in a later letter, "Little Raimund is so like me that everyone immediately remarks it. It is just as if my face had been copied."

Leaving Raimund with a wet nurse, Wolfgang and his wife

went to Salzburg at the end of July and stayed three months. The visit was not a success. Leopold was unyielding. Since Wolfgang's babyhood, he had believed himself to be entrusted by God with the development of the boy's genius. Now, convinced that Constanze would ruin Wolfgang's life and that his own held nothing more, he became bitter.

For once, Loveday agreed with Leopold. Constanze was a selfish wife, a disgraceful mother, an opportunistic widow. What happened when Wolfgang and Constanze returned to Vienna from Salzburg was so tragic that Loveday couldn't bear to write about it: they found that little Raimund had died.

She'd become a participant in this story, living in it, just as she'd always lived in Mozart's music. The sufferings of these people filled her with such pity that she wept.

Was it right for an historian to be so subjective?

But, from the first, she hadn't approached this like an historian. She wanted to prove her theory and now she found it didn't work. She had let her anger slant the story. Why this anger? Bill never made her feel inferior. He'd treated her with respect. Why was she so bitter?

Oliver had tried to improve conditions. He'd made great sacrifices. But he hadn't operated out of anger. His whole motivation was love.

If only Loveday could talk to him now! She was losing her grip.

What she needed was her coffee. She left the house, passed the Franciscan Church, and came to St. Peter's.

On an impulse, she entered the Precincts and walked through the cemetery, looking for Nannerl's marker among the monuments in the Arcades.

Nannerl hadn't planned to be buried here. She'd stated in her will that she wished to rest beside her father and her daughter Jeanette in St. Sebastian's Churchyard, across the River. But three years before she died, something happened that outraged Nannerl and she changed her will. Her detested sister-in-law Constanze had remarried and settled in Salzburg with her second husband, Georg von Nissen. Constanze hadn't attended Mozart's funeral and never visited his pauper's grave, but when Nissen died, she had him buried with lavish pomp in the Mozart family plot and erected a huge tombstone on it bearing Nissen's name, omitting Leopold's and Jeanette's. This was too much for Nannerl. She asked to be buried elsewhere.

Loveday passed the monument commemorating Sigmund Haffner, for whom Wolfgang composed the D major Symphony. Beside Michael Haydn's marker, she found the modest, wooden cross. Affixed to it was a small, weathered portrait of Nannerl holding a bunch of flowers.

This had been painted shortly before Nannerl died at seventy-eight — just Oliver's age.

Styles had altered by the late eighteen twenties. Gone was the ridiculous pompadour Nannerl balanced on her head in the earlier portraits. This picture, set against a dark background, showed her with hair curled into tight sausage rolls, resembling the fluted pleats of her fichu. She was growing blind. She stared back from the world she was currently in to the one she had left, possibly regretting, now that she possessed the vision of eternity, that she hadn't been more loving while she was here.

Such a contrast between this pathetic marker and the stone bas-relief at St. Gilgen, from which Nannerl had looked down in the prime of life and demanded that the world be notified of its failure to appreciate her!

What this old woman was trying to communicate was of quite another order. It seemed less personal, yet more immediate. If Loveday could only decipher the message —

She turned away, shivering. Five years from now, how would *she* feel about herself?

An icy wind swept through the cemetery as she hurried off to the comfort of her coffee, glancing back at the acres of graves, wondering where they had executed the witch.

5.

ON THE FOURTH of December, Loveday's landlady came to her room with a tall jar of wintry branches.

"*Barbarazweige*," Frau Scheibl announced. "They will bring you luck." She set the jar on the table, brusquely pushing aside the pile of index cards with Loveday's notes, as if they were of no consequence. The cards went flying across the room.

Stooping to help Loveday retrieve them, the landlady babbled on. It was St. Barbara's Day — the saint who protected people in thunderstorms. On her day, one must cut cherry branches and take them indoors. If the branches bloom by Christmas, she explained, straightening up and pushing a wisp of skimpy, white hair out of her eyes, Loveday will have good luck.

To the simple woman, this clearly wasn't superstition. She believed it.

"*Ach*," Loveday murmured, nervously shuffling the cards she'd picked up, "*Weihnachten*."

By Christmas she'd no longer be here. "*Die Kinder*," she explained. They wanted her home. She'd be leaving in a couple of weeks.

Was she really going? But her book —

Frau Scheibl didn't conceal her disappointment. She'd thought Frau Mead was staying till spring, when the tourists would be returning and she could rent the room again. She started to leave, but stopped at the door to observe with a smirk that if Loveday would write the name of the man she loved on one of those little cards and tie it on a Barbara branch, she could almost surely count on being married within the year.

Loveday laughed. Did she take her for a gullible country girl? "I? Marry?" she cried, as the door closed on the foolish woman. "I have no wish to."

Still, the conversation made her think of Oliver again.

"I'm going to rewrite my life," she remembered telling him, when Serenity came back from New York with the job offer. "Even before I write Nannerl Mozart's."

They had been standing in the doorway at Firbank, watching the reunited Hollands clasping each other in a three-way embrace.

What had Loveday meant, anyhow, by that peculiar remark? The past couldn't be altered. Mistakes haunted one forever.

But even history is rewritten, she argued with herself. As new insights develop, events are interpreted differently. If I had reviewed my life first, discovering what made me want to write this, I wouldn't have gone off on the wrong track.

She scolded herself for indulging in reverie, when she had a book to write.

Nannerl had another suitor — Baron Johann Baptist von Berchtold zu Sonnenburg, the prefect of St. Gilgen, her mother's native village. He was fifteen years older than Nannerl, twice widowed, in need of a mother for his five unruly children. He was well off and had that title, which made him eminently desirable in the eyes of Leopold, the son of a humble bookbinder. Nannerl didn't love Berchtold but she was thirty-three. She married him on August 12, 1784, and went to live in St. Gilgen in the very house in which her mother was born. Leopold found her stepchildren — the youngest was still a baby — "naughty, ill brought up and ignorant." And he —

he!—complained that his son-in-law was "too absorbed in the
spirit of economy."

The following July, Nannerl went back to Salzburg to have
her baby in her father's house. She named him Leopold Alois
Pantaleon, in honor of her father.

Then something occurred that Loveday found extremely
puzzling. She tried not to let her feelings show through as
she stated matter-of-factly:

When Nannerl was ready to return to her husband, she left
the baby behind with his grandfather.

The child's father must have demurred, for the day that
Nannerl left, Leopold wrote to him, "Once again I implore you
not to worry about the baby. We have no need to rush about
anything. You have five children at home and the sixth is
well cared for here...you shall have the child, if God spares
him, when he is nine months old... That I shall gladly do all
this at my own expense goes without saying."

This mystery had intrigued Loveday ever since she first read
the Mozart letters: Why did Nannerl part with her firstborn?
Was she still so under her father's thumb that she would
even give him her child, if this was what he wished? Was
her husband violent, perhaps? There was nothing to shed light
on these questions.

We just don't know her side of the story, Loveday had to
admit to herself. It certainly *seems* bizarre.   ✓

Now Leopold had something to live for. No young parent
was ever more fatuous. Each "bla, bla, bla" was recorded. "I
can never look at the child's right hand without emotion," he
wrote to Nannerl, when the baby was three months old.
"I wish he were three years old, so he might begin to play
at once." Later, Leopold wrote, "I'm keeping Leopoldl. You
needn't worry about him." In a postscript he added, "So that
you may know my whole mind, I'll tell you that I shall keep

Leopoldl with me as long as I live. This is and was my intention from the first."

There was a second, even more tantalizing mystery: why did Franz D'Yppold, Nannerl's real love, come to see the baby every day?

Loveday refused to draw conclusions that could not be verified. She would not be guilty of innuendo. Still, it was hard not to wonder —

"I haven't let Leopoldl hear a fiddle yet," the grandfather reported, when the baby was six months old. "But I made an experiment with a brass bowl, striking it with a little key, first pianissimo and then forte, while I sang. Instantly, he became motionlessly attentive... He just stared at me and the bowl."

Poor, self-deluding Leopold!

If Wolfgang irritated him by not accepting parental advice, Nannerl must have delighted him by asking for it. Even as a married woman she sought his help for every ailment. He sent her pills and powders. He always knew exactly what to prescribe, until Nannerl's hair began to thin — that hair in which she had always taken such pride. For once, Leopold was baffled. "About hair falling out — I don't know what to advise, but I'll find out," he promised.

Loveday was having the same problem. Her hair kept growing thinner. She could still comb it so the bare spots on her pink scalp didn't show, but before long — Anyhow, she wasn't going to get a permanent. It would change her whole appearance and Oliver seemed to like her the way she was.

She ran her fingers through her hair, recording the birth of another little Leopold in Vienna. This one was only a couple of weeks old when Wolfgang wrote to his father, telling him that he intended to go to England with Constanze. Might he leave his two babies in Salzburg?

Papa, who was feeling old on his sixty-seventh birthday and unwell enough to dose himself, sent Wolfgang an indignant refusal.

"Not at all a bad arrangement!" Leopold expostulated, when he told Nannerl. "They could go off and travel—they might even die—or remain in England—and I should have to run after them with the children. As for the payment which he offers me for the children and for maids to look after them, well—"

Leopold admitted to Nannerl that he had never told Wolfgang about caring for her baby. A silhouette-maker, who had gone from Salzburg to Vienna, "said a lot of nice things about little Leopold to your brother. That's how he heard that the child is living with me."

The grandfather would have been spared part of his outrage, could he have known that on the very day he wrote this letter, his Vienna namesake was being buried, having died of suffocation.

The following spring, Leopold was taken very ill. Nannerl came to take care of him, but as he seemed to be improving, she left again. Her little son stayed behind. By Whitsuntide, Papa's condition had worsened. Nannerl hurried back. He died in her arms.

At long last, Leopold von Berchtold zu Sonnenburg was taken to his parents' home. He was barely two years old—too young, fortunately, for his grandfather to have discovered that the child was totally unmusical and destined for a military career.

Nannerl notified Wolfgang of their father's death only indirectly. "Be assured, dear," he wrote to her, "if you wish a good, loving and protecting brother, you will find him in me."

But when it came to settling Leopold's tiny estate, the old sibling tensions reappeared. With Nannerl's husband—whom even Leopold hadn't considered generous—acting as executor and Constanze egging her husband on to demand as much as he could get, there was a good deal of negotiation.

It was almost noon. Loveday had become so involved in writing that she'd forgotten about her coffee and the carillon. But the letter from home — surely by now — She locked up the manuscript and went to the post office.

Not since she arrived had Salzburg looked so enchanting, with sunshine restoring the buildings to their proper glory.

6.

PEOPLE were milling around the Cathedral Square, patronizing the stalls of the Advent Market.

Loveday walked on slowly. She had to glance, in passing, at the displays: wreaths and garlands, candles and miniature lanterns to hang on the tree, toys, colorful calendars with little windows for impatient children to fold back, one each day, till Christmas.

Endearing, Loveday thought. None of that tawdry stuff we so often go in for.

Many of the things looked handmade. They were lovely. But it was the childlike faith of the women in shawls, who were purchasing the articles, that transfigured them. The women's eyes seemed to be saying that they were carrying something precious in their market baskets, something that would sanctify their homes.

At another stall, there were gingerbread figures of St. Nicholas, dressed as a bishop with miter and staff. His only resemblance to Santa Claus was a benign expression and flowing beard, iced in sugar. Unlike Santa Claus, the Saint had a diabolical companion — a figure made of dried fruit. Loveday had never seen anything like this. The head was a fig. It had currant eyes, a cherry tongue and curved horns — what they were made of, she couldn't guess. Nuts, maybe. The trunk and legs were of prunes, strung on wire, with toes turned up. This evil-looking person carried a raisin-chain and a twig for a switch.

The Devil? But what has he to do with Christmas?

"Was ist dass?" Loveday asked the old woman behind the counter, pointing.

"Krampus."

Seeing that Loveday was puzzled — obviously a foreigner — the woman explained that on December fifth, St. Nicholas and Krampus went from house to house together. The Saint brought presents to the good children. The Devil switched the bad ones and rattled his chain to scare them.

Loveday was horrified. What kind of parents would let the Devil in to scare and beat their children, if only with token blows? She hurried away.

But she couldn't resist glancing at one last stall. Along with an assortment of carved animals, there was a little box no bigger than a matchbox, containing a Nativity scene. Against a landscape typical of the Salzburg countryside, were set tiny, tiny figures, with hands and faces made of wax. They were dressed in bits of cloth that must have been soaked in paste and molded. Mother and Child, ox and ass, shepherds — all looked at Loveday with gentle, trusting eyes. And she looked back at them, unable to tear herself away.

Only an accomplished artist could have created such beauty. It would have had to be a person of great simplicity, too — noble simplicity, like Oliver's.

If Loveday were to take the little box back to her room and put it on the work table, maybe she'd be less lonely. It might even inspire her. She'd been having a lot of problems with her writing, the past few days.

As she handed the money to a smiling girl, dressed in a dirndl and embroidered sweater, Loveday asked herself why the little box meant so much. Even before she carried it off in its tissue wrapping, it had become essential to her, as if it were capable of working miracles.

She wasn't superstitious. She knew it wasn't going to help her writing. Why did the little box mean so much?

She was crossing the Square in front of the Cathedral when all the bells struck noon at once, harmonizing, quarreling, captivating Loveday all over again. She stood still until the last one had sounded. Then she walked on, hearing the resonance which always seemed to linger on the air after the clappers came to rest — an aftertone far sweeter and more serene than the pealing turbulence.

At the *Postlagernd* window, she asked timidly whether she had any mail. By now, the clerk must think her some sort of nut — the way she kept inquiring several times a day, when there never was anything for her. She was losing hope herself.

But, this morning, she was in luck! She was handed an envelope — not the aerogram she wished for. She turned the letter over. It was from Oliver!

She must rush back to her room, read the letter in private, not in the somber, impersonal post office. But she couldn't control her impatience. Halfway to the door, she stood still and tore open the envelope. It was a long letter.

My very dear friend, it began.

Thee will, I trust, not take it amiss if I address thee in the plain language. The request I am making is so intimate that the form intended for the world seems quite inappropriate.

I can now ask thee with all my heart to become my wife.

Loveday's fingers shook as she quickly refolded the letter and put it back into the envelope. Then she stuck it in her coat pocket and stumbled out of the post office. She had to get back to her room. But she hardly knew where she was going. Her vision was blurred by tears.

No, she kept crying to herself. No, I can't.

As she walked on, she touched the letter tenderly, convinced that her fingers could feel the emotion with which Oliver's had written on the paper, just as she'd felt it, back in Boston, when he declared that he loved her.

That declaration had required no response. But this one Loveday had to reply to and her answer must be, No. How could she follow in Daphne's footsteps? Given companionship, Oliver might stop hankering for Daphne. Still, wouldn't he expect to find the same qualities in Loveday? If he ever started comparing — No!

It was out of the question. She had a book to finish. If she didn't, she'd never be able to send him an autographed copy.

But he wasn't asking for a book. He was asking for her.

She must be definite, not leave him in doubt. She couldn't bear to picture his disappointment. He would be sitting in his study at Firbank, opening the letter he'd waited for so eagerly; he'd read her negative reply and — It was too painful to contemplate.

As she rounded the back of the Cathedral and passed under the north wall, she heard singing. It didn't seem to be coming from inside. She turned into the Square and found herself wedged in a crowd of people. Heads tipped back, they were looking up at the balcony which joined the Cathedral towers. There, partly hidden by statues on the balustrade, a choir was singing Christmas carols.

The hushed crowd below seemed transported. So was Loveday, standing there a moment, listening to a glorious arrangement of "Silent Night." That, she'd been told, was composed around here. Then came, "Lo, How a Rose E'er Blooming!" Loveday didn't know the German words, but the familiar tunes made her homesick. So many Christmases, when the children were small —

It was freezing in the room when she got there, carrying the little treasure — colder than outside. The traveling clock said one-thirty. She should have stopped to eat before coming in. But she couldn't have waited another minute to read Oliver's letter. Standing by the window, she removed the envelope.

I am now free to ask thee to become my wife, she read again. Her heart was pounding.

This, thee surely knows, has long been my desire. I felt constrained from asking thee earlier by the need to make certain that we would become more than a couple living in isolation; that we would truly be joined to our families. On my side, way has now opened.

Heather returned to London, assuring me that she would be in accord. But she's convinced that such an able woman as thee is would never want an old codger like me! I fear she may be right. Only my strong leading compels me to ask thee, anyhow.

Old codger! Loveday all but blurted out. That Heather doesn't deserve such a sweet father.

At our age, time is very precious. Otherwise, I would not have mentioned the matter until thee has had a chance to finish thy book. I regret burdening thee with making a momentous decision while thee is working on it.

At the moment, all I ask is that thee stop here on thy return from Austria. Together, we could talk over the questions we shall have to consider before thee can decide. Thee could then discuss them with thy children.

Discuss a proposal of marriage with her children? With Emily and Will, even Toby? Indeed not! They'd never take it seriously. At her age — Just because Oliver was under Heather's thumb, Loveday didn't have to expose herself to ridicule; did she?

Suppose she did tell the children and they disapproved? Would she pay any attention?

But why was Loveday asking herself that, when she didn't intend to marry, anyway? She mustn't stop at Firbank on her trip home. That would be cruel. It would raise Oliver's hopes. She must simply write and tell him as kindly as she could that it was better for her not to come, that she was flying right through to Kansas.

Her mind was made up. But her heart ached as she read on.

I've been out in the field the past few days, husking the corn that was still standing and carrying it to the barn. Slow work. I miss Ross. He used to "help."

So the Hollands have already left, Loveday thought, troubled. He doesn't say whether that Judy is keeping house for him. Is he alone? Why didn't he tell me?

She knew why. He wouldn't have wanted to play on her feelings, persuade her to come, just because he needed her. Unless she returned his love —

In closing, Oliver wrote, *I am prepared to make any adjustments within my power that might contribute toward thy happiness.*

Say, No? Say, No, to someone like that? How could she?

I hope I am not pressing too hard. Just knowing that I might have a visit from thee to look forward to would sustain me during the agony of waiting.

But Loveday mustn't visit Oliver. If she did, she wouldn't be able to resist him. They might fall into each other's arms again, the way they did on Beacon Hill, when he came to her apartment. She would feel his slender frame through his jacket, as she pressed against him. His love would enfold her and she'd never be free again.

All I have to offer, dear Loveday, is a heart filled with love and regard for thee.

Thy,
Oliver

7.

THE FOLLOWING MORNING, bells woke Loveday — not the sedate, rhythmical chimes that she'd grown accustomed to. These were jerky, high-pitched sounds, mixed with boisterous shouts.

She hated to get up. Most of the night, she'd lain awake, regretting what she'd written to Oliver. But curiosity dragged her to the window.

Down in the Green Market, young men were racing over the cobblestones, balancing top-heavy crowns of flowers on their heads, playfully shaking cowbells at the cheering bystanders.

Another Advent custom, Loveday figured. Whoever concocts the tallest one and can run without toppling it wins.

Chilled, she turned back into the room, envying the young men's high spirits.

As she was dressing, she noticed something white sticking out from under the bed. It was an index card — one of those Frau Scheibl had knocked on the floor. Recovering it, Loveday read:

> Dec. 4, 1791, 2 p.m. Rehearsal of the unfinished Requiem
> M. sings the alto part from his bed
> Dec. 5, 1 a.m. M. dies

So, today — *today* was the anniversary of Mozart's death! As if Loveday needed anything more to depress her —

Ever since she'd written that letter to Oliver, telling him that she had a commitment to this book, that, anyhow, marriage was out of the question, that she'd better not visit him, and so on — ever since, she'd been in a highly emotional state.

She had taken the letter to the post office, not entrusting it to any outlying box. Returning at dusk, she'd sobbed in the street, telling herself that she had just thrown away the most precious gift she'd ever been offered. But what else could she have done?

It had been a dreadful night. Nevertheless, after breakfast, Loveday made herself get down to work, moving the jar with the cherry branches to the bureau, so she could spread out her cards. What would Frau Scheibl say, if she knew that, even without tying one on a branch, Loveday had received a proposal?

Luck isn't what I need, she thought, gazing at the branches. A leading — that's the only thing that will help me now.

She started by recording the birth of Nannerl's second child, Jeanette, in 1789, and of the third, who died in infancy.

So engrossed was Nannerl in child bearing, rearing and burying, that she neglected to communicate with Wolfgang. Having been out of touch for two years, she was stunned when she heard of his death.

Loveday was crying again. Was she breaking down? If something happened to her here —
She managed to continue.

A few months later, Nannerl was asked to supply details for a biography of Wolfgang. She described the tours they took together as children and her brother's subsequent travels. About his last years, she knew nothing.

"For the events of his later life, you must inquire in Vienna," she declared, spitefully rejecting Constanze, "who his wife was, how many children they had, how many survive." Then she described herself, explaining that she lived "in contented retirement, devoted to the noble duties of wife and mother."

"Noble duties" — ha! Loveday thought contemptuously. She was beginning to dislike Nannerl.

"In the last years of her spinsterhood, which she passed at home with her father," Nannerl continued, still focusing on her own story, "she gave instruction in the clavier to a few young ladies...even now," she bragged, with a flair for publicity that would have delighted Leopold, "one can tell the Nannerl Mozart pupils by their delicacy, precision, and devotion to the music."

"In their day," she added, "the Mozart parents were the handsomest couple in Salzburg. The daughter was also considered a regular beauty, when she was young, but the son Wolfgang was small, thin, pale, completely undistinguished. Except in his music, he remained a child...he always needed a father's or mother's care or some other person to look after him. He could not manage money. Against his father's wishes, he married a girl who was altogether unsuitable, which accounts for the frightful disorder at his death."

Loveday pushed the index cards away. She couldn't take any more of this. The docile daughter, who never forgave her brother for displeasing their father!

Unreconciled with herself — that was the trouble with Nannerl, Loveday decided. When she was asked to tell about her brother, she had to remind the world that she was an eminent musician herself, as well as a former beauty, now nobly domestic. Wolfgang lived on in his music; Constanze achieved lasting notoriety. Only Nannerl was forgotten. Why? Hadn't she been a dutiful daughter?

Why was Loveday wasting her time on such a petty character? Maybe she ought to give up — go home, explain to her publisher, return the money.

Thinking of Nannerl's inability to accept herself, Loveday was reminded of what Oliver had said after the silence, that morning at Firbank: that her name endowed her with a gift for reconciliation.

She could see him standing before her in the living room, holding her hands, looking down on her in a way that made her feel she possessed a treasure of which she was unaware, but which he recognized. He had made her feel young.

In actual fact, she was an old woman. Oliver couldn't seem to grasp that. Marriage — she'd been celibate so long — how would she respond? Well, at their time of life, sex probably wasn't an issue. Or was this one of the things Oliver wanted to discuss? Heavens, no! With his old-fashioned chivalry, he'd never talk about sex to a lady.

Anyhow, it was too late. She'd written that letter. It was already on its way to the States. Even if she were to write another, telling him to disregard the first, Oliver would never forget that her initial impulse had been to reject him. He wouldn't understand that there were these two people inside of her who sometimes were at war with each other.

The conflict was tearing her apart. She'd better fly home before she broke down completely. Fortunately, she had an open ticket. All she had to do was decide when she wished to go.

Rummaging in her suitcase, she hunted for the ticket. It wasn't there. She hunted and hunted, growing more and more worried. The ticket finally turned up, just where she'd put it — carefully hidden with her passport in the bottom of her bag.

At the airline, she discovered that a number of flights had been canceled. Lots of other people wanted to go to the States for Christmas. The best the agent could do was put Loveday on the waiting list. That was the final blow. She couldn't get home. She needed to go and she was stranded.

She left the office feeling distraught. What she needed was a decent meal. She went to a restaurant and ordered *Wienerschnitzel*, finishing with *Salzburger Nockerln* — mounds of soufflé, higher than they were wide, toasted golden brown. Delicious.

A brass band was playing in front of the Palace as Loveday walked by on the way to the room. It reminded her of the Salvation Army, playing in downtown Emporia at Christmastime, when she was a kid. That used to thrill her. This music was unfamiliar — some Baroque fanfare — yet the sound of the trumpets uplifted her now just as it had in her childhood. Only, then, she never had to think about her feet. Now, they hurt.

She went into the Cathedral and sat down at the back to rest a few minutes.

The lofty, white-and-gold interior, with the painting of the Resurrection on the high altar, the inlaid marble floor, the huge font, resting on those thirteenth-century copper lions awed Loveday. She thought of Leopold Mozart, anxiously running through the January cold with newly born Wolfgang in his arms, to have him quickly baptized at that font, lest, like five previous babies, he should die, any minute.

Loveday was going to die — not any minute, probably, but without ever experiencing again the elation that took her by surprise, when Oliver arrived at the apartment on Beacon Hill and they fell into each other's arms.

A verger was fussing with candles on the altar. Otherwise, Loveday seemed to be alone in this vast edifice. If only Oliver were here to share the silence with her! Companionate silence — when she shared it with him, the better of those warring people inside her seemed to win out. She wanted Oliver. She was suddenly overwhelmed with longing for him.

Was it irreverent to be sitting in church, wishing for someone that way? But if it was someone as pure in heart as Oliver —

Suppose she had let her feelings run away with her; suppose she'd accepted his invitation to go to Firbank and talk things over. Could she have lived up to his exalted concept of marriage? Was she capable, as Daphne'd been, of becoming a loving servant, one who would find greater freedom in selfless giving than she'd ever known?

How unworthy of her to think that Oliver would compare her with Daphne! No doubt Daphne had faults, too, only he didn't elect to dwell on them the way Loveday had dwelt on Bill's. For that matter, Oliver had faults, himself. They didn't make him less dear.

He had invited Loveday to enter with him into a relationship that her life experience didn't prepare her for. Unprepared and scared — that's why she'd said, No.

But Oliver was no fool. When he proposed, he must have realized that she was unprepared. Yet, he was ready to take her as she was, bestow his life on her, become her servant, convinced that she would quite naturally reciprocate. If he believed in her capacity to grow into such a relationship, shouldn't she believe in it herself?

Growing took time. One couldn't change direction overnight. Loveday needed time to think things over. But that was the one thing she and Oliver didn't have much of. *At our age,* he'd written, *time is very precious.*

It was now or never, all or nothing.

8.

TIME!

Assuming that she had said, Yes — how much time could they reasonably have expected to enjoy together, she and Oliver? He was seventy-eight. The infirmities of age might make themselves felt any day. And she knew all about nursing a sick husband. Would she be willing, if necessary, to do it again? With better grace?

But Oliver was in excellent health. Loveday might go to pieces first.

As a matter of fact, right now, her heart was acting up, lurching the way it did that evening in the ell at Firbank, when Oliver turned from the window, looking as if he wanted to embrace her. She'd told herself then that she must see her doctor.

She leaned back against the pew, terrified. With her family history —

Why was she holding her breath? She didn't have pain. Only fear. Was it all in her head?

She tried to center down, as Oliver called it, to quiet her emotions, to open her mind to the order and beauty of this place, the aspiration of the vaulting; the figures of Faith and Charity over the pediments on the altar; the golden tabernacle.

This vast Cathedral made her homesick for the little Friends Meetinghouse in Kendal, which was as plain as this was ornate. But the feeling she had, sitting here in the silence, was the same. Not peaceful, exactly, though she did feel more relaxed — hopeful, rather, confident of finding her way somehow, of having it "open," as Oliver would say.

Yes, she would gladly have cared for him, in sickness or in health, instead of wasting her substance on writing about a peevish woman. She would gladly have loved his grief away, freely offering him that treasure that he seemed to think she possessed.

If only she'd waited till today to answer his letter, instead of dashing off what she didn't really mean! If she'd waited for a leading, as Oliver did, in his withdrawal from the fuss of the world, her answer would have been different. Now, she'd disappointed him.

The comforting silence was suddenly shattered. The bells of Salzburg were sounding the hour. Loveday had been in the Cathedral a long time.

What would her children think? she wondered, as she walked out and crossed the Square. When their mother announced that she wished to marry again —

"How long have you known this man?" Emily would probably ask. And when Loveday admitted that it wasn't even five months, Emily's eyebrows would shoot up, the way they usually did, and she'd observe, "Isn't that an awfully short time?"

What would the children say when Loveday told them that Oliver had gone to prison instead of to war? She thought she could just hear Will's remarks and she cringed.

Oliver was right. Unless her children were comfortable with her decision, she'd have to give it up.

What decision? Hadn't she already said, No?

Her children loved her the way Heather loved Oliver. They wanted to protect her. If she could just tell them what he was like, maybe they'd understand. Communicating his gentle strength, explaining why he had chosen peace as a way of life would be hard, but if the children could meet him, they'd surely be won over. If only they could come to Firbank!

There was one of those ancient questions Oliver quoted — "Queries," he called them — something like, "Are you endeavoring to make your home a place of friendliness, refreshment and peace?" Loveday longed to have her children know such a home, especially Emily, whose disastrous marriage had left her embittered.

When Loveday got back to the room, she wrote to Emily, telling her she'd be home for Christmas, if she could get a flight. She didn't mention Oliver's proposal. No need to, now that she'd rejected it, though, if she still was in this nervous state when she got to Emporia, she might be forced to explain the reason.

She put down her pen a second, imagining Michael and Jed, running along the beach at Firbank in the summertime, discovering, as she'd done, only a few months ago, the gulls and sandpipers, the terns circling overhead — all those wonders they'd only seen on television.

This dream, which could never be realized now, saddened Loveday so much that she couldn't go on writing. She signed off. Her feet still hurt, it was growing dark outside, but she felt driven to take the letter to the post office that night.

As she rounded the corner by St. Peter's, she bumped into a black figure. A chimney sweep? No. He didn't have a top hat, just horns and his tongue was so long, it hung down over his chin.

Krampus! Of course! December fifth was his day, as well as Mozart's anniversary. Loveday had collided with the Devil!

He rattled a chain in her face, frightening her to death.

Krampus, she thought immediately, he was the villain! Salieri didn't poison Mozart. Krampus snatched him away while he was composing the Mass for the repose of his soul.

Loveday felt relieved when Krampus had passed her. He made her feel guilty for hurting Oliver. But she couldn't take her eyes off him. Halfway down the block, he was joined by a man in a bishop's miter, carrying a staff. St. Nicholas! In the dim light, he looked like a gingerbread man.

Then Loveday saw that, in every window, children were peeking through the curtains, waiting for him.

When she reached the post office, she mailed Emily's letter, thinking how, only last evening, she'd dropped Oliver's in this same box.

The airline was still open. She went in. Maybe — She wanted so much to get home.

There'd been a cancellation! Would the fourteenth be too soon?

Too soon? How could she wait nine days?

Elated, she headed for her room. She was going home!

She had almost reached the house in the Sigmund Haffnergasse when, by the light of a street lamp, she saw St. Nicholas again. He was alone. Maybe Krampus had gone home to his supper.

At Firbank, it's almost noon, she thought irrelevantly. Oliver's having lunch in the kitchen.

Who cooked for him? He must be lonely.

Loveday was thinking this when St. Nicholas turned and saw her. He smiled over his shoulder and waved. He made her feel the way Oliver had — young and full of promise. She waved back, but he was already walking on, drawing her after him. She made an about-face and followed, gaining on him till she could hear his boots hitting the cobblestones, echoing in her heart, *Now* or *never, all* or *nothing; now* or *never, all* or *nothing.*

St. Nicholas was leading her back to the post office, the one place where she could telephone. Was it still open?

Why had she waited so long? When time was so precious — Did she have enough money? She knew the number. She just didn't know what she was going to say.

Was this what Nannerl had tried to tell her, back there in St. Peter's cemetery, she wondered, as she waited for the call to go through — not to make the same mistake, not to deceive herself and turn away from selfless love?

Was Loveday such a fool that she'd had to spend months running to libraries, suffering with the Mozarts, when she wanted to be home for Thanksgiving, putting up with Frau Scheibl's cherry branch nonsense, just to learn this?

Yes, she'd been a fool. But she was grateful to Nannerl for opening her eyes.

Way off at Firbank, the phone was ringing. Oliver was getting up from his lunch and going to the study. In a minute, Loveday would hear his voice! But hers — would her vocal cords work? Her heart was doing that again. It wasn't Oliver who answered.

"Serenity?"

"Loveday! Where are you?"

"I'm calling from Austria. Please let me speak to Oliver."

"He's not home."

"He's *not?* Where is he? Is he all right?"

"Yes, he's fine. He went to Cambridge for that committee. We just came to pick up Peter's books. Loveday, guess what! He's got a job in New York — a fabulous job. It just fell in his lap."

"That's wonderful. I'm so glad. Listen, the reason I'm calling — I wrote to Oliver yesterday and I wish I hadn't mailed the letter. I don't want him to open it, just to throw it away. Will you tell him, please?"

"Okay. He'll be back tonight. We aren't leaving till tomorrow."

"You'll be sure to tell him?"

"Loveday, this isn't a very good connection. Did you say, *throw your letter away?* Oliver wouldn't do that."

"Please, Serenity, tell him to. I don't want him to read it. How's the job going?"

"Great. It's harder than I expected. I get tired. But I'm meeting interesting people. Isn't it wonderful about Peter?"

"Who's taking care of Ross?"

"Well, we don't know yet. Maybe Judy will. We're working on it."

"Something else, Serenity. Tell Oliver I'm flying to Boston the fourteenth. I'll rent a car and drive straight to Firbank."

"Oh, Loveday, he'll be *so* happy! We'll try to come while you're here. We've been going weekends to keep an eye on him and help Ross over the break. But with both of us working full time — "

"I've got to hang up, Serenity, or I'll run out of money. *Please,* tell Oliver — "

Loveday walked out of the musty post office into the cool

of the evening and inhaled the pure air that came down from the Alps. It was as if she'd been holding her breath all her life and, at last, she could let it out. She could fill her lungs and live to the utmost.

After all, she wasn't breaking down. She was breaking out — out of that dark place she'd locked herself into years ago, with her unexamined theories about prerogatives, her need to direct others, when she didn't know how to run her own life. She was breaking out into the light. Just in the nick of time, Oliver gave her a second chance.

To be unto thee, she repeated to herself happily.

She was going to Firbank! Not to talk over the questions that he said needed considering before she could decide. Those were irrelevant. She was going in order to give him her self, unconditionally — her whole self, as freely as he'd offered her his.

She'd barely taken a few steps before her heart started jumping again. But now she knew what made it jump like that. Not angina. Joy!

Taking another deep breath, she almost skipped over the cobblestones, already seeing herself leaving the airport in Boston, entering Rhode Island, driving along the Old Post Road. Between Perrytown and Kendal, she'd come to the arch of maples. Late afternoon light would be shining through the bare branches, crisscrossed against the sky — the light Loveday had broken out into in the afternoon of her life.

She would turn off the Salt Pond Road, feeling the sand and scallop shells crunch beneath her tires, slowing down, in case Ross or Lion should be wandering in the lane. But when she reached the house, she'd jump out of the car and run. Oliver would be waiting for her on the doorstep, the way he always did. She'd jump out and run to him.

Now she was humming the theme with which the oboes, horns and strings introduce the glorious Motet that Mozart composed when he was barely seventeen, *Exultate, jubilate!* Then she began to sing. Joyously, as if she were seventeen herself, she sang the opening bars of the soprano solo: *Exultate, jubilate!*

Exult, she sang under her breath, though she would have liked to let her voice drown out the bells, just then striking six. Rejoice! I'm going to Firbank.

PART FIVE

Oliver
and Loveday

1.

*H*ER COMING made Oliver so happy that there were moments when he wondered whether his aged frame could bear such intense emotion. Even after Loveday left, at the end of three beautiful days, this ecstasy persisted.

He was still glowing with it when he went out to cut the Christmas tree. Tramping over a thin crust of snow between rows of white spruce, looking for the perfect one to grace the Firbank living room, Oliver thought of Loveday — how she had unexpectedly appeared in the dooryard.

He hadn't heard the car coming up the lane, so when Lion announced her arrival, Oliver wasn't on the front step to greet her. He was out back, filling the bird feeders. When he suddenly saw her, running toward him like a young girl, he rushed to meet her and caught her in his arms, almost knocking over the can of bird seed in his excitement.

Through her coat, he felt the spontaneity with which she nestled against him as he held her tightly.

In this moment, he thought, elated, we've become joined.

All that would follow — preparing for the wedding, making the legal arrangements, reorganizing the household, the meeting for worship in which they actually entered upon marriage — would be but a confirmation of the fact, a public declaration that, in this precise moment, Loveday Mead and Oliver Otis had taken each other for as long as they both should live.

The conviction was so strong that he felt almost physical pain when, a second later, she detached herself, looking a little self-conscious.

As she backed away, he studied her. She seemed changed.

He took her arm and drew her into the house. Helping her off with her coat, he had the impulse to kiss the back of her neck.

Watch out, he cautioned himself. Don't be too forward.

But the eagerness with which Loveday came to him in the dooryard left no question about her feelings. That revelation was intoxicating.

In the living room, she took the chair she'd always chosen and he sat down on the other side of the fireplace, the way he used to do when she was here. It was almost as if she hadn't been away.

She leaned forward and looked at him anxiously. "Did you get my letter?"

"No. Not yet."

She appeared to be relieved. "I didn't want you to read it," she confessed.

"Serenity mentioned something," Oliver murmured off-handedly. "But I was sure she had misunderstood. I couldn't believe thee wouldn't want me to read thy letter. She said the connection was poor, so I decided to disregard the message. But the letter hasn't come."

Loveday stared into her lap.

"You think you know me," she told Oliver, still avoiding his eyes. "But you really don't. Sometimes I say and do things without thinking them through — things I don't really mean. It's as if there were two people inside of me, pulling in op-posite directions. When I got your proposal, my first reaction was that I couldn't possibly marry — I don't know why, now. I just dashed off that letter. Soon as I'd mailed it, I wished I hadn't. Please understand. It takes time to get used to some-

thing so amazing as your love. If it hadn't been for St. Nicholas — " She looked up anxiously. "Can you put up with someone like that? There'll be times when you'll find me impossible."

He went over to her and reached for her hands, looking
down reassuringly. "There'll be times," he answered, smiling,
"when *thee'll* find *me* impossible. Can *thee* put up with someone like that?"

Tears were rolling down her cheeks.

He took out his handkerchief and dabbed her face. "There,"
he whispered, as if she were a child. Then he bent and kissed
her.

She needed his loving care, just as he needed hers!

Oliver relived this tender memory as he chose the one tree
out of the many he had planted in the years when Christmas
trees were his cash crop — the one particular spruce whose fra-
grance and glowing branches would delight Firbank throughout
this Christmas season.

While he was hacking off the lowest branches, he scolded
himself for not having asked Loveday to explain her reference
to St. Nicholas. Wasn't he the patron saint of children and
sailors? What would he have to do with them?

But, at supper, he had asked the question that weighed on
him: how would her children take to the idea of her remarrying?

"I don't know," she had answered. "They've been so used
to having me around. It'll make quite a change in their lives.
You're right — if they aren't content, it would be a mistake.
At first, I couldn't see this. But I don't want to lose them."

"I'm glad thee agrees," he'd told her. "Most people would
say that the children's wishes are irrelevant. But how can there
be harmony in the world, if even parents and children disregard one another? We shall have to be patient. It may take
time for thy children to understand. If thee thinks their seeing

what kind of character I am would help, I'll fly out. Oh, Loveday, thee makes me so happy! If thee shouldn't come back — "

"I'll come," she promised. "Whatever happens, I'll come. But if things work out and we do" — she hesitated, obviously finding it difficult to say the words — "get married, it'll take me a while to clear out the house in Emporia and pull up stakes. I've lived there all my life."

"How long does thee think it will take?"

She shrugged. "A couple of weeks, maybe."

"Thee must have found it hard to leave Salzburg."

"No, I was dying to. I got fed up with Nannerl. She was a jealous, self-centered person, unreconciled with herself. Well, in her old age, she did — But I never got that far. I'm thinking of giving up the whole thing."

Oliver felt conscience-stricken. It was all his fault. He had ruined Loveday's book by proposing before it was completed. He should have waited.

"I don't mean to play down what I learned," Loveday assured him. "Living through the Mozarts' experiences woke me up to the priorities in my own life. Hadn't been for them, I might not even be here. But now, I'm putting them behind me."

"Think it over," Oliver begged.

The letter Loveday had sent him from Salzburg arrived the next day. He handed it to her unopened.

"Go ahead, read it," she told him, handing it back. "You might as well know the worst about me."

He took the letter, walked to the fireplace and dropped it on a smoldering log.

As they watched the paper burst into flame, she said, "You're nice."

The spruce he finally decided to cut was seven years old. It had been planted the year after Daphne had her stroke, when he was trying to help her develop the muscles of her left hand, so she could return to painting, and when he was searching for a formula that would revitalize the ravaged soil in Vietnam. He recalled now how nearly defeated he'd felt that year. Success in both endeavors seemed completely out of reach. Yet, with time, it came. He did hit on the formula. And Daphne not only began painting again, she made the portrait of Serenity, which the critics called her finest work.

Dragging the tree home in the snow — it was more of a struggle than he liked to admit — Oliver remembered the presents which Loveday brought back from Salzburg. As soon as the tree was up, he'd place them under it.

She had explained that they were for the Hollands — an embroidered blouse for Serenity and a jaunty Austrian hat for Peter, gray-green felt with a cockade.

"Looks like a shaving brush," she said, laughing. "I realize, Peter never wears a hat, but I couldn't resist it."

"He may wear one now," Oliver observed. "He has to wear a suit to work. Can thee picture our Peter in an office on the forty-second floor of a skyscraper in New York?"

"What kind of job is it?"

"Research satellites. Studying ways they can be used for gathering astronomical data and radioing it down to earth. Maybe some meteorological data, too. Nothing to do with spying — he looked into that before he took the job. It's not exactly what Peter's been trained for, but his knowledge of astronomy is useful. The professor he worked for here is interested in this new concern. It's through him that Peter got the job."

Loveday was unwrapping a tiny package to show Oliver a beautifully made box containing a Nativity scene. "This is for Ross," she said. "I fell in love with it in the Advent Market and kept it on the work table to cheer me when I was feeling low. But I don't need it any more."

Oliver looked at the tiny figures, the wax faces, the animals' trusting eyes.

"Ross will be delighted," he exclaimed. "He'll take good care of it. If it has the power to cheer, it's just what he needs. He's finding life in New York very hard. No place to play. And for six months, his bed was dry. Now, even in the daytime — The accidents upset him."

Loveday looked troubled. "That's hard on Serenity," she commented. "Having to clean up before going to work — She said she felt tired."

"Yes, she shows the strain. Thee sees, when they moved, Peter was planning to take care of Ross. They'd hardly arrived when he was offered this job. Since then, they've had to make all kinds of stopgap arrangements."

"Serenity said Judy Young — "

"That's only temporary. Judy's tired of New York. They've applied to a very superior private school. If Ross is admitted to the nursery department, he'll automatically be promoted to the kindergarten, which is very hard to get into. With two incomes, they can afford it, though an exclusive school like that is the last thing they would have chosen for Ross. Anyhow, it won't accept him till he has better control of his bladder."

"Seems a little unfair."

"Very. Each time they come, I have the feeling that the Hollands' situation is deteriorating. Ross isn't the only one who's suffering. Serenity is beginning to regret having chosen what seemed best for her rather than for all three of them."

Loveday set the little Nativity box on the coffee table with the other presents. Then she took a step closer to Oliver. "I hunted and hunted for something you'd like," she told him, "something that would tell you how I feel about you, but nothing was good enough. All I've brought you," she said gravely, "is myself, my whole self."

Overjoyed, he put his arm around her and drew her to the

couch, so they could sit close together. "It's all I wish for," he assured her.

"I'm not the same person I was when I left," she said softly, resting her head on his shoulder. "Maybe you think, at our age, people can't change. But I have."

"I know," he whispered. "I saw it the moment thee arrived."

"In Salzburg, I went through an awful time, suffering with the Mozarts, especially Mama. Some day, I'll tell you about her. I was scared something might happen to me, the way it did to her, dying among strangers, far from home. And I was afraid I'd make the same mistake Nannerl did. A lot of my old notions were shaken up. I'm still sorting them out."

Thinking about the endearing way Loveday had tried to communicate her innermost feelings, Oliver reflected that he had changed, too. That was one of the things he'd told Heather: since Loveday's first visit, he hadn't been the same.

When he lost Daphne, he also lost a certain buoyancy. He remained convinced of God's goodness, despite the violence and hatred that seemed to be mounting in the world; he still rejoiced in the unfolding of each returning season and the fellowship of his friends. But his feelings seemed muffled.

Now, life was coursing through him again. His dormant emotions were roused. The transforming power of love!

He leaned the tree against the wall of the house, close to the kitchen door. He couldn't get it in by himself. Tomorrow, Johnny Smith was starting work. Together, they'd put up the tree. Then, Oliver would trim it and place the presents under its branches. Ross would be enchanted!

Ordinarily, the Hollands spent Christmas with one or the other of their families, but this year, they'd told Oliver, they needed to be at Firbank. Might they invite Serenity's parents and her brothers and their wives and children? They'd bring the food. The house was going to bulge with people and festivity.

Oliver went to bed early. The exertion of cutting the tree had made him only too aware of his limitations. Tomorrow, he'd be stiff and sore.

Peering into the darkness, watching the signals from the lighthouses flashing across the water, he savored the joy of Loveday's short visit.

But it was symbolic. Should way open, they would have a blissful life together. Then, ultimately, they would be parted again. That would be for good. The thought of being separated, not for an interval like this, but forever, seemed unbearable.

That was perhaps why the practical matters Oliver had meant to discuss with Loveday slipped his mind until she was about to drive away.

"I've saved a little," he told her, sticking his head through the open window of the car. "If inflation doesn't erode it, this should provide for thy needs, in case I — Firbank would be thine as long as thee lives, but after that, it would have to go to Serenity. Grandmother left it to all her descendants."

Loveday waved the whole subject aside. "I wouldn't need money. I have a pension. As for Firbank — naturally, it has to stay in the family. Anyway, what makes you think you would go first? I should have told you: there's a history of heart disease in my family. Why worry about those things now? First, I have to convince the children. If I win them over, we'll take our chances. But, Oliver, whatever happens, just remember," — she craned her neck to kiss him — "I love thee."

It wasn't until she had disappeared down the lane that Oliver recalled one of the main things he had meant to ask her: where and under what auspices she wished to be married.

That is, he reminded himself, as the Watch Hill light pierced the darkness, assuming that way opens.

For the present, it was rapture enough that she loved him,

that she'd declared it in the plain language. She must be feeling, too, that they were already joined.

2.

IT WAS SIX MONTHS since Loveday left home, intending to stay away two, innocently believing that she would merely discover something about Nannerl Mozart. Arriving home, she realized that she had discovered more about herself than about Nannerl, learned the most important thing of all — how to receive and return selfless love.

The night she reached Emporia, her family congregated at Emily's house for dinner, all except Emily's children, who were away at college. Toby was there, looking very happy to see her, though a little drawn — was his love affair getting him down? — and Will and Sara Ann, with Michael and Jed, who even kissed their grandmother.

Loveday was shocked to see how bald Will was becoming. Always the least demonstrative, he merely said, "Hi." As if his mother hadn't just returned from *Europe!* But she knew him. She couldn't have had a warmer welcome.

As soon as they were seated at the dinner table, Loveday announced solemnly that she was thinking of marrying a man called Oliver Otis, who lived at Firbank Farm in Rhode Island. She had rehearsed the words while she was above the clouds, imagining the sensation they would make.

Down on earth, they fell flat. No one said anything.

Loveday talked on and on, trying to impress her children, describing Oliver — what a lovable man he was, how vigorous and enterprising. "And handsome," she couldn't resist adding.

No one spoke. They looked uninterested. They didn't seem to believe she meant it.

"That part of Rhode Island is very much like this — farming country," she continued, "only, it has the ocean and sand dunes. They're so beautiful. We don't realize how much we're missing, living inland."

This brought a rebuff from Will. "What's the matter with Emporia? We have two rivers, don't we? Who wants to go some place else? For a vacation, sure. But — "

"Oliver doesn't live in Emporia," Loveday countered.

"What does he do?" Toby asked. "Well, of course he's retired."

"No. He still farms, just fewer acres."

Toby looked surprised. He probably thought it strange that his scholarly mother should fall for a farmer.

"He's published a book," she added. "His first wife was one of the foremost artists in America, Daphne Otis. You've probably heard of her."

They all looked blank.

"The Otis family is highly respected in that part of the country," Loveday persisted. She saw no need to mention that Oliver was a Harvard man. It wouldn't improve his standing around here.

"How long have you known him?" Will asked, frowning, obviously disapproving. "Seems like a whirlwind courtship."

"I suppose. But at our age — he's seventy-eight — time is very precious. At first, I couldn't imagine marrying again. Then I thought it over carefully and I realized how much he's come to mean to me. Before going ahead, though, I also want to be sure that you all are satisfied."

"You don't have to ask our permission," Emily told her. "It's not like we're your parents." She giggled.

"I know I don't have to ask you. But how can there be peace in the world if parents and children disregard one another?"

No one had given Loveday the assurance she craved before the awkward meal came to an end. She told herself it would be wise to let the matter rest.

But as they were clearing the table, Sara Ann asked, "Will you be married in church? Which one? You don't belong to any."

"A wedding!" Emily sang out, beginning to enjoy the idea. "What fun! We're going to have a wedding in the family! Toby won't oblige, so Mom has to. Everybody in town will want to come."

She made it sound like a carnival.

As usual, Loveday was struck by the contrast between her thoughtful, conventional daughter-in-law and her flighty though warm-hearted daughter.

She recalled the awesome promise she intended to make: *In the presence of God and these friends, I take thee, Oliver, to be my husband, promising, with divine assistance —* How convey this solemnity?

Is it my fault? she asked herself, distressed. Did I fail Emily when she was young, not presenting marriage as desirable, so that, expecting little, she invested less in it and ended up with nothing?

Following Emily into the living room, Loveday noticed that either her tan slacks had shrunk or she had gained weight, which she certainly didn't need.

When they were all seated, Sara Ann, raising her voice so as to be heard above Michael and Jed's television program, repeated her question: "Will you be married in church?"

"Oliver and I haven't discussed details," Loveday said wearily. "First, I want to be sure my children are comfortable with the idea. Then we can begin to plan."

Loveday thought of Kendal Meetinghouse, with the sea gulls flying over the ridgepole; of the Hollands, Ludlows, Hills, and all the children, worshipping quietly in the unadorned room, of the many others who had given her the heart-warming feeling that she was part of their fellowship, though actually she was a stranger. In their presence (and God's) she and Oliver would make their promises to each other. Everyone would sign the certificate.

"Oliver's a Quaker," she explained, "like our ancestors. Only, a hundred or so years ago, one of them 'married out,' as they called it — married a person of another faith and was disowned."

"Will he be disowned for marrying you?"

Loveday laughed. "Oliver? Friends don't do that any more. I'd like to be married in his Meeting."

"You mean," Emily cried, "in Rhode Island?"

"Yes. I hope you'll all come. Oliver wouldn't want to marry me without my family being part of the gathered silence."

Loveday was obliged to define that. Put in her words, competing with the jingle of a television commercial, this mystical experience sounded downright queer.

"Michael!" she shouted. "Jed! Turn down the TV."

The nervous rasp of her voice sounded more offensive than the commercial.

"Why doesn't he come to Emporia?" Emily inquired. "That's the usual way. The groom goes to the bride's hometown. There's a Quaker church here. I've seen it in the paper. Why do we all have to traipse east?"

"Lay off of Mom, Emily," Toby urged. "Naturally we'll go. You can't tell me you wouldn't love a trip. If Mom really wants to marry this man — "

"Do I have to give you away?" Will asked, as if he'd rather die.

"I'll be the matron of honor!" Emily exulted. "I've always wanted to be one."

It seemed cruel to disappoint her. "A Quaker woman is her own person. She gives herself to the groom and he gives himself to her. They don't need a minister or any attendants. Everyone present is a participant. Even the children sign the certificate."

Loveday was relieved when it was time to say good night.

Walking into her own house after all these months, she was struck by the loyalty of her possessions. They were exactly where she'd left them. The only thing that hadn't kept faith was one light bulb, which burned out during her absence. She knew where to put her hand on a new one. It was comforting.

She was worn out, but before going to bed, she wrote to Oliver.

I don't think the children are taking my desire to marry seriously. They aren't saying they're opposed, but they treat it as sort of a passing whim, that I'll get over.

Dear Oliver, I do want to marry thee, but thee can't guess how hard it's going to be, leaving my home and the children. I'm only finding this out myself. I guess I more or less took them for granted.

Reading what she'd written, Loveday discovered that, quite unconsciously, she'd fallen into using the plain language. Well, how could she address Oliver any other way?

She snuggled down in her own bed gratefully. How good to be home! Did she really want to leave again, to sleep in another strange bed? Which? The one in the Firbank ell? Oliver's? After all these years, it would require adjusting to share a bed. And yet, to fall asleep curled up against him, with his arm around her—

How naive she'd been, imagining that, at his age, physical love was out. When she ran to him the day she returned from Salzburg and found him feeding the birds, he had caught her in his arms with an ardor that his correct behavior couldn't conceal. And she'd been surprised by the vigor of her response.

In the morning, Loveday got out her Bible. She'd scarcely

looked at it since college. She must get in the habit of reading and having a quiet time, after breakfast. Goodness knows, she needed it.

Sitting in the living room, she tried to center down, but her eyes traveled around to the furniture, the pictures, the rugs. Once the children were in accord with her marrying, she must dispose of everything. They wouldn't want much of it. What would she do with the rest? She couldn't cart it to Firbank.

When she and Bill got married, all they took with them was their clothes, a few books, a portable typewriter and the wedding presents they liked. The others they left behind. Loveday had walked out of her parents' house, leaving anything she didn't want in their attic. Now —

It was too hard, centering down alone. She needed Oliver to share the experience with her.

That morning at Firbank, when she had ostensibly gone there to babysit Ross and they had settled into a silence after breakfast, she had had what amounted to a revelation — the discovery that she had misrepresented their father to her children. She had resolved to go home and tell them the truth.

She remembered telling Oliver afterward that the silence had made her realize some awful things.

"We all have regrets," he had said, standing before her, holding both her hands. "Beginning over is all that's asked of us."

Beginning over!

With Oliver standing there, holding her hands, it had seemed altogether possible. The very prospect exhilarated her. All of life took on a new glow.

She was determined then to return to Boston, pack up quickly and go home. She couldn't wait to tell the children what she had come to see that morning.

Yet, instead, she went to Austria. On the way back, she lingered in Firbank. Now, at last, she was here and she still hadn't told her children the facts. She was so wrapped up in herself, so eager to have them accede to her wish that she had disregarded them.

The very next time they were all together, she would right this wrong.

But how was she going to say something so damaging to her self-esteem? What would they think of her? Communication at a deeper level had never been very good between them.

She didn't open the Bible.

Had she always been this way with her children? she asked herself, as she put it back on the shelf. Taking care of them when they were small, doing the proper motherly things, had she, all the while, been too absorbed in herself to come to know them at a level that would have made it easier now to set the record straight?

Wearing her down coat and ear muffs, Loveday spent the whole day in the attic, going through stuff she hadn't seen in years — things she and Bill acquired, then decided they didn't like, but wouldn't part with. When Bill's mother died, he brought over the contents of her attic. Loveday surveyed the iron beds, the antique trunks, Bill's first shoes, his high school yearbook, some buttons from a Civil War uniform, her mother-in-law's treadle sewing machine.

Sitting on Aunt Beatrice's wedding present, a record player of the nineteen twenties that had to be cranked up — what had she kept that for? — Loveday thought of the Query which Oliver's Committee was reviewing. It asked whether you were living in simplicity and moderation. She felt a surge of anger.

In Salzburg, when St. Nicholas led her to the telephone, she was gloriously happy. *Exultate, jubilate!* And when she reached Firbank and saw Oliver in the dooryard, she knew she had finally come home.

Now, all she felt was anger and defeat.

Why couldn't she walk into her new life without first hav-

ing to dispose of the remains of the old? It would take weeks
— months — to decide what to do with these possessions and
time was the most precious possession of all.

Oliver was waiting for her.

3.

WILL was right about Emporia's charm.

All the years Loveday had lived here, she'd hardly noticed
the place, unless a new building went up or something extraordinary happened, like the time the Cottonwood River almost overflowed. She'd been too busy to take in her surroundings.

Now, as she walked around town, everything looked attractive. When she passed William Allen White College, where
she'd studied and taught, when she came to Peter Pan Park,
where she used to take the children to play, she felt nostalgia
and the pain of separation, although she was actually still here.

The checkout girl in the supermarket greeted her like an
old friend. Several of her former students stopped her on the
street. They'd heard she was writing a book.

"What's the title?" they asked, openly admiring. "When's
it coming out?"

Would it ever? At the airport in Boston, Loveday had
started to phone Mary Day. "I'm back in the States," she was
going to announce, "catching a plane for Kansas!" She'd tell
Mary apologetically that she had decided to give up writing.
The book wasn't very good. No one would want to read it,
anyhow. She dropped the money in the slot. Then she remembered Oliver, begging her to think it over. She hung up.

But wasn't it unreasonable of him to expect this of her?

How could she write if she was going to keep house for him, clean, cook three meals a day, preserve mounds of garden produce in the summertime?

She didn't see the children again till Christmas Eve. Will and Sara Ann had decided to have Christmas dinner then because, they said, the house would be uninhabitable, once the boys opened their presents.

Loveday wrapped the things she had brought from Salzburg: dirndls for Emily, Sara Ann, and Emily's girls, who were spending Christmas with their father in California; Austrian hats for Will and Toby, leather breeches, with stags embroidered on the suspenders, for Michael and Jed. She also had a box of *Mozartkugeln* — chocolate balls, wrapped in gold foil, with a picture of young Wolfgang in his wig and scarlet coat.

Loveday arrived late. As she walked in, Emily started humming the wedding march. "Da, da, da-da!"

This irritated Loveday. Then it struck her funny. What would Emily say when she learned that Kendal Friends didn't celebrate weddings with music?

The house had a festive air. Even the grown-ups were imbued with holiday spirit. The troubling tension Loveday had felt when she spoke to her children about Oliver seemed to have eased. But, apart from Emily's silly welcome, there was no reference to what Loveday thought of as the only gift she wanted for Christmas. Were they hoping that the whole thing would blow over?

As she placed her presents under the tree in their respective piles, she pictured Oliver putting the little Nativity box under the Firbank tree. Ross was going to love it! How ardently she had meant it when she told Oliver that she was simply giving him herself, her whole self! But how long must she wait till she could bestow it in the flesh?

After dinner, before the boys went upstairs, they all gathered around the piano and sang a few carols: *Silent Night, O*

Little Town of Bethlehem. Sara Ann played the piano and Jed tried his trombone, but mercifully gave up after one or two ear-splitting notes.

Loveday thought of Salzburg, of the choir singing on the balcony between the Cathedral towers, when she was rushing to her room with Oliver's letter. And dear St. Nicholas — how, in some inexplicable way, the thump of his boots — *now* or *never, all* or *nothing* — had led her to follow what her heart wanted her to do all along.

"And praises sing to God the King," Loveday sang with all her might, as Sara Ann thumped out the beat, "and peace to men on earth."

In the past few years, she had been critical of the sexist, feudal language still tolerated in these carols, though she knew in her heart that peace and good will were invoked for her, too. Tonight her soul felt shaken by the meaning. These carols were a cry of desperation from the heart of the world. Threatened by its total annihilation, how could one quibble about words?

"Peace on earth" made Loveday ache for Oliver. She thought of the wine-colored tablecloth in that restaurant, where he had confided to her something he had kept bottled up all his life — what it had cost him to uphold the Quaker Peace Testimony.

She must tell the children, as soon as things quieted down. If Oliver had ever had a chance of winning their approval, his refusal to bear arms sixty years ago would surely spoil it. But Loveday couldn't keep that part of his life from them.

"There's something I must tell you," she began, when they were sitting down again. She braced herself for their reaction. "Oliver was a conscientious objector in the First World War. He was only eighteen."

"Is that how he got into farming?" Toby asked. "Guys who wouldn't fight were assigned work like that."

"Not in the First World War. There was no provision for

conscience. Every man who was drafted had to serve in the Army or go to prison. Oliver took the traditional Quaker position and was court-martialed."

Loveday looked at each of her children in turn. The outrage she had anticipated wasn't forthcoming. They had evidently given some thought themselves to the futility of war.

How little I really know them, she thought sadly. All these years —

"He isn't only against war," Loveday explained. "He's *for* peace. So when he got out of the stockade, he went to France and helped farmers there rebuild their homes."

"It's a beautiful ideal," Will observed. "We'd all like to live that way. But when you have a super-power that's out to destroy you, that's not the time to refuse to defend your country."

"I don't know," Toby argued. "Where's the arms race getting us? So we have enough warheads to blow each other off the face of the earth — Who's going to win?"

Loveday put in earnestly, "At first, I thought the way you do, Will. But I'm beginning to see that it's his courageous gentleness that has made Oliver the fine person he is. I just wish you all could know him."

"Lots of good folks are going to jail these days," Sara Ann observed. "They're not criminals. They're simply protesting injustice."

"Yes," Will said. "And hazardous waste. Guy I know, over in Langley, where they want to build a disposal plant, got arrested, picketing the site with his neighbors. All he wants is to protect his children and grandchildren from getting cancer. I'd do the same thing, if it happened here."

"How about your safety, Mom?" Emily asked. "I'd be worried about you. The crime rate in the East is something awful. Suppose you're attacked — would Oliver just stand there and watch while you're being stabbed?"

"No. I think he'd place his body between me and the assailant. He'd take the violence without striking back. He'd be friendly, try to reason calmly. You see, he takes that command about loving our enemies seriously. He believes there's something of God in everybody, even gunmen. It's a matter of reaching that something, instead of retaliating."

"I don't see what good being friendly would do," Emily said, shrugging. "Those gunmen mean business."

Will changed the subject. "What makes you think you'd like living in the East, Mom? They're so different, those people. I've met some of them."

His tone implied that he hadn't cared for those he'd met.

Loveday gave him an enthusiastic description of Kendal people, particularly the Hollands. She told about their fabulous jobs.

"Before they went to New York, they lived with Oliver. Ross, their little boy, is devoted to him. He's having a pretty bad time, making the break." She paused, wondering how Serenity and Peter were taking it, themselves. "Ross has blue eyes and red curls," she went on. "He's very cute. Reminds me a bit of you, Toby, when you were three."

Will snickered. "Toby? Cute? He was a pain, always bawling."

Toby grinned.

"It wasn't his fault," Loveday cried. "When Daddy was sick, I had to leave you all with anybody who'd take you and he was afraid of strangers. I wish now — "

There was no use going into that. But it reminded Loveday of some unfinished business. This was the moment. Could she face it without breaking down?

"One morning at Firbank," she began, "we had one of those Quaker silences, Oliver, Ross and I."

"You mean, the little kid? He does that, too?"

"Yes. He was perfectly quiet, sitting on Oliver's lap. It was a three-way communication."

Loveday recalled how it had struck her that morning that she'd never had communication of this kind with her own children. If only she'd known, when they were young, what she'd learned the past few months!

"The silence sometimes results in what Oliver calls a leading — a whole new perspective on life," she explained, looking down at her fingers, which were contracting and stretching in agitation. "That morning, I realized that — "

She couldn't go on. Imploring for help, she glanced at the children. They were listening, waiting.

"I realized," she finally managed to say, "that Daddy was a much nicer man than the one I used to talk to you about."

And Loveday started to cry, sitting there, surrounded by her children, on Christmas Eve.

"I meant to come home right away," she sobbed. "I wanted you to know."

They said nothing. But she felt their love enfold her, as it had done all along, when they refused to respond in the way she desired, though she hadn't understood that till this minute. They weren't giving up their mother lightly. They valued her.

She couldn't tell them how thankful she was. She just cried.

Toby took her home.

By the time they got there, she had herself under control. She switched on the light in the living room and collapsed into an armchair. Toby stood, looking at her.

"All this stuff," she told him, waving her hand. "What'll I do with it? If I really go to Firbank — I don't know whether to start taking the house apart. It'll take me forever."

"Mom, why don't you leave everything, lock the door and just go? The taxes aren't that high. We'll keep an eye on the place. You're in no shape to deal with moving. Getting married's enough to handle."

"But you and Will and Emily don't want me to," Loveday wailed. "That's what's upsetting me."

"It's not that we don't want you to, just that we feel you're not acting like yourself. You were always — well — in charge. And now you're asking us for our consent. It's like something's come over you."

"I guess it has. I've — what you'd call — fallen in love."

"That's just it. That's why we're worried. You were always so independent. We thought you were down on marriage — that you felt gypped, when we were kids, because you couldn't get out and do things, like Daddy. And now you want to go clear across the country and live on a farm with a man you barely know. You make him sound — well — sort of queer."

"Quakers are," Loveday admitted, laughing. "They're called a Peculiar People. Maybe he's a little more than most. Else, why would he have fallen for me?"

"Well, you seem to be taking an awful lot on faith."

"Isn't that what marriage should be — an act of faith? I wish I'd made you all feel that when you were young, instead of what you say I did. How can I convince you now, so you won't have all those objections?"

"I don't have any objections, just that I hate to see you go so far away. Usually, it's the kids who leave the old folks. Kids don't see anything wrong with that. For us, it's the other way round. If you're real sure you'll be happy, I'm satisfied. You mustn't mind Emily — you know how she is. I think Will's the only one who really objects. He wants to size up the guy. Sounds reasonable."

"Oliver said, if I needed him, he'd come. Maybe I should ask him to. Only then, if he doesn't pass muster — That would be cruel."

"No, don't do that. Will says, he's the head of the family and it's up to him to be sure you aren't getting into something weird. He wants to case Firbank, says he'll take a few days off and drive you out, so you'll have your car there."

Who was in charge now? Loveday resented having plans

made for her. Why hadn't she been consulted? Then she saw how loving it was of Will to look after her. She was no longer in charge; she was being cared for.

Stop trying to run the world, she admonished herself. You shouldn't have yelled at the boys about the TV.

To Toby she said, "You mean, Will's going to do all that for me?"

"Yes. Soon as he can get way. Some time after New Year."

New Year, Loveday thought with gratitude. A new beginning! A new life.

How could she make up to her children for her early failures, awaken in them what Oliver had evoked in her?

"Get some sleep, Mom," Toby urged, moving toward the door. "Just leave everything. Then, if things don't work out after you're married, you can come back."

"If things don't — Toby! How can they not work out? Oliver is the most wonderful man."

"Sure," Toby conceded, "but he's old. How long can he expect to farm, even live? So, if something happens, you can always return."

Loveday was shaken. Of course, Toby was right. But if she and Oliver were given only a short time together, what a benediction on her life it still would be! She thought of what she had told him, when they parted.

"We'll take our chances," she declared now, standing up and grasping Toby's hand. "Oh, Toby, I wish you would — That you'd have faith — " She kissed him, fighting back the tears again. And then she said something she'd never said before, though she knew she should have, long ago. "Will you bring Jean here to supper tomorrow night?"

4.

It wasn't till the end of January that Loveday finally returned to Firbank. Will drove her car. He scarcely spoke. On the long stretches of road, Loveday felt as though she were traveling beside a stranger, instead of her firstborn.

But he had things in hand. He, who had never taken responsibility for her, made motel reservations, decided when it was time to eat, picked the restaurants. He was looking after Loveday.

She was amused. Hadn't she just gone alone all the way to Europe?

They reached New England Friday noon. Loveday hadn't approached Firbank from the west before. She missed the arch of maples beyond Perryville. Everything was unfamiliar till they turned into the Salt Pond Road. Then she could barely contain her excitement. "We're nearly there!"

Oliver, bundled up in a parka and stocking cap, was on the front step as they drove in. He greeted Loveday with restraint, but reached out to Will with such cordiality that she wondered how he could resist it. How could anyone not be attracted to that endearing person — the love, accepting of all, which radiated from his eyes and crinkled in his smile?

"The Hollands are due any minute," he announced, when they were indoors. "Coming to see thee, Loveday. They both left work at noon."

His way of addressing her seemed to startle Will, although she had tried to prepare him for the plain language.

"I told you about the Hollands," she said. "Hadn't been for Serenity, I wouldn't be here. She picked me up. That's how it all started."

Will looked as if he would have been pleased if it had never started. But he seemed to be taking everything in — the spaciousness of the house, the antique furniture, the walls of bookshelves.

He deposited Loveday's things in the ell. Then Oliver took him up another flight to the top floor guest room.

"Thee'll have a good view of the ocean from there," Oliver promised.

Loveday's belongings filled the little room and there were more in the car. Where was she going to put everything? The house was fully equipped.

Will had laid the garment bags across the bed, obscuring the irises and daffodils on the blue spread. After the wedding, would Loveday continue to use this bed? Did Oliver expect her to share his room? Maybe he snored. If she had trouble falling asleep, she'd come back here.

She went downstairs, hoping to get in a word alone with Oliver. They'd scarcely spoken to each other, though, the way he looked at her, words weren't necessary.

But Will was already down, watching Oliver make tea.

There was an array of food on the counter, presumably for supper — a large casserole, two pies, a beautifully braided bread. Who had done all that?

As they sat down at the table, Loveday noticed that the plastic cloth had been removed.

Will was rubbing his finger over the polished surface of the wood, examining the grain. "What's this?" he asked Oliver. "Walnut?"

"Yes."

That was about the extent of the conversation. But Will was sizing up his host, whose hand seemed a little unsteady as he poured the tea. Loveday thought of Heather coming to Beacon Hill. Now it was Oliver's turn to be looked over.

The tension was broken by the arrival of Serenity and Ross. The child rushed to Oliver, then to his box of toys. His happiness in being back was touching.

"Where's Peter?" Oliver asked.

"He's just taking Judy over to Periwinkle Farm. We brought her with us."

Oliver showed surprise.

"Don't get your hopes up," Serenity cautioned. "I worked on her. The children are home this weekend. It'll give Austin a chance to express regret, if that's what he feels. Knowing Austin, I can't imagine him expressing anything."

"Does thee think she might stay?"

"She'd better not. We can't do without her. Ross still — "

Will was whispering to Loveday. "Doesn't he have a television set? Can't see one anywhere."

Loveday shook her head. Had Oliver flunked already?

When Peter arrived, things went better. He inquired how the car had behaved coming across the country. Will gave him a detailed account of its idiosyncrasies.

With Ross between them, Oliver and Peter took Will out to show him the farm before it got much darker.

Serenity went to the kitchen to prepare supper.

Loveday followed. "Anything I can do?" Without waiting for an answer, she blurted out, "I can't take the suspense any more. Emily and Toby both said all they want is for me to be happy. But Will won't commit himself. If he doesn't come around before he leaves, I'm going ahead, anyhow."

"I don't blame you feeling the way you do," Serenity said, lighting the oven. "But you can't do that to Oliver. He couldn't live with himself if your children didn't want to be part of our family."

"I guess you're right."

"You've got to realize, Loveday — you're dealing with a man of very high principles. Things most people think okay, he sticks at. There'll be times when it'll get to you. But, if you're like me, you'll eventually see it's what makes him so great. Matter of fact," she murmured, putting the casserole in the oven, "I've got a man like that, myself."

Loveday was setting the table. "Where does all that food come from?"

"I guess Johnny Smith's wife made it. I think her name's Alison."

"Who are they?"

"Johnny was a research assistant in forestry, but funding for his project got cut off the end of the year. Professor Anselm — he gave Peter his start — asked Oliver if he could use Johnny. There's nothing much to do here in winter, but the Smiths were hard up, so Oliver let them have the cottage at the end of the lane. Come spring, Johnny will be a real help. Alison comes a few hours a day and takes care of the housekeeping."

Loveday stood still with a stack of plates in her hands. "It'll be nice to have her help. I mean — if we get married. I was expecting to do everything."

Serenity stared at her. "You didn't think Oliver wanted you to do all the work? He's hoping you'll write. He took Daphne's canvases out of the woodshed and fixed it up as a study for you."

"Just when I was thinking of retiring!" Loveday cried. "I'm fed up with that book. Domesticity looks good to me." She laughed at herself.

Oliver suddenly appeared in the doorway. "My dear," he said, going up to Loveday. "It's a joy to have thee here and to have the chance to make friends with Will."

The others came in and they all sat down at the table.

Recalling how supercilious she had been about the Quaker grace, when she first came, Loveday wondered how Will would take it. Peeking at him during the silence, she thought he was more reverent than his mother had been.

In fact, she wasn't altogether devotional now, resting her hand in Oliver's. The little squeeze he gave it before letting go roused a passionate response in her.

The only person Will seemed willing to talk to at supper was Ross. He told him about Michael and Jed, the Little League, and how the family suffered while Jed practiced the trombone, illustrating this with sound effects, which his mother considered rather too realistic, but Ross laughed so hard, he nearly fell off the chair.

"Tell me about your jobs," Loveday asked Serenity and Peter.

"I love mine," Serenity answered. "The Museum has the most fabulous art treasures stashed away — pictures visitors never see. If it weren't for Ross — "

"I've no complaints," Peter added. "The firm I'm in is just starting. Even junior staff, like me, know what's going on at the top. That's nice. It might change when we grow, but for now — We're both lucky, only Ross — "

Peter and Serenity exchanged glances.

There was something in the way they looked at each other that jolted Loveday — a unity she'd never experienced, never even witnessed in a marriage. These two young people liked their work, but it wasn't what fulfilled them. Their oneness with each other and with Ross took precedence over everything.

And Loveday asked herself anxiously, Do I have what it takes to make that kind of marriage? I love Oliver, but can I ever be that giving? I want to be. I want to so much. Is it in me?

The men washed the dishes.

As Loveday followed Serenity into the living room, she recalled how assertive Serenity had been when she returned from New York after her interview, all fired up over the job offer. Loveday had identified with her completely. But the woman who looked at Peter that way a few minutes ago had changed.

"You're going to love living here," she said, as she and Loveday sat down by the fire. She spoke as if it were a foregone conclusion. "We miss the country and the community, the Meeting, our friends. If Oliver couldn't stay with Ross while I was at school, Ross would go to the Ashaways. The Hills used to take him out on their boat. He'd let John Ludlow do anything. We don't know people in New York. We've gone to meeting. We've been invited places, but we don't have much time to socialize and we hate dragging Ross out at night."

"I can see that. He reminds me of my younger son, Toby, at that age."

"There's another problem — we have to move. The apartment we took over from Judy's too far from the school we're trying to get Ross into. He isn't used to the place we have and already he's got to go somewhere else."

Loveday's heart went out to Serenity. The beautiful young woman, who had looked uncommonly serene only a few months ago, was drawn and troubled. It made Loveday feel guilty.

Suddenly, Serenity said defiantly, "I know this is going to disappoint you, because you were so keen to have me take the job, but I'm not sure I'm going to stay. I come home tired after a day's work and riding the subway in rush hour, with dinner to get, the laundry, and there's Ross, who's been waiting for me all day. When we went, we thought Peter was the one who'd make a sacrifice so I could have a career. He could have handled it. But as it's turned out, Ross is the one. I don't want that." She broke down.

Loveday went over to Serenity and put her arm around her. "I'm sorry," she said. "I was so stupid, urging you to take the job. I never stopped to consider what it would do to your family. You wouldn't believe how I've regretted sounding off. I've changed."

"I know," Serenity said, wiping her eyes. "You used to call

me Rennie and now you say, Serenity, like Oliver." She giggled.

"Do you mind?"

"Oh, no. I like it. I should be serene."

"At first, I wanted Oliver to use my nickname — Lowdy — the way my friends do. They think Loveday's some kind of bad joke. He gave me respect for it. Serenity, till you can work things out, would you leave Ross with us? He loves Oliver and he won't have him forever."

Serenity looked startled.

"I'll be more understanding than when I came to babysit. Christmas Eve, Toby told me that when he and Will and Emily were small, they felt I wanted to get out more than I wanted to be with them. I felt awful, because it's true. Later, of course, working was an economic necessity, but at that time, when Bill was still living, it was just that I didn't feel fulfilled."

"I know," Serenity said, nodding. "A job looks so attractive when you're tied down at home. Then, when you're working, you wish you could spend more time with your child."

"Think about leaving Ross with us," Loveday pleaded.

"Thanks," Serenity said, standing up, "I'll speak to Peter. Right now, I'm going to put Ross to bed. It's sweet of you to offer — " She looked thoughtful. "I couldn't come home and not find Ross there." She started for the door, then stopped and turned. "Be still and cool," she urged Loveday. "That's a pet phrase of Oliver's. Sooner or later, Will is bound to cave in."

"But he's leaving in the morning."

Serenity laughed. "Don't underestimate Oliver's charm."

When the men came in, Loveday took Will around the living room, showing him Daphne's portrait of the First Serenity. He was indifferent. She showed him the sampler, trying to explain the meaning of the words. It didn't interest him. Only the two wedding certificates attracted his attention.

"You see," Loveday said. "This was the marriage of Oliver's grandparents, Serenity Millburn and Edmund Otis. This, the marriage of Serenity Ross and Peter Holland. Over a hundred years apart. Nice, having the two together, isn't it? If our ancestor hadn't married out, we might have one."

Will was reading the words under his breath. "And Peter Holland, taking Serenity Ross by the hand, did on this solemn occasion declare that he took her to be his wife, promising with divine assistance to be unto her a loving and faithful husband as long as they both should live; and thereupon Serenity Ross did in like manner declare that she took him — Phew!"

As soon as they were all seated, Oliver attempted to draw Will out, inquiring about his work, the farming conditions around Emporia, the state of the economy. Little by little, Will began to talk.

Just when he was loosening up, the telephone interrupted, over and over.

"Sorry," Oliver murmured, coming back after the third call. "It's all about the Friends Hostel. We've been working hard, drawing up plans to remodel the house and tidy the grounds. I've been charged with coordinating the work."

Peter was listening eagerly. "When do you expect to open?"

"In June, we hope. But there's still a lot to be done."

"I wish we were here to help," Peter said. "It's just the kind of thing we'd love to do."

Oliver turned to Will and explained: "This is property that was left to our Friends Meeting. It's a nice old house, close to the beach. At first, we intended to turn it into a place where city people, coming here to enjoy the swimming, could spend the night simply and inexpensively. Now, the scope has broadened."

"How?" Loveday asked. "Last I heard, that was the plan."

"I know. But with the cutting back of funds for social programs, a great many people in this area are experiencing hardship. Some welfare allowances are so reduced that the recipients have to choose between housing and eating. On top of that, people are being released from prison and mental institutions who have no home to go to and hardly any prospect of finding work. They don't know how to take care of themselves. Sooner or later, they get into trouble again. We're not equipped to help them on a long-term basis. But we care. We can provide shelter for a few homeless people until a better arrangement can be made."

"That's a huge undertaking!" Loveday exclaimed, looking worried.

"We're well aware of it. We've considered the matter prayerfully and it seems the only right thing to do. At first, I was one of the cautious Friends, who was frightened by the magnitude of the job. But then, I looked at the Nativity box thee brought Ross — that homeless family in the manger with the animals — and I knew we had to do it."

Loveday noticed that Will was listening intently. He stared at Oliver with what she took to be admiration.

Soon after that, they said good night. Will didn't refer to the matter that was uppermost in Loveday's mind.

The next morning, when she was getting ready to take him to Providence, he still hadn't given her reason to think that he felt easy about her marrying.

"Want to come along?" she asked Oliver.

He must have realized that it would be better if she and Will went alone. He declined.

As he stood on the doorstep, shaking hands, Will asked him, "When's the wedding?"

Oliver looked as though he were having trouble maintaining his composure. "We don't know," he answered. "First, we want to be sure that thee and thy sister and brother feel completely comfortable about my running off with your mother. I promise to take good care of her."

Will nodded. "It's okay," he muttered.

Loveday understood. This was his way of expressing approval. She threw her arms around his neck and kissed him.

He looked at her affectionately, a little embarrassed. "Can I bring Sara Ann and the kids?"

"Of course!" Oliver exclaimed. "We want all of you — all. Plenty of room in Kendal to put everyone up. As for the date — we can't set it till we pass Meeting. That takes several months."

"Why so long?"

"The Meeting appoints a Committee on Clearness, which tries to make sure that nothing is likely to interfere with the permanence and happiness of the marriage. It usually consists of two men and two women."

"What kind of people are they?" Loveday asked, sounding anxious. "Marriage counselors?"

"Oh, no. Just Friends who seem to understand the art of making a good marriage. When the Committee has reported back to the Monthly Meeting that all is satisfactory, a meeting for worship is appointed in which the marriage is to be accomplished and a Committee of Overseers is named to attend the marriage and see that it is conducted with dignity, reverence and simplicity. Only then can the date be set."

"Wow!" Will exclaimed, grinning. "If I'd have had to go through all that to marry Sara Ann, let me tell you — I'd have stayed single. I'm sure glad that Quaker ancestor of ours married out."

5.

HEATHER, Oliver thought, as he watched Loveday leave with Will. I must write at once and tell Heather the joyful news.

He went to his study. But instead of sitting down at the typewriter, he flopped into the armchair by the window, suddenly overcome with fatigue. It had been an anxious time.

A tiny, squeaky whistle drew his eyes to the door. Ross was standing there, signaling his wish to be invited.

Oliver called him in and drew him close.

"Ross, remember how I told thee long ago that I loved Loveday? And thee told her one time, when she was driving away?"

The recollection seemed to trigger a twinge of conscience. Ross frowned.

"It was kind of thee to do that for me, a big help. And I want to tell thee something surprising: Loveday loves me, too! Isn't that wonderful? We love each other. So we're going to be married. Will thee come to our wedding? Thee knows what a wedding is. Thy parents have talked about theirs. Will thee come? *Please.*"

Ross nodded gravely.

"That's good! We wouldn't think of being married without thee. We'll have a certificate, like the ones in the living room. Everyone at the wedding will sign it. Thee must, too, now that thee's big enough to write thy name. Does thee know why Loveday gave thee the little Nativity box? It's because she loves thee very much."

"Will she die?"

He must be thinking of Daphne.

"Oh, some time," Oliver answered casually. "So shall I. But not, we hope, for a very long while. In the meantime, we'll be living right here and thy parents will bring thee to Firbank whenever they can. They haven't heard the good news yet. Will thee run and tell them?"

Ross flew out of the room. When he came back, bringing Serenity and Peter, there was exuberant rejoicing.

"We were so hoping," Serenity said, hugging Oliver. "May

we be Overseers at the wedding? After all, thee was one at ours."

Oliver reached out to both of them. "I trust the Meeting will appoint you."

"With Heather and Stephen and maybe their children arriving," Serenity said, taking the chair by the typewriter, "and all those people from Kansas, there's going to be a lot to do. I'll come and help." She turned to Ross. "Let's make a paper chain to decorate Loveday's chair at lunch, like the one thee made for my birthday. Thee go and find the colored paper. I'll come in a few minutes. Daddy and I want to say something more to Uncle Oliver."

"I'll help thee get started," Peter offered, ushering Ross to the door. "Be right back," he promised, over his shoulder.

"Last evening," Serenity told Oliver, "Loveday asked me if we'd like to leave Ross here till we can make a better arrangement for him."

"I needn't tell thee how happy we'd be to have him."

"And he'd be happy with you. He never has accidents here. Peter and I talked about Loveday's offer till late last night. The way things are now, it would be better for Ross. If we don't do something soon, we'll have a serious problem. He's pretty bad, already. But I've about decided, instead of leaving him, I'm going to resign from the Museum. We can live on Peter's salary, even in New York. When Ross is in school all day, I'll go back to work."

Peter had returned. "Someone else may have thy job," he warned, perching on the edge of the desk.

"So — " Serenity cried, shrugging. "If I can't go back to the Otis Collection, I'll work in another wing. Or I may finish graduate school first. Then I'd be in a higher salary range."

"Is thee sure, Rennie? Is thee sure thee won't regret it? I could give up my job again. Thee wants a career so badly."

"I'm not giving it up. I'm only postponing, to give Ross the care he needs. After all, I'm barely twenty-five. And I want *thee* to stay in *thy* job. This is the best arrangement for the whole family."

"Thee knows, I'm sure," Oliver put in, "how heartily I concur in thy decision."

"Actually," Serenity admitted, "I'd been thinking about it in a vague way, not really facing how deprived Ross feels, till Loveday suggested leaving him here."

"Thee mustn't think we don't appreciate the offer," Peter told Oliver. "It was real nice of Loveday. But — "

"Yes," Serenity added, "and it did something for me. The idea of coming home from work and not finding Ross there — Suddenly, I realized that's how he must be feeling all day, without me."

Oliver looked sympathetically from one to the other. "After you and Will had gone upstairs last evening, Loveday and I discussed something, too. She was afraid Will would never be comfortable with her marrying. I was more hopeful. I could see that, in his inarticulate way, he cares for his mother and I felt sure, when he saw that she's happy here, he'd be satisfied. On that assumption, I asked her to tell me candidly how she would feel, should you ever wish to come back to Firbank."

Glancing at them, Oliver was surprised by the intentness with which they seemed to be awaiting his next words. Until then, he hadn't realized how much they needed the assurance he was about to give them.

"I don't think I'm overstating when I say that Loveday would welcome you as warmly as I would. This always will be your home, no matter where your work may take you. If I should predecease Loveday, I wish her to continue living here as long as she chooses. But she indicated that her children would want her to return to Emporia. In any event, thee, Serenity, will inherit Firbank. Thy great-grandmother left it to all her descendants and thee's the only one who has shown an interest in it."

"That's what thee told me the first time I came here! Till that weekend, I didn't even know Firbank existed, outside of Daddy's childhood dream world. I never thought it was a real place. Then I discovered it. Thee and Daphne made me feel good about myself for the first time. As I was leaving, thee said, 'Wherever thee and Peter happen to live, remember that Firbank's thine, waiting for thee to come home to, any time in thy life.'"

"She rushed back to college and told me," Peter said, grinning. "She didn't think thee meant the farm was going to belong to her, the way thee's saying now, just that it was a refuge, a spiritual home. And we needed it." He reached down to put his arm around Serenity's shoulder.

"We still do," she said.

"We all need Firbank," Oliver declared. "And it needs us, if it is to continue being 'a place of friendliness, refreshment and peace, where God becomes more real to those who dwell therein and to all who visit there.'"

"Thee and Loveday can count on seeing us often," Peter promised. "We miss what we had here. But it looks as though we'll be living in New York for some time. My prospects in that firm seem very good."

Serenity stood up and hugged Oliver. "We love thee," she said. "We're so happy about Loveday. I'm going to see what Ross is up to."

"And I must write to Heather. I think she's going to be pleased."

"Why doesn't thee phone?" Peter asked, following Serenity to the door. "This is a pretty special occasion. Forget that Query about frugality."

"Thee's right."

"What a relief!" Heather exclaimed, when Oliver told her

his news. "I was sure something terrible had happened or you wouldn't ring up." Then she laughed. "Yes, we'll all come. When are you thinking of getting married?"

"We don't know. We haven't written our letter yet. Heather darling, even though we're separated by such great distance, I do hope we can become a united family."

When Loveday returned and they sat down to lunch, it was impossible, Oliver thought, to assess whether she or Ross derived the greater pleasure from the garlanded chair. She looked altogether radiant. It was indeed a festive meal.

"Let me show thee something," Oliver said to her afterward, leading the way to the woodshed.

He had lit a fire in the potbellied stove.

"How cozy and cheerful!" Loveday exclaimed.

"All these years since Daphne died, I never made a fire in here. I knew I ought to clean out the stove, but something held me back. Now I realize I was waiting for this day, keeping a bed of ash in readiness to build a new fire on. I hope thee will make this thy study."

Daphne's canvases, easel and paints had been removed. In their place were two cretonne-covered armchairs. A little, old-fashioned desk stood by the window.

"My grandfather made this for my grandmother," Oliver said, running his hand over the top of the desk. "She treasured it and I thought thee might enjoy pressing it into service again."

"Oh, Oliver," Loveday exclaimed. "It's lovely."

"Thee will, at least, look over thy manuscript, won't thee? Perhaps when thee reads it, thee will change thy mind about finishing."

She looked at him shyly. "Could we read it together? If I heard thee read it, I might feel inspired again. Will spoke of it, too, this morning. He said they were all proud of me.

When I left in the spring, he thought it a crackpot idea. I don't understand what made the change."

Oliver took Loveday in his arms. "Thee," he whispered, "thee made the change. Shall we write our letter to Kendal Meeting, requesting to be married under its care?" He stepped back, holding her at arm's length, so that he could look into her eyes. " 'Do you recognize marriage as a sacred, loving, and permanent relationship, requiring mutual consideration and adjustments?' That's the Query we shall be asked to answer in our own minds. I feel quite clear about it. Does thee?"

"I do."

They kissed solemnly and again Oliver had the conviction he'd had when Loveday came back from Austria and surprised him in the dooryard, as he was feeding the birds — that they already belonged irrevocably to each other.

"But you're — thee's — more of a handful than I bargained for," she said, when they let go. "That plan for sheltering homeless people — it's very nice, but it would be too much for a younger person. How can I take care of someone so impractical?" Although she laughed, Oliver saw she was uneasy.

"I'm not doing it alone. The whole Meeting is engaged in the effort. And once others in the neighborhood see what we're about, they'll surely want to help. There's great concern about the needs of less fortunate people. I don't think of it as optional. We have to do it because it's the right thing to do."

"Thee's such a good man and I — When I was home — I mean, in Emporia — this is home now. When I was there, Toby told me the children felt they took second place with me when they were little. It made them mistrustful of marriage, all but Will — thanks to Sara Ann. Can I ever make it up to them, Oliver?"

He thought a long time. "I don't know. But offspring aren't

all that love begets. Hope, understanding, sympathy — we're not too old to beget these. When thy children come and feel our love, maybe —"

Loveday's face lit up. "It may be happening already! Toby brought Jean — she's the girl he's living with — to my house one evening. I'd never met her. She's lovely — just right for Toby. But he's had this stop in his mind about getting married. And yet, they really seem to belong together. He told her about us that night and, for some reason, the thought of two old people being in love stirred her. 'It gives one hope,' — that's what she said. Toby nodded gravely, as if he agreed. Oh, Oliver, wouldn't it be wonderful if our love turned out to mean something to them, as well as to us?"

"I think," he whispered, then paused to kiss her. "I think that's the crucial test of love — whether it generates new life in others."

6.

THE DAYS that followed were supremely happy ones. From breakfast until they kissed good night and retired to their rooms, Oliver and Loveday savored the joy of being together.

Oliver wanted to redecorate the room Loveday was going to move into after they were married, but he felt diffident about asking whether she wished to share his or have one of her own. She might prefer to stay in the ell.

Sometimes, when he was sitting up in bed in the morning, reading the Bible, he could hear her creeping past his door on her way to the kitchen to make coffee. Was she wearing the pale green robe she'd worn months ago, when she took him by surprise? Hearing her footsteps, he was tempted to jump out of bed, open the door, and embrace her. But in his pajamas —

He asked himself whether he must indeed observe the propriety that governed his youth. Then, society prescribed behavior. Now, men and women made up their own rules. Did Loveday think him stuffy? These days, where did people draw the line?

The fact that convention had changed so that it was considered proper for Loveday to be living under Oliver's roof without the Hollands' presence was a distinct improvement. It gave them an opportunity to get used to each other.

It also, Oliver realized, thinking about it, put a responsibility on him to be scrupulously correct. His young friends believed in his integrity.

He had always let them know that, whatever lifestyle they elected, they held no less a place in his affection, but that of himself he demanded celibacy. His friends would expect him to adhere to his principles, even when he was in love.

He thought of those early Quakers who told the king that the spirit by which they were guided wasn't changeable, "so as once to command us from a thing as evil and again to move unto it."

No, neither popular opinion nor a change in personal circumstances justified forsaking those principles on which Oliver had built his life. But he knew something now that he'd all but forgotten: how dearly a man must pay for upholding them. And he was more sympathetic toward those of his young friends who didn't try to repress their instincts.

He also saw the humor of his dilemma.

Before breakfast, he always lit a fire in the woodshed stove, so Loveday would be comfortable while she was working on her book. Her interest in it seemed to be returning. After Oliver had read the first chapters aloud, she exclaimed, "Thee makes it sound better than it is."

"No, it's better than thee thinks. Letting the characters speak for themselves through letters brings them to life."

"The part I'm coming to — Nannerl's old age — is fascinating. Her nephew, who was only four months old when his father died, came to see her. He'd been baptized Franz Xavier, but his scheming mother changed his name to Wolfgang Amadeus Mozart, Junior. She thought the illustrious name would further his musical career. Just the opposite happened — he was constantly compared to his father and declared an inferior musician. Oh, Oliver, I must be boring thee. Shall we go for a walk?"

"Yes. Come, Lion."

Loveday was still thinking about the Mozarts as they went through the woods.

"Wolfgang, Junior, was thirty and Nannerl was seventy when they met for the first time and discovered that they had a bond — both their lives had been embittered by failure, not for lack of ability but because they happened to be next of kin to a genius."

"What a tragedy," Oliver exclaimed.

The pond had a thin crust of ice. On a piling at the end of the dock, a great cormorant was spreading his wings to dry.

"When I came here last summer," Oliver recalled, forgetting the Mozarts, "all I did was dream about thee. I was very moony."

How wonderful that he and Loveday should be laughing about this now! At the time, it hadn't seemed funny.

In the afternoon mail, there was a letter from Heather, addressed to Loveday. It was a touching expression of approval. *I wanted Father to come and live near me,* she wrote, *but he would have been sad, so far from Firbank. After the Hollands left, I worried terribly. Now I know he's in good hands. Bless you, Loveday, for making him happy.*

On First Day, when they were driving to Kendal, Oliver confided to Loveday that nothing had been so painful after Daphne's death as going to meeting alone. "Now," he rejoiced, "I have thee."

Still thinking of Daphne, as they sat in the deepening silence, he realized how much more reconciled he had become. He could think of her without aching.

Across the aisle, Lucas Lang was getting to his feet, buttoning his jacket, the way he always did when he was about to speak in meeting. His message, urging Friends to live fully in the present, went straight to Oliver's heart.

On the way home, he told Loveday how moved he had been. "That verse from Paul, which he quoted — 'forgetting those things which are behind and reaching forth unto those which are before —' Thee's brought me this peace."

Joy overspread her face. Then she looked embarrassed. "I was thinking about my book in meeting. Is that awful? I mean, shouldn't I have been more religious?"

"I see nothing wrong with that. All of life ought to be sacramental, particularly our work. If it isn't, maybe we ought to engage in something else. One Query asks whether our spiritual growth integrates our life's activities."

Loveday shook her head incredulously. "I'm always amazed by thy way of looking at things. I'm glad it was all right to be thinking of Nannerl. Something nice happened at the end of her life. I want to write about it."

"Would thee care to tell me?"

"An English couple came to see her — Vincent and Mary Novello. Vincent was an organist and music publisher in London. He was the first to publish Mozart's scores at a price most people could afford. In eighteen twenty-nine the Novellos made what they called a 'pilgrimage' to Salzburg, bringing Nannerl sixty guineas, which had been contributed by a group of English musicians because, as they said in a covering letter, they'd heard that the composer's sister was in poor health and poorer means.' "

"The Novellos came all the way from England to bring her this comfort!" Oliver exclaimed. Concern for a needy old woman was an aspect of the Mozart story he could identify with.

"When they reached Salzburg, Wolfgang, Junior, happened to be there," Loveday went on, visibly gratified by Oliver's interest. "He took them to his aunt's house. They were impressed by his deep affection for her. She was paralyzed, blind, barely able to speak. But the English visitors and the gift they brought gave her enormous pleasure. Vincent reverently touched the keys of the clavichord on which her brother had played. Then he and Mary kissed Nannerl's emaciated hand and said farewell. After her death, he conducted the Mozart Requiem in her memory at a church in Grosvenor Square, only half a mile from Buckingham House, where, sixty-five years earlier, the Mozart children performed on the accession to the throne of George III. Doesn't thee think this will make a touching ending?"

"I do."

"I guess," Loveday admitted, "it appeals to me because it's a bit like my life story. Nannerl and I both tried to impress the world, instead of doing what we should have done. Still, in the end, she had Wolfgang, Junior, and the Novellos. I have thee, who gave me my self — the self I want to be."

They had arrived at Firbank.

Smiling tenderly, Oliver turned to Loveday. "Welcome home," he said.

The next evening, John Ludlow telephoned to say that the Nominating Committee was proposing four names of members for the Committee on Clearness. Before asking these Friends to serve, he wanted to know whether Oliver and Loveday would be comfortable meeting with them.

"First," he said, "there's Neil and Alice Hill."

"They would be fine," Oliver told him. "I've known them both since they were children and they've been friendly toward Loveday."

"The other two," John went on, hesitating a little, "are Austin and Judy Young. I expect this will come as a surprise."

"Well, it's unusual to ask Friends whose marriage is in trouble. Does thee think they'll do it? Thanks, anyhow, John. I'll speak to Loveday and let thee know." Impatient to tell her, Oliver was about to hang up, but John detained him.

"While I have thee, I just want to report that plans for the Friends Hostel have been submitted to the Town. There shouldn't be any hitch."

"First-rate! Soon as they're approved, we'll start work. Good-bye, John."

Loveday found the Quaker process baffling. "I thought these were going to be people who had a satisfactory marriage. I know Austin. I haven't met Judy."

"She's a good woman. She put up cheerfully with him until she became a feminist. Then she left."

"Quite right. Why should a woman put up with an impossible husband?"

"*Thee* promised to. Has thee changed thy mind?"

Loveday burst out laughing. "It's too late. We've written the letter!"

"Austin's good, too," Oliver added, becoming serious, "only he's not very perceptive. According to Serenity, the separation isn't making Judy happy, either. I wish we could help them."

Loveday put her arms around Oliver's neck. "Remember what thee said about us not being too old to beget hope, understanding, sympathy? Maybe when the Youngs are around us, they —" Her last words were cut off by a kiss.

All four nominees agreed to serve on the Committee on Clearness. They were appointed at the meeting for business in Second Month. Neil Hill was named Clerk. He and Alice offered to have the interview take place at their house the following Saturday.

At lunchtime on Saturday, Ross bounced joyfully out of the car, followed by Serenity. Peter drove on to Periwinkle Farm with Judy.

"I invited her to stay here, if she preferred not going to her own house," Serenity told Oliver, as she was hanging up her coat in the entrance hall. "But she said she didn't mind. She made a point of telling me that living there doesn't mean she has to act like Austin's wife. Anyway, they're talking. That's something."

"It's a lot."

"At the last minute, she decided to bring most of her stuff. She says she'll stay home till she decides what she wants to do."

"That's wonderful news! But what about Ross? Who'll be with him?"

"I will. I quit work."

"Serenity! Thee really did? It must have been hard."

She looked down at the floor. "A lot harder than when I talked to thee about it, last time we were here. When I was with thee" — she looked at him squarely — "I knew it was the right thing. But when I got back to New York and had to do it — hand in my resignation, leave Daphne's pictures, give up the prestige of working there —" She was blinking back tears.

"Come in and sit down," Oliver urged.

Ross had to show off his new shoes. "Look, 'cle Oliver, boots! Just like Daddy's." He held up his foot. "See?"

"First-rate! We'll take them out walking later."

Bursting with pride, Ross went off to play.

"He'll be much happier," Oliver assured Serenity.

"He already is. It was all right while he had thee, but in New York, we were heading for pretty bad trouble. Some kids don't mind being left with strangers. Ross still needs his family. There's a good side to the situation, too. With him not going to that school yet, we don't have to move. And parts of the job were boring — entertaining important people, going to cocktail parties — stuff that has nothing to do with art, just raising money."

Loveday came in, dressed to go out.

Serenity told her that she'd resigned from the Museum. "We've been thinking," she added, "now that Peter's getting a good salary, it's the time to have another baby. Wouldn't that be nice?"

"No wedding present could give us greater pleasure. Isn't that so, Loveday?"

"Yes. Oliver, if we don't want to be late to our final exam, we'd better leave."

Serenity giggled. "Quit worrying, Loveday. Friends are a pushover. If Peter and I could pass meeting, the two of you won't have any trouble."

7.

DRIVING in to Kendal, Oliver pondered Loveday's remark. *Our final exam!* Did she really look on the meeting with the Committee on Clearness as an inquisition? Or was it just a collegiate joke, intended to amuse Serenity? He struggled with himself, feeling obliged to face this, yet afraid to ask Loveday whether she had any lingering doubts.

She seemed withdrawn.

"Thee knows," he ventured finally, as they neared the River Road, "religion isn't static. It's a living organism, always growing and maturing. Things have changed drastically since those eighteenth-century Friends sat in judgment on their hapless fellow members. Today, the Queries ask us simply to have a living concern for the welfare of each person, even to the sharing of one another's joys and burdens. That's the spirit in which this exercise is supposed to be conducted." He paused, more and more uneasy. If, when they met with the Committee, Loveday appeared reluctant —

"I know."

Oliver was so disturbed that he almost pulled off the road so he could stop and study Loveday's face. But they were already late.

"It's also," he added, choosing his words with care, "an occasion for looking into our own hearts once more; a time to make certain we truly wish to enter into this marriage. Thee understands — it's not too late to change our minds. Unless we're completely clear — "

She said nothing.

"Even during the wedding," Oliver persisted, frantic now, "the groom makes his promise first. The bride is uncommitted right up to the very last minute. Until she makes the promise, the marriage is unaccomplished. Remember that, dear Loveday. Everything in me already feels joined to thee, but if thee has any hesitation — "

They had reached the Hills' house. It stood beside the boatyard, tucked into a cove on the Kendal River.

Oliver's hand was shaking so, he had trouble pulling on the brake.

Loveday changed the subject. Was she trying to reassure him?

"What a beautiful spot," she said, as they walked to the door.

But Oliver thought she was dragging her feet.

The Youngs had already arrived. Oliver's first impression of Judy was that she had aged. Or was it just the city veneer

— those murderously high heels and the loss of country color in her cheeks? He introduced Loveday and they exchanged a few words.

Austin was standing across the room, looking glum.

Oliver went over to him. "Only another month and we'll be putting in our peas!"

"Yup."

"Yesterday, Loveday and I had fresh carrots. Can thee believe it? Thee knows that southern slope at the corner of my garden? Last fall, I covered it with salt marsh hay and, to my surprise, they made it through the winter. The ground has thawed there. That's the very end of harvest."

Returning to Loveday, Oliver drew her to the window to show her the view of Little Narragansett Bay at the mouth of the river. She still seemed apprehensive.

"These are our friends," he whispered, pleading with her to understand. "They're not here to pass judgment, only to participate with us in our search for Truth, to make us sensitive to any problems we may not have faced. Actually, we've pretty well covered the ground ourselves, doesn't thee think?"

"I guess so."

How would she respond when Friends asked those probing questions it was their duty to bring up at this point? Would her replies be half-hearted? All her working life, Loveday had been in the position of determining the future of others. Now other people were considering her future — people who held Oliver in great affection, while she was a newcomer. It had never occurred to him that they would have the slightest difficulty in convincing Friends of their clearness for marriage. But now, he was uncertain himself.

"Be still and cool," he murmured, trying desperately to encourage himself.

Loveday heard him. The incredible happened: she smiled and patted his sleeve.

They turned back into the room. Everyone looked at them expectantly. Judy seemed pleased when Oliver took the chair beside her. Neil offered Loveday the armchair. Then everyone settled into silence.

In it, Oliver tried to figure out what had happened. He couldn't recall ever having quoted those words for Loveday. Yet, hearing them, she became her old self. They worked like a charm. Puzzled, he gave thanks for her return.

"Seems funny," Neil said, breaking the silence, "to be counseling thee, Oliver, when thee's done that for us all these years. Thee must have served on dozens of Clearness Committees and this is my first experience. I don't know where to begin, except to say that we're here to help the two of you forestall any possible difficulties."

Oliver glanced at Loveday. She looked relaxed. Neil's quiet, informal manner helped. Or had those words of Fox made this wonderful change?

To his surprise, it was taciturn Austin who began the discussion. "What about property? Firbank and all. Have you made your wills?"

Oliver explained that the marriage would change nothing as far as property was concerned. Loveday's would go to her children and his to Heather, apart from Firbank, which she didn't want. Serenity would inherit that.

Judy waved this aside impatiently. "What happens after they die isn't important now. It's how they're going to live together that we should be concentrating on."

Austin looked slapped down.

"You've both lived alone so long," Alice said thoughtfully, "are you prepared to share your innermost feelings?"

"Yes," Judy broke in. "That's what I want to know. Without communication at a deeper level, a marriage is no good."

Oliver stared at the Hills' rag rug, following the coils of colored braid till his eyes reached the center. His conscience hurt. To his relief, Loveday felt moved to answer.

"We're communicating," she said, sounding more assured than she had all day. "Maybe not as well as we shall when we're married. I don't know about that. I never experienced the Quaker silence before I came to Firbank. It's made me more sensitive. I used to be afraid to say what I think. Oliver's understanding has given me courage."

But Oliver was thinking of his indefensible reserve. Loveday didn't know how badly he had failed her.

"Men think," Judy muttered bitterly, "they don't have to show their feelings. Wives are there to do things for them, not to be told what they feel."

Oliver turned to her gratefully. "Thank thee for the warning. I'll take it to heart."

On the way home, he'd ask Loveday which room she would like to have. Then, on Monday, he could call in the painter.

Alice had another question, this one just for Loveday. "I understand thee's writing a book. Isn't it going to be difficult to pursue thy career and devote thyself to Oliver, too? I know Alison Smith's a big help with the housekeeping. Still —"

Everyone seemed to be looking at Loveday, hanging on her reply. Oliver had the impression that this matter must have been discussed in the Meeting. Friends wanted to be sure that he was going to have adequate attention.

"Oliver's first in my life now," Loveday said placidly. "The rest will have to be worked in, if I can do it. I've written to my editor, explaining that I'm getting married and publication will have to be postponed." She laughed. "Anyhow, I have to have something to do while Oliver's poring over those seed catalogs."

This seemed to allay all fears. For a few minutes, there were no more questions.

Then Austin suddenly asked, "What'll you do when you have a fight?"

The Hills looked amused. They appeared to consider that improbable.

Supposedly counseling Oliver and Loveday, the Youngs were obviously talking to each other, airing grievances. Maybe this was the Nominating Committee's wish when it chose them.

"That's a good question," Oliver told Austin, "one we hadn't ever considered. I'm glad thee brought it up. I'll tell thee what I hope I'd do. I'd just take Loveday in my arms and let her feel I love her. Then I'd ask her to sit down and talk. But every few sentences, I'd find some way of reminding her that I want to make her happy."

Austin was listening to him intently.

"What we do," Neil said, grinning at Alice, "we go out in the boat and sail up and down the River. It's so beautiful — how can anyone stay mad? I'll be holding the tiller and Alice will be sitting opposite, in the cockpit, and suddenly we'll begin to laugh at each other. Then we know it's all over. Well, as far as I'm concerned, Oliver and Loveday are clear for marriage."

The other members of the committee agreed.

Neil heaved an audible sigh of relief.

Oliver and Loveday exchanged glances. He thought she looked quite herself again.

"Come in the dining room, Friends," Alice urged. "We'll have some tea."

As they were going in, Judy went up to Loveday. "I'm glad to know you," she said. "Daphne Otis was the person I admired most in the whole world. When I heard Oliver was going to get married again, I got worried. I couldn't believe anyone would live up to Daphne. And I couldn't understand why you wanted to give up your independence. Now I see, you're very different but okay, too. I hope you're going to be real happy."

Oliver was touched by the way Loveday reached out to Judy. "I've learned a lot," she said. "That's the one good thing about getting old. You begin to get sense. Wait and see. I hope we're going to be friends." She turned from Judy to Alice. "Now, about the reception — With my family so far away, I've got to start arranging —"

"Leave that to the Meeting," Alice told her. "Between us, we'll take care of everything. We usually do. It gives us pleasure. You can just forget about it and enjoy the happy occasion. Have you set a date?"

"Oliver and I thought, if we pass Meeting, we'd like to have it the twenty-first of March — the vernal equinox."

Neil was trying to get Oliver's attention. "Now that we've settled your marital affairs," he said, "I'd like to talk to thee about the Friends Hostel. We're running into trouble with the neighborhood people. They claim a shelter will bring in all kinds of questionable characters who'll endanger their wives and children and depreciate the value of their property. Go locate some place else — that's what they're telling us to do. I'm afraid they're going to cause trouble for us with the Planning Board."

This was alarming. "The danger," Oliver contended, "lies in *not* taking care of unfortunate people. By our inattention, we drive them to desperation. We'll have to go from door to door and explain this to the neighbors."

Just then, Oliver couldn't quite concentrate on the Friends Hostel. He was trying to overhear what Loveday was asking Judy and Alice.

"What does an elderly Quaker lady wear at her wedding? Now that we know we can go ahead, I'm thinking of driving to Providence next week to shop."

"Excuse me a minute," Oliver said to Neil. He went over to Loveday and whispered, "May I come?"

"I was counting on it."

"Oh," Alice answered, "I don't know — wear whatever thee'll feel comfortable in. As long as it's simple — We don't really care."

"Thee'll be lovely," Judy said, smiling for the first time, "whatever thee wears." She was using the plain language. Loveday was no longer an outsider.

Oliver recalled Thoreau's admonition to beware of all enterprises that require new clothes. But he didn't repeat it aloud. Why spoil Loveday's pleasure in the prospect of her wedding dress? She looked so happy.

Was he already ignoring the counsel he'd received a few minutes ago? Was he keeping his secret thought from her?

No. It wasn't his thought; it was Thoreau's. And what did Thoreau know about the joy of preparing for one's wedding? He never got married.

8.

AT THEIR MEETING for business in Third Month, Kendal Friends appointed a meeting for worship to be held on the twenty-first to solemnize the marriage of Oliver Otis and Loveday Mead. John and Clara Ludlow and Peter and Serenity Holland were named Overseers.

For Oliver, this was a busy season. He began sowing seeds in the hotbed — lettuce and beets, most of the annuals. He brought his bulb plants into the house, along with branches of fruit trees and flowering shrubs. Forced, he assured Loveday, they'd proclaim the beauty of spring by the time the guests arrived.

"Goldfinches are showing splotches of yellow, changing into summer garb," he reported, coming in with his arms full of lifeless-looking branches. "And I heard fox sparrows scratching in the leaves under the brush, like chickens."

Watching him tend the still-closed buds, Loveday amused him by recalling her superstitious landlady in Salzburg. "But those cherry branches she brought in on St. Barbara's Day did come through," she gloated. "Wouldn't I have been surprised, back then, if I'd known I was really going to get married!"

When the phoebes returned and nested under the eaves by the back porch, Oliver could scarcely contain his excitement. "They'll welcome our travelers with their clear, *phoe-be*."

Serenity and Ross came first.

"We're going to have a baby!" he shouted, before he was even out of the car.

"First-rate!" Oliver shouted back with all his might.

Ross helped him fill the kindling box and remove remnants of salt marsh hay from the flowerbeds. He was a happy little boy.

But his mother looked peaked. She confided to Loveday that the first weeks were rough. Still, she insisted on giving Alison Smith a hand with the cooking and baking.

Then, Heather and Stephen and their children had to be met at the airport. They filled the whole of Firbank's top floor.

Meeting Stephen, Loveday thought she understood Heather better. He was gracious, but reserved. Their children had beautiful manners. They were also brimming with fun. Heather kept assuring Loveday that this was the happiest of occasions for her.

Nevertheless, Loveday was nervous. How would her children fit in here? What would Oliver and Heather make of Emily? As for Emily's sophisticated daughters — And Michael and Jed's manners!

Loveday needn't have worried. Oliver's joy in welcoming his stepchildren and stepgrandchildren was contagious. Everyone was eager to meet everyone else. Differences were dis-

cussed with humor. Heather's and Emily's children took pleasure in mimicking one another's accents.

"These are my big children," Loveday said, introducing them
to Ross, fearful of his reaction to strangers.

But Ross was growing up. He accepted the newcomers, who
all made a fuss over him.

Will and Sara Ann and their boys stayed with the Ashaways;
Emily and her girls with the Hills. Toby was at the Ludlows.
He never stopped talking about them. What great people!

It was one glorious house party. They took turns providing
meals and washing up. Loveday wasn't allowed to do a thing.
In the background, Serenity and Peter quietly managed the
large household. When Oliver discovered that Michael and
Jed had never seen the ocean, he asked Heather's Ollie to row
them over.

He devoted himself so wholeheartedly to the guests that
Loveday feared he was overdoing. Then the Friends Hostel
demanded his attention. It had been broken into during the
night. Oliver seemed equal to it all.

But Loveday became exhausted. She had to retreat to the
ell. Resting on the spread with the irises and daffodils, she reflected happily that her children were discovering Firbank, as
she'd done — the beauty, the tranquillity, the unusual caring.
And, at the center of it all, the wonderful man, who was reaching out to them with a love they'd never known. Toby was the
one who seemed to feel this the most.

On the day of the wedding, when it was almost time to
leave for the Meetinghouse, Oliver drew Loveday into his
study and shut the door. He was wearing the nice suit he'd
bought to visit her in on Beacon Hill.

Taking both her hands, he looked searchingly into her eyes.
"Loveday Mead, does thee truly wish to marry me?"

"Yes." Why had she hesitated? How could she have been
uncertain?

"With all thy heart?"

"With all my heart. I'm sorry about the other day — when we went to the Clearness Committee. I had cold feet, not about marrying you — thee. It looked like an adversary situation. When thee said, 'Be still and cool,' I suddenly realized they weren't out to test me."

"Will thee allow me to remove thy old wedding ring? In just a little while, I'll put another one in its place." Without waiting for permission, Oliver took off the band Bill had put on Loveday's finger, all those years ago. He kissed the finger reverently and backed away to admire her. "Thee looks lovely."

She glanced down at her dress, the soft challis with little white flowers on a delphinium ground. Oliver had fallen in love with it when he spied it through a shop window.

Now he did something he'd never done before: he reached out and gently touched the front of Loveday's dress.

She grasped his hands and pressed them to her. "After today," she whispered, "we won't have to be proper any more."

The embrace with which he responded to this conveyed his passionate impatience.

"Remember what thee asked me on the way home from the Hills that evening," she went on, when he let go, "whether I wished to have a room of my own or whether I'd like to share thine?"

"Indeed I do."

"And I said I didn't know. Can thee understand that? I guess I want intimacy and privacy, too. Is that trying to have it both ways? I'm so used to being alone. Do we have to decide yet?"

"Well, I was going to send for the painter. My room is in need of freshening up. It's not fit to invite thee into."

Loveday smiled. "Just try inviting me. Tonight. But I'd still like to leave my things in the ell. Maybe later —"

"Gracious!" Oliver broke in, noticing the time. "We'd better leave."

From his desk he took a little polyethylene envelope containing a corsage he'd made for Loveday of Firbank blossoms — apple, forsythia, scilla — the color of her dress — and downy shadbush.

"Oh, Oliver!" she exclaimed, as he handed it to her. "How beautiful!"

His boyish eagerness, as he waited to see how she liked the corsage, was as much evidence of spring, Loveday thought, as the flowers. He, too, was burgeoning with new life. He made her think of his grandmother's portrait — the old woman who radiated such zest, such anticipation of the future, that, looking at her, one could only think of youth.

Can *I* have done this, Loveday asked herself, awed. Can I have made him so happy?

And she found herself praying, even before the wedding, praying that she might be worthy of his trust and the gift she was about to receive. Never had she prayed so fervently.

The gift she was *about* to receive? No. She already possessed it. Hadn't he told her weeks ago that everything in him felt joined to her?

There was a knock on the door. "We're leaving," Serenity called.

"Coming," Oliver replied, without opening. "Go ahead, all of you."

Loveday looked at him anxiously. "I just hope she makes it through the ceremony. She feels awful."

"And she has a lot on her mind," Oliver murmured. "With all our guests, I haven't had a chance to tell thee — just when we're so happy, the Hollands are in serious trouble. I only discovered it early this morning. After the wedding, when we're finally by ourselves, I'll explain." He opened the door for Loveday. Lion was standing there. "I wish we could take him with us."

"Why not? That's what I like about Friends — you're not formal. Why can't Lion come to our wedding?"

"I did take him on First Days, after Duffy died. He was so desolated. I couldn't bear to leave him. Both dogs came along after Daphne — They lay quietly at my feet. No, today I want to feel alone with thee."

But as he shut the front door from the outside, Oliver looked back regretfully. In deference to the occasion, he took Loveday's car instead of the truck. Will had warmed it up. About to turn on the ignition, Oliver stopped a moment. He had seen an early osprey flying straight inland with a fish.

"I just hope Michael and Jed behave themselves," Loveday said on the way to Kendal.

"Trust that they'll feel God's presence in the meeting," Oliver answered placidly. "We needn't trouble ourselves about that. So long as *we* come in the right spirit — "

"There I go again! Always trying to run things. Oliver, will I ever learn?"

When they reached the Meetinghouse, he pinned the corsage on Loveday's dress. Then he stood off to admire the effect. His face was glowing.

They lingered in the vestibule, greeting their guests, just as they would have done in the entrance hall at home, except that they kept their voices low. In the meeting room, the people who'd already arrived were establishing the hush which would sanctify their union.

A small table stood in one corner. On it lay the long wedding certificate which Oliver and Loveday would sign, after they'd made their promises — she with her new name!

But we're already joined, she thought. I feel that, too. This ceremony is just a confirmation. From the very first, we belonged together.

Oliver took her arm. "Let's go in," he said.

9.

SITTING on the narrow marriage bench, facing the Meeting, Oliver dedicated himself to Loveday, praying that he might possess the insight and selflessness to be unto her a loving and understanding husband.

Through the hallowed silence, he became aware of a faint rustling.

John Ludlow had risen to speak. Some of those present, he said, might not be familiar with Quaker practice. Friends wished them to know that everyone here was a participant in the accomplishment of this marriage and free to speak out of the consecrating silence. Since they were all witnesses — even the children — they were all asked to sign the certificate during the reception.

"May we uphold Oliver and Loveday in their union," John concluded, "and as we share in their joy, may their faith and love strengthen us."

Moved as much by the quiet grace with which he spoke as by his words, Oliver recalled that it was John who urged him to run after Loveday months ago — run and not be weary, mount up, if need be, with wings.

Hadn't been for him, Oliver thought gratefully, it would have taken me a lot longer to screw up my courage.

The Meetinghouse looked lovely with the sun streaming through the south windows, lighting the faces of friends and loved ones, giving the room an air of ethereal joy. On every sill stood a slender vase containing a daisy and a daffodil, set off by the dark red buds of a maple branch, announcing the arrival of spring.

Anyone was welcome to attend and there were so many people that some had to stand at the back.

Looking at the sea of faces before him, Oliver was touched by the number of Kendal folk who had never been here before, yet who, like old Annie Carr, had simply come to wish him well. Annie seemed to be so impressed by the importance of the occasion that she was wearing a hat, the only one in the Meetinghouse. Whenever she ran into Oliver, she recalled the time her husband was taken ill and Oliver kept their farm going, though that must have been twenty years ago.

In the front row, on Oliver's side of the aisle, Heather and Stephen and the children filled a bench. Sunshine delineated their dear faces. Oliver let his eyes rest a second on each one, hoping to transmit his thankfulness. Their coming from England was a magnificent wedding gift.

He felt concerned about Heather. She'd been charming all week, assuring him that she was pleased with the outcome of events. And yet, Oliver knew that she was finding it painful to accept his love for another woman.

He glanced sideways at Serenity and Peter, whom he thought of as his children, too.

Grandchildren, to be exact, he corrected himself. What they feel like, though, is contemporaries. How troubled they look!

Turning, he hunted for Ross, who'd been told in advance why his parents were going to be sitting on the facing bench, next to Oliver, while he would have to sit with the Youngs.

Spying the top of his bright head, near the aisle, where he was sitting between Judy and Austin, Oliver thought he seemed content.

But Judy and Austin — Oliver's heart went out to them. Their faces showed the struggle they were going through.

What must they be feeling, attending his wedding, recalling their own! It would take so little, he thought, carried away by his happiness, for them to recapture the magic that drew them together originally. No, it would take a great deal. They would, with God's help, have to recognize that marriage requires mutual consideration and adjustments.

Loveday's children and grandchildren were sitting across the way. Would they believe this was a bona fide marriage, even if no minister declared Oliver and Loveday to be man and wife?

Will and Sara Ann looked very solemn. Michael and Jed were fidgeting. They must be finding the unaccustomed quiet tedious. From morning till night, their world was filled with sound. Still, contrary to their grandmother's fears, they were behaving. Emily and her girls gave the impression that they felt a little out of place. But Toby—he seemed absolutely transported.

Although Oliver had resolved to be a good father to all three of Loveday's children, Toby was the one who particularly appealed to him. When the news came about the damage to the Hostel, it was Toby who offered to go there and take care of things.

"Thank thee," Oliver had answered. "Peter's already gone. When thee comes this summer, I hope the Hostel will be in running order."

Toby's face lit up. "Could I? Could I come? But—" He looked embarrassed. "I mightn't be by myself. I've been thinking, if Mom can get married, why not—Would that be okay? You and Jean would hit it off great." Then he added quickly, "I'm not sure. Don't say anything to Mom yet."

How happy this news would make her, when Toby saw fit to announce it!

Right now, it was time for Oliver and Loveday to declare their promises. They stood up and faced each other.

Oliver's heart was racing. Loveday appeared to be serene.

Taking her right hand, looking at her with his whole spirit, Oliver said clearly, "In the presence of God and these friends, I take thee, Loveday, to be my wife," — overcome with emotion, he had to stop and catch his breath — "promising," he went on, "with divine assistance to be unto thee — "

When he had finished, she gave him her promise, speaking more softly, but with assurance, although earlier, she'd been afraid of forgetting the words.

Oliver took the ring from Peter and placed it on Loveday's finger. The way she looked at him then brought tears to his eyes.

He thought, If she's ever impatient with me or a bit thoughtless, I'll remember this moment — the way she looked at me, as we stood face to face, in the presence of God. I'll forget everything but this bond of perfectness.

They kissed and sat down. Loveday reached for Oliver's hand to squeeze it.

In planning the wedding, they'd decided that Heather should have the honor of reading the certificate. Michael and Jed were to carry it in on the little table. Oliver nodded to them now.

Responding to the signal, they stomped up with the table and slammed it down.

Oliver and Loveday signed their names. Heather walked up to the table and took the certificate to read it to the witnesses. Her hands were shaking.

"Whereas," she read in a low voice, "Oliver Otis of Firbank Farm — "

Oliver wasn't thinking of the words but of Heather herself, as she read, "and Loveday Austell Mead of Emporia, Kansas, having declared their intentions of marriage with each other — "

Her voice was unsteady, but she persisted bravely, "And

Oliver Otis, taking Loveday Mead by the hand, did, on this solemn occasion, declare that he took her to be his wife, promising — "

To proclaim publicly the finality of an event which she regretted, even while she rejoiced with her father — what devotion to him this bespoke!

I must find some way to assure her that Loveday isn't taking her place, Oliver told himself; that no one can. Unless Heather's comfortable — That must be the first order of business in my new life.

When she'd finished reading, Heather put the certificate down and returned to her place beside Stephen. He grasped her hand.

The boys removed the table and the meeting settled into silence again.

For Oliver, it was a time of such inwardness that he only vaguely heard someone offering prayer. His spirit had drifted to a place words couldn't reach.

Suddenly, a throaty explosion warned him that someone, who was terrified by the prospect, was about to speak. Glancing around, Oliver couldn't believe his eyes. It was Austin! But Austin never spoke in meeting. Now that he was on his feet, he didn't seem to know what he wanted to say. He looked around helplessly. Then he blurted out, "Live and learn," and hastily sat down.

Before Oliver had a chance to figure out what this meant, titters drew his attention to the other side of the room.

Over by the window, Michael and Jed were nudging each other and shaking with giggles. Then Oliver saw why: while Austin was on his feet, Ross had quietly slid out behind him and escaped into the aisle. He headed straight for Oliver and climbed up on the narrow bench beside him. Squeezing in, he grinned happily.

Not in the least ruffled, Oliver moved closer to Loveday

and, putting his arm around Ross, returned to his meditation. But now it was clouded by anxiety. The child's unscheduled arrival reminded him of what Peter had said early this morning.

Before Peter joined Serenity at Firbank, she had been radiant about her pregnancy, even when she was battling nausea. But after he came, she changed visibly. He must have brought bad news.

Early this morning, Oliver took Peter into the study, opened a little box, and handed him the ring.

"Will thee take care of this and give it to me at the appointed time? Otherwise, I'll forget which pocket I put it in and Loveday will be standing there, waiting, while I turn out my loose change onto the Meetinghouse floor, hunting for it — "

Peter laughed and stuck the ring in his pocket.

Oliver thanked him for taking care of the damage at the Hostel. "We've been careless," he said. "Property like that ought not to be left uninhabited. Our thought was to wait till summer, but with things of this kind happening — If we could just find the right people to live there — "

"What about the Hollands?" Peter asked, smiling diffidently. "Would Friends consider them?"

"Why, Peter! Thee isn't thinking of commuting from there?"

"No."

"Thee can't be giving up thy job."

"I didn't want to bother thee, when thee s so busy with all these folks and it's such a happy time. I thought maybe after the wedding — " Now Peter looked downright frightened. "Remember how I was assured before I took the job that those satellites weren't going to be used for spying? Last week, the firm was offered a multimillion dollar contract and reversed its policy. I don't think I can live with that. Rennie feels the same way." Distracted, Peter scrambled the papers on Oliver's desk. "Thing is, she's pregnant."

"I know."

"Seems irresponsible to throw up the job now. What does thee think?"

Oliver said nothing. Peter knew what he thought. Peter must decide himself.

"If we just had a place to live while I'm hunting for something else, it wouldn't be so risky. With the baby coming — We were feeling so good about that. Now it's scary."

"Loveday and I would welcome you back any time. Thee and Serenity know that. But it would be a real service to the Meeting if you were to take care of the Hostel. It would help us."

"And us. From the first, we were excited about the project. We'd be happier living in the country. But the main thing is, our children would know that we were willing to sacrifice our security in order to uphold what we believe."

Thinking of the Hollands' dilemma, it struck Oliver that nothing would bring them so much clarity and confidence now as the child beside him.

He stood up and, with a reassuring smile, lifted Ross onto the neighboring bench, where he was joyfully received. A noticeable change had come over Peter and was reflected in Serenity's lovely face. Could they have made their decision in the past few minutes? They seemed at peace.

Greatly relieved, Oliver sat down again. Loveday gave him an approving smile. Far from disturbing the decorum, Ross had brought them a blessing. They were still gazing at each other when Serenity began to speak. Oliver turned to her swiftly.

"Listening to Oliver and Loveday make their promises," she began slowly, "I couldn't help thinking about when Peter and I were in that same place, saying the same thing."

Although she stood erect, facing the people before her, she kept hold of Ross's hand.

"I didn't come from a religious home, like Peter," she confided, "so when we first talked about being married in meeting, I had trouble with the words, In the presence of God. How could I say that, when I didn't know what God is? Peter argued that I was taking him on faith, so why not God?" She paused and took a deep breath. "I was scared, too, of that awful phrase, As long as we both shall live — so many couples were breaking up. Peter told me one had to promise that on faith, too."

Serenity looked back to him and smiled. Then she turned again.

"My parents wanted me to have a big, snazzy wedding," she continued, laughing nervously. "I wanted to be married here. I'd just discovered Firbank and Oliver and" — she lowered her voice — "Daphne. This is where the great-grandmother I was named for got married. So my parents finally gave in. I crowed to Peter, And they lived happily ever after! I thought we'd never have to face anything again as bad as that struggle with my parents. Little did I know!"

A wave of sympathetic amusement rippled over the room.

"I was just a kid, you know," Serenity said. "I didn't know the first thing about life. I couldn't understand why Oliver told me that, while we'd won the freedom to make our own decisions, it would depend on what we did with that freedom. I remember his saying, 'Firbank will help. The pond and the dunes and the ocean will counsel you.' Well, they did. But mostly it was Oliver."

She turned toward him and he felt her affection reaching out. He remembered the young girl who had been led to Firbank. Daphne had seen beyond her momentary confusion to the person she believed would emerge — the one whose likeness she painted in that portrait which now hung in the Museum in New York. In it, Daphne was foretelling the dawn of a day she hoped the whole of Serenity's generation would wake to. Serenity and Peter had!

"Thanks to Oliver," Serenity was saying now, "Peter and I are making decisions as a family and I know we couldn't do it without divine assistance. Because doing what you feel is right sometimes means taking big risks. You don't know how it'll work out. You may not even be able to feed your children. Taking risks is leaving the outcome to God."

Looking as if she might break down any minute, Serenity said, "I think it's even more wonderful for old people, who know how rough life can be sometimes, to make this commitment." She got hold of herself and added, "Oliver often quotes a verse about 'the Indian summer of the heart.' He says it makes him think of my Great-grandmother Serenity. I didn't know her. It makes me think of Oliver and Loveday."

She turned to them with a radiant smile, although there were tears in her eyes. Then she sat down.

Barely able to contain his joy, Oliver said to himself, My whole life has been a continuum of love.

He was just a little boy like Ross when his mother died and his grandmother took him into her love. She made Firbank home for him. When the time came, she passed him on to Daphne. Now, Daphne was passing him on to Loveday.

We may not have many years, he conceded to himself, as he and Loveday walked jubilantly out of the Meetinghouse together, while the guests lingered in the silence a few minutes longer. But love isn't measured by time. It may be the only thing in the universe that lives forever.

CHRISTIAN HERALD ASSOCIATION AND ITS MINISTRIES

CHRISTIAN HERALD ASSOCIATION, founded in 1878, publishes The Christian Herald Magazine, one of the leading interdenominational religious monthlies in America. Through its wide circulation, it brings inspiring articles and the latest news of religious developments to many families. From the magazine's pages came the initiative for CHRISTIAN HERALD CHILDREN and THE BOWERY MISSION, two individually supported not-for-profit corporations.

CHRISTIAN HERALD CHILDREN, established in 1894, is the name for a unique and dynamic ministry to disadvantaged children, offering hope and opportunities which would not otherwise be available for reasons of poverty and neglect. The goal is to develop each child's potential and to demonstrate Christian compassion and understanding to children in need.

Mont Lawn is a permanent camp located in Bushkill, Pennsylvania. It is the focal point of a ministry which provides a healthful "vacation with a purpose" to children who without it would be confined to the streets of the city. Up to 1000 children between the age of 7 and 11 come to Mont Lawn each year.

Christian Herald Children maintains year-round contact with children by means of a *City Youth Ministry.* Central to its philosophy is the belief that only through sustained relationships and demonstrated concern can individual lives be truly enriched. Special emphasis is on individual guidance, spiritual and family counseling and tutoring. This follow-up ministry to inner-city children culminates for many in financial assistance toward higher education and career counseling.

THE BOWERY MISSION, located at 227 Bowery, New York City, has since 1879 been reaching out to the lost men on the Bowery, offering them what could be their last chance to rebuild their lives. Every man is fed, clothed and ministered to. Countless numbers have entered the 90-day residential rehabilitation program at the Bowery Mission. A concentrated ministry of counseling, medical care, nutrition therapy, Bible study and Gospel services awakens a man to spiritual renewal within himself.

These ministries are supported solely by the voluntary contributions of individuals and by legacies and bequests. Contributions are tax deductible. Checks should be made out either to CHRISTIAN HERALD CHILDREN or to THE BOWERY MISSION.

Administrative Office: 40 Overlook Drive, Chappaqua, New York 10514
Telephone: (914) 769-9000

F   #216

New   Newman, Daisy.
         Indian summer of the
    heart